Energy and Environmental Issues

Energy and Environmental Issues

The Making and Implementation of Public Policy

Edited by
Michael Steinman

The University of
Nebraska—Lincoln

LexingtonBooks
D.C. Heath and Company
Lexington, Massachusetts
Toronto

Library of Congress Cataloging in Publication Data

Main entry under title:

Energy and environmental issues.

    1. Energy policy—United States—Addresses, essays, lectures. 2. Environ-
mental policy—United States—Addresses, essays, lectures. I. Steinman,
Michael.
HD9502.U52E449   333.7   78-13871
ISBN 0-669-02699-9

International Standard Book Number: 0-669-02699-9

Library of Congress Catalog Card Number: 78-13871

For Linda and Jonathan

Contents

List of Figures and Tables

Preface

There are few questions of more interest and importance to the general public today than those dealing with energy and the environment. Even the most mundane behaviors—breathing, drinking a glass of water—make us aware of complex problems lying beyond our individual powers of resolution. This almost compels us to follow, understand, and perhaps even try to influence government efforts.

This book brings together two areas of study. It first describes and analyzes various problems and concerns related to energy and the environment. Nine original chapters cover the following: citizen participation in water quality planning; structural and procedural correlates of utility rates; the future role of solar energy; the regulation of industrial discharges; air pollution control; how representative state senators are and can be with respect to energy development and environmental issues; administrative reorganization; the effects of using different standards in evaluating a federal agency's implementation of congressional energy policy; and the difficulties of making and implementing a comprehensive national energy program.

In addition, this book contributes to a larger understanding of the way in which government works. Political science and public administration have long dealt with such matters as public opinion, legislative behavior, planning, and enforcement. Only recently have these and other foci come together into a widely used, empirically based theory that attempts to describe and explain political and related phenomena. This is not to say that this theory of the public policy process is complete and all-explaining; but it does promise greater explanatory power and has attracted much professional attention. The chapters of this book deal with issues covering the entire policy process: what kinds of actors participate and with what effect; how does government make policy when confronted by different kinds of demands; and what are the impacts of bureaucratic factors on policy, outcomes, and future policy.

This theoretical diversity is not artificial. Energy and environmental issues are very complex. Consequently, efforts to understand government's responses to these issues must be commensurately complex.

There is, however, a natural special emphasis among the theoretical concerns discussed. Eight chapters deal to some degree with bureaucratic agencies, either as policy makers, implementing agents, or arenas of political competition involving nonbureaucratic combatants. This is appropriate given the degree to which energy and environmental policies are made in administrative agencies. Such agencies are integral objects of study in any policy area. They are especially pivotal in energy and environmental matters, because these issues are extremely complex, technical, and controversial.

David Howard Davis's concluding chapter discusses the utility of various perspectives on these subjects. He concludes that although political frameworks of analysis are more "untidy" than others, they nevertheless provide the best means for understanding the policy linkages between energy and environmental matters.

I want to express my gratitude to each of the contributing authors as well as to Caroline McCarley and Mike McCarroll of Lexington Books for their help and cooperation. Thanks go also to Ramona Farmer for her assistance in preparing the manuscript.

Themes in Energy and Environmental Policy

Michael Steinman

This book examines the ways in which energy and environmental policies are fought over, made, diminished, strengthened, implemented, and ignored. Few recent issues have excited as much attention and concern as these have. The purpose of this chapter is to connect and comment on the various contributions of the following chapters. These contributions are of two kinds. The first deals with discussions and analyses of real policy problems related to energy and the environment. The second offers theoretical lessons about the public policy process based on the more substantive materials. The nature of this process and the degree to which it enables us to understand and resolve public problems are our major concerns.

Substantive Themes

There can be no denying that energy and environmental issues have been salient in the 1970s. The guess here is that they will continue as such into the 1980s as well. There are a natural tie and a natural tension between them. The more crowded and technological our society becomes, the more many of us will worry about the availability of sufficient energy to keep things moving. As the demand for and use of various energy resources increase, many others will worry also about the not-always-beneficial consequences of using our technologies and resources in certain ways. This is not to say that sincere people do not exist who concern themselves with both problems simultaneously. Nor does this mean that it is impossible to pursue energy development and environmental protection at the same time. The history of these issues, however, indicates that contestants for political power usually concern themselves with either problem instead of both. Furthermore, this history suggests that each side is rarely satisfied by any policy containing the slightest hint of compromise.

Three explicit and implicit themes run through the substantive discussions of this book: the politics of energy and the environment are now directed toward rearranging government's action agenda and affecting the way in which public authorities handle issues rather than persuading government that particular problems are public ones; political competition over these issues is sustained and intense, and extends into every political arena; and, underlying all the themes, is a diversity of deeply felt values. The rest of this section is devoted to discussing these themes and relating them to particular chapters.

1

Energy and environmental issues did not appear de novo on our political agenda in the 1960s and 1970s. Teddy Roosevelt's concern for what he called conservation, Woodrow Wilson's efforts to help settle a coal miner's strike, and the New Deal's interest in generating hydroelectric power through the Tennessee Valley Authority all testify that such issues have been around for some time. Pelsoci's contribution draws effectively on the structural and procedural traditions of state public utility commissions in this century to make some conclusions about rate setting. The analysis of Illinois's attempts to reorganize energy-related agencies by Nelson et al. reveals a long history of alliances among agencies, legislative committees, and clientele groups with complementary interests.

The 1960s and 1970s nevertheless represent a bench mark in the relationship of government to energy and environmental issues. Masses of rank-and-file citizens became concerned about the damaged and declining quality of our natural environment, our dead and dying streams, and the often noxious atmospheric conditions of our industrial centers. Vig's discussion of efforts in Minnesota to control industrial discharges into Lake Superior reflects this as does Anderson's study of air pollution control in Ohio. In the early 1970s, after years of warnings from lonely voices in the wilderness, the finite quality of many of our energy resources also made a profound impression on the national psyche. The oil embargo of October 1973 was obviously a key factor in this. All of a sudden, the energy resources that many had taken for granted were much more expensive, limited in extent, difficult to find and exploit, and often controlled by foreign powers. Chapters by Daneke, Rycroft, and Tobin and Cohen are focused around these newer givens of the energy scene.

The events of this period made energy and environmental problems, in all their diversity and complexity, legitimate concerns of government. That they were public problems was undeniable. Individuals could not cope with them using their own private resources. Major interests could not agree about solutions. The gravity of the problems and the profound societal ramifications of efforts to deal with them led most people to look toward government for satisfaction. The "imperial" powers of the Johnson and Nixon presidencies and congressional aspirations after Watergate for more legislative clout made government a willing recipient of additional responsibility. Political debates increasingly concerned what government should do rather than whether government should do anything at all.

Walter Rosenbaum writes that the 1960s and early 1970s were years of "... noisy, acrimonious, and widely observed mobilization ..."[1] He rightly notes that this phase is now largely ended, replaced by a period emphasizing efforts to formulate and implement particular policies. Although it is impossible to separate a mobilization phase (including aggregation, organization, and representation stages of the policy process using Jones's labels[2]) from the formulation stage in the real world, it is possible to speak of emphases and tendencies. This book's topics and discussions reflect this.

The politics of energy and the environment today are essentially directed toward two related general goals. The first is to alter the priority rankings of public problems and policies already on government's action agenda. Chapters by Anderson, Tobin and Cohen, and Vig document the jostling of environmental and economic goals on the nation's hierarchy of needs. Daneke's contribution discusses a particular policy option (solar energy development) that many believe should have a higher priority.

The second general goal is to influence, if not control, the way in which government formulates and executes policy. Nelson et al., Pelsoci, and Rycroft discuss the complex organizational milieu in which these steps of the policy process often take place as well as the various benefits and deprivations they produce. This concern for means also includes an interest in individual participants, their motives, and their interrelationships. Czarnecki and Kamieniecki examine citizen intentions to participate in water quality planning, and Ingram et al. investigate the uncertain linkages between state senators and citizens in the Four Corners area with respect to energy and environmental policy matters.

The first theme leads to the second: political competition over these issues is sustained and intense and extends into every government arena. Energy and environmental issues have especially powerful appeals because their handling affects practically everyone. If we have reason to believe that the purity of our air and water is threatened, we are interested and want protection. If the availability and/or cost of gasoline restricts our mobility, we are concerned. If our household budgets have difficulty handling the costs of heating and cooling, we worry about our comfort and health. These matters affect the quality of our lives so directly and thoroughly that we are led, as a society, to pursue our interests beyond bringing problems to government to influencing and monitoring government's responses.

More specifically, competition is sustained and intense for a number of other reasons:

1. Some parts of the country export more energy than they use, and other parts use more than they generate themselves. This creates a built-in tension leading to continuing competition. Chapters 2 and 10 provide some background for understanding this.

2. A very large and complex technological infrastructure already exists, supplying us with energy from a variety of sources in a variety of ways. It is not easy to change these arrangements significantly, because a great deal of money, costly capital equipment, and people are involved. Consequently, there is a tremendous momentum working to the advantage of the status quo, inhibiting the development of new sources of energy that many think are necessary to continued prosperity. Chapters 8 and 10 discuss this.

3. Energy and environmental problems are very complex. Consequently, people often disagree in defining them and in anticipating the results of using alternative strategies to deal with them. A majority of the contributors touch on this to some degree.

4. Economic problems such as inflation and unemployment will be with us for some time. We do not always agree about when each of these becomes a problem nor do we agree which is worse. This leads to a continuing battle over economic policy, which must include a concern for the costs of energy and environmental protection. Again, more than one chapter raises these matters.

Our problematic understanding of energy and environmental problems puts them effectively beyond our capacity to solve once and for all. This does not diminish their importance, however, nor the confidence of some that they are on the one, right track. This produces sustained, intense efforts to influence and control government action.

The policy process of a modern technological society is a maze of direct and indirect routes to power interlaced with many dead ends. Casual and once-only efforts to influence events are rarely productive. Czarnecki and Kamieniecki's chapter suggests that sustained political participation may be more related to individual concerns with specific problems than standard correlates of involvement. The opposition of various interest groups to a vaguely worded bill, described in chapter 3, implies an insecurity about the future and the end of an era of positive-sum, distributive politics. Daneke's discussion in chapter 8 of the difficulties of getting and using more objective projections of the future role of solar energy is based on a view of vested interests repeatedly frustrating the development of new energy sources.

The persistent politcs of energy and the environment occurs in every nook and cranny of government. This book analyzes policy-related events in all levels and branches including the judiciary. Chapter 5 analyzes the impacts of different levels of courts on the regulation of industrial discharges into Lake Superior. Thus, even the courts are drawn into these matters, although, in strictly technical terms, they may be the least competent agents to decide them.[3]

The third theme—the existence of a diversity of deeply felt values—underlies all of the earlier observations.[4] Energy and environmental politics are extremely complicated because of the following factors:

1. The number of different energy sources.
2. The number and technological complexity of different ways of exploiting energy resources.
3. The number and heterogeneity of people and organizations involved in energy production and supply (heterogeneity in expertise, degree of organization, socioeconomic characteristics, residence in different parts of the country, and size of economic stake in more traditional or newer energy sources).
4. The number and heterogeneity of energy consumers.
5. The relatively uncertain impacts of individual energy sources and technologies on our way of life and the environment.
6. The relatively uncertain amounts of nonrenewable energy reserves that remain unexploited.

These are only generally stated categories that break down into many more specific ones. Suffice it to say that a great many people, perhaps all of us, operate in sufficiently different circumstances and ways to produce many different perceived needs, definitions of social and technological problems, and possible solutions.

A concern for value differences permeates this book. For example, Ingram et al. look at the degree to which senatorial opinion in a number of states represents views expressed by samples of citizens. Anderson's chapter examines the competition between environmental values and energy/industrial/utility interests in Ohio. Rycroft's sophisticated analysis of the old Federal Energy Administration (chapter 9) highlights the many aspects of one agency's operation, its multiple impacts, and different ways of evaluating its success or failure simultaneously. He (along with a few other contributors) comments critically about the powerful influence of economic standards in conceiving and evaluating energy and environmental policies.

The great diversity of values in these matters reflects more than a heterogeneity of people, places, and technologies; it is also envidence of the central and pervasive role of government. Government has two general functions in these and other issues. The first is to dispense advantages and disadvantages. The second is to serve as a forum and marketplace of ideas. People and organizations with different visions of the future compete with each other to have government embrace and promote their own more-or-less unique preferences. Before they can compete over actual public policy they must obtain some minimal credibility for their definitions of public problems and the public good. This first task has already been accomplished by most energy and environmental interests. There has been a byproduct with this accomplishment however. In mobilizing large numbers of people behind such causes as purifying the air and water and making utility rate setters more accountable, the new, the old, and the aspiring powers that be communicated a message: that government is a necessary and very powerful potential partner. The more that this message sank in the more it in turn fostered a desire to control government's seemingly great power.

Theoretical Themes

The growth of the public policy literature is a welcome development having a number of benefits.[5] Students of government are traditionally compartmentalized into a slew of specialties and subspecialties, for example: comparative government, legislative behavior, international relations, and public opinion. Each area and subarea often has a somewhat specific literature denoting its own importance and, by implication, its relative independence from the others. The growth of policy studies has begun to reverse this history by cultivating a larger view of the potential interrelation of different political behaviors and arenas. This is not to say that more focused perspectives are becoming irrelevant and useless. Rather, their subjects of study must increasingly be considered as both dependent and independent variables in larger systems of political phenomena.

An appreciation for the interrelatedness of political phenomena leads to two other productive emphases of the public policy literature. First, the typical dependent variable is a function of many explanatory factors. The more complex and involved it is, the more analysis of it must be grounded on a larger number of independent variables. Thus, several chapters in this book criticize the dominance of economic criteria in policy analysis and the exclusion of other, equally important factors. The potentially large number of considerations an analyst must make in turn leads to uncertainty. The good policy analyst should always worry about his assumptions and the quality of his work. Good analysis flourishes in a state of creative insecurity.

The following concerns of the public policy literature tie the chapters of this book together: participation and representation, incremental and nonincremental modes of policy making, and the importance of bureaucratic style and action. The remainder of this section is devoted to discussing these subjects and relating them to particular chapters.

Americans often display a split personality in their view of government. On the one hand, they have a very low opinion of it. It is slow and inefficient. It is responsive primarily to the rich and a few corporate interests. It is corrupt and for sale to the highest bidder. Polling organizations periodically ask national samples to rate various types of occupation, and "politician" is usually near the bottom or dead last. Some students of government have described it as a powerful tool that interests try to control. Many private citizens probably see it as a screwdriver they would like to avoid.

On the other hand, there is a tremendous amount of pride in this country about our democratic institutions, traditions, and opportunities. Even those who recognize our system's faults compare it favorably with others elsewhere. People have died for it in the past. People will probably fight for it in the future.

A reconciliation of these two views is possible. The more pessimistic view concerns the way in which government seems to operate: the kinds of people seemingly attracted to government work, what they seem to do, and why. The more optimistic view evaluates the quality of our political structures and constitutional-legal procedures. Reconciling the two, then, leads to a positive evaluation of governmental forms but a negative evaluation of the way they are used.

The literature on political participation partially confirms this interpretation. Prevailing tendencies are for people to be minimally informed about government and its operations and disinclined to participate in it.[6] This is not surprising given the negative views described earlier. It is also understandable given the hard work and long hours usually associated with productive participation. This helps to explain findings that those who tend to participate often have more resources (in terms of income, education, community contacts, and so forth) and substantial motives (an awareness of what "good citizens" should do and/or a profound sensitivity to a particular problem). In chapter 4, Czarnecki and Kamieniecki discuss various ways of understanding political participation and its correlates.

This is not to say that mass participation does not occur. In chapter 7, Anderson describes the impact of Earth Day in Ohio. Jones's book on the politics of pollution control gives a more complete description and analysis of the environmentalist upsurge of the late 1960s and early 1970s.[7] The Clamshell Alliance in New Hampshire and other antinuclear energy movements around the country are more recent examples of grass roots concern.

Mass participation and the mobilization of public opinion are not major emphases of this book however. Going back to an earlier observation, the politics of energy and the environment today are more focused on formulation and implementation of policy than on getting new problems on government's agenda. Given that formulation and legitimation require well-informed (substantively and strategically) representation, negotiation, and analysis of policy options, they are more likely to be performed by experienced leaderships and staffs of experts. This is reflected by the fact that seven chapters describe the politics that swirl in and around bureaucratic agencies, and an eighth concerns how representative state senators are of citizen opinion in their areas.

Most of the participation examined in this book is engaged in by relatively few people (given the numbers they say they represent) with higher-than-average levels of information and expertise in matters at hand. They have already defined their problems and positions and now aim their efforts directly at those actually making or carrying out policy. A major question raised by this kind of participation concerns the responsiveness of leaderships to their constituents. In chapter 2, Ingram et al. deal with this matter by examining the opinions of both state senators and samples of their constituents. They conclude that the ties between the two are not very clear or certain. Interest groups emerge as a major linkage between the elected and their electors, and this is reflected in many of the other chapters. For example, Anderson sees air pollution politics in Ohio as heavily influenced by interest groups; Vig's case study of judicial decision making has interest groups among the protagonists; and the discussion of efforts to reorganize Illinois bureaucracies in chapter 3 describes the effectiveness of defensive interest group action.

It may be too early to conclude that this type of participation has led to problems associated with Michels' iron law of oligarchy.[8] However, it probably has transformed the nonincremental policy preferences of many participants into more modest incremental goals to obtain favorable policy adjustments. Chapters 7 and 10 describe and discuss nonincremental and incremental policy styles.

Public interest in energy and environmental matters is relatively new. More recent arrivals in these issue areas have a relative lack of expertise and experience in formulating policy goals. Representing a heterogeneous public only recently excited about these problems has led to the development of total or utopian approaches to problem solving. Some of the great nonincremental policy ambitions of the last decade or so show this: to purify the air and water; to develop economically viable, renewable energy sources for mass use in the short term; and to establish social equity in the distribution of energy resources and costs.

The enactment of nonincremental policy revealed government's inability to implement it. Chapters 5, 7, and 8 discuss this development, which Jones has labeled "speculative augmentation" and "administration beyond capacity."[9] Government simply was unable to live up to the utopian expectations created for it by the new arrivals. It lacked the technical and administrative capacity to resolve complex problems vulnerable to different and competing definitions. In addition, powerful political actors—major industries, labor unions, utilities—were aligned against these policies with expert and experienced staffs. Further inhibiting implementation efforts was a relatively swift decline in national grass-roots demand to deal with energy and environmental problems comprehensively.

Government agencies did what they could to implement these utopian policies but were forced by necessity to take a cautious and incremental approach. Resulting compromises showed the purists among us the public's lack of representation in government and the general corruption of the system. "Realists" saw, however, the problems of bringing about wholesale change when powerful interests combine in defense of the status quo; when intense popular interest is sporadic; when problems are difficult to define; when huge investments have already been made in more conventional energy technologies; and when other problems intervene (energy development against conservation, inflation, unemployment, and regional competitions for control over energy resources and costs).

Incremental policy making consequently functions as a defense of the status quo and of the interests benefitting from it. Efforts to fashion comprehensive policies by centralizing government decision making in executive and legislative branches have become increasingly misleading.[10] They communicate a sense of nonincremental policy movement to a population only poorly to moderately well informed, when actual policy is made through almost invisible incremental maneuvering. They also imply that comprehensive, that is, nonincremental, policy making can be productive in the near term when issues are complex and divisions are many and deep. It is little wonder that people are increasingly distrustful of those in government and pessimistic about their ability to resolve public problems.

Some public servants seem more likely to have nonincremental policy styles than others. Those possessing a considerable amount of expertise and a commitment to apply it as "scientifically" as possible may be more likely to concentrate on ultimate goals. This may be true particularly in issue areas heavily influenced by the hard sciences, where variables appear more tangible and measurable. Other officials, however, with responsibility for the cohesiveness and self-maintenance of policy units (agencies, bureaus, committees), tend to approach their work in more incremental ways. They are more concerned with the general health of their units and relations with others. They may consequently be more sensitive to differences of opinion and anxious to prevent them from developing into threats. This concern leads naturally to an openness to compromise.

Regardless of the style policy makers employ, they probably use bureaucratic factors to make their choices look good. We all like to think we are rational actors, able to identify our true interests objectively and select the best strategy for satisfying them. We are children of the Age of Reason who try to ignore, or at least subordinate, our biases in an effort to know the world as it is and deal with it efficiently and effectively. It is the rare political figure who adopts a position because lightning hit when he thought of it. Again, this is especially the case in issue areas containing visible, tangible, measurable problems seemingly susceptible to resolution through application of the scientific method. More traditional descriptions of bureaucracy are very sympathetic to this desire to be, or at least appear, rational.

A reading of Frederick Taylor or Luther Gulick and Lyndall Urwick and a misreading of Max Weber have led many people to conclude that bureaucratic ways can maximize, maybe even perfect, our collective ability to solve problems.[11] Behavioral norms that stress objective planning, assigning people to jobs solely on the basis of their competence, and requiring regular communication to coordinate and evaluate performance are terribly attractive to those wanting to be or appear rational and unbiased. The aspiring rational actor need only experience bureaucracy and its impersonal standard operating procedures to recognize its awesome apparent potential.

Policy makers in highly conflictual issue areas can rarely resist the temptation of bureaucracy. A great deal is written about the inability or disinclination of elected policy makers to enact specific rules and regulations themselves. Instead of making specific policy, they often delegate the authority to do so to administrative agencies. These allocations of discretion are sometimes quite broad and include only very general goal statements that agencies can specify according to their own expert lights and their readings of the political climate. Lowi has called this "policy without law."[12] This abdication of immediate, specific impact allows many elected officials to:

1. Shift responsibility for information generation and analysis to bureaucrats, thereby diminishing their own workload and avoiding the chance of coming up with politically unacceptable findings.
2. Appear more dispassionate and less self-promoting if they entrust discretion to putatively objective agency experts.

3. Make themselves appear less like wheeler-dealer politicians and more like action-oriented pursuers of the public good.
4. Deflect competing interest group demands onto agencies where incremental policy adjustments can develop more easily out of the public eye.
5. Avoid being held responsible for policy outcomes.
6. Advertise their representative contributions more easily by interpreting enacted general goal statements to include the interests of a wider diversity of constituent groups. That is, they are able to support contradictory goals and thereby broaden their own power base.
7. Keep their options open for the future.

The cumulative effect of these advantages is to give some policy makers an opportunity to avoid problems emanating from their own highly politicized situations. Legislators and elected executives usually lack the expertise to understand technological problems and develop appropriate responses themselves. This justifies their use of bureaucratic knowledge, skills, and analyses as necessary functional aids. They can manipulate these bureaucratic factors either to portray themselves or actually serve as effective mediators between their constituents' needs and expert judgments of what is possible and proper.

A major problem with these arrangements is that agency operations and decisions are themselves often compromised by political considerations and insufficient knowledge and expertise. Thus, Nelson et al. in chapter 3 and Tobin and Cohen in chapter 10 portray bureaucracies as representing legislative and clientele interests. Chapters 8 and 9 analyze the built-in biases of agencies and comment critically on the narrow economic standards that typically dominate their decision making. In chapter 7 Anderson describes the inefficacy of bureaucratic action when agencies lack the technical capacity and political support to implement policies. And in chapter 6 Pelsoci examines structural and procedural correlates of public utility commission policy.

Taken together, these chapters describe policy processes that have changed significantly since the early 1970s. Given the availability of enough resources, the United States has historically had a distributive style of politics precluding the need to engage in zero-sum games.[13] It is now clear, however, that the game has changed.

There is more uncertainty now about our energy supply. Many actually fear running out of energy resources that we have come to depend on heavily and consequently promote the development of renewable sources. Others believe it will be some time yet before we begin running out of natural gas and oil and point to our huge coal reserves as justification for taking a slower more gradual approach. Still others see nuclear energy as a major source and look forward to its becoming a more economically viable option. Whereas ten years ago the country could worry about environmental problems because its energy supply seemed plentiful, it is now less sure of its energy future and divided about which course or courses to follow.

Although energy problems appear more salient today, they have not pushed environmental considerations out of the public consciousness. Many still worry about the impacts of various energy and industrial uses. In addition, laws protecting the environment are on the books, and particular agencies are responsible for implementing them. A General Accounting Office analysis estimates that we will spend approximately $423 billion on air and water pollution control between 1975 and 1984.[14] There are, therefore, popular and bureaucratic incentives for pushing environmental goals now and in the future.

In addition, demand for goods and services has not abated. If anything, our wants are more numerous (witness our inflation problems) and difficult to reconcile. We want big-car luxury and small-car mileage, more energy-efficient housing without higher home prices, and more electronic gadgets (television recorders, electric toothbrushes) and lower utility costs.

These conditions have produced a collective uncertainty with respect to what national values should be, which energy resources are most plentiful, and how we should exploit them. Although distrust of government is high, as manifested by the passage of Proposition 13 in California and the popularity of its clones elsewhere, it seems reasonably certain that people will still look to government for the answers. Realistically and traditionally, government policy will reflect the interests of those who mobilize the most persuasive expertise and the greatest evidence of popular support. What is different today, however, is a growing sense that government support of particular policies now means less and less opportunity for other, bypassed options in the future. There is, in other words, a more general appreciation for the long-term nonincremental policy consequences of short-term incremental policy making.

Today's environmental and energy situations did not develop overnight. However a set of nonincremental expectations has enveloped current incremental policy adjustments. It was created by the almost utopian goals of many environmentalists to cleanse the air and water without considering some harsh technical, administrative, and economic realities; the grand dreams of some advocates of renewable energy sources; and the distribution by government of vast resources according to the prescriptions of supposedly comprehensive programs. The resulting tension between nonincremental expectations and actual incremental movement has generated an intense and continuing interest in every aspect of public policy that seems to benefit one solution, one vision of the future, over another. This tension is at the center of the political questions examined in this book.

Notes

1. Walter A. Rosenbaum, *The Politics of Environmental Concern,* 2d ed. (New York: Praeger Publishers, 1977), p. 11.

2. See Charles O. Jones, *An Introduction to the Study of Public Policy,* 2d ed. (North Scituate, Mass.: Duxbury Press, 1977).

3. For an analysis of judicial involvement in the "softer" arenas of social policy, see Donald L. Horowitz, *The Courts and Social Policy* (Washington, D.C.: The Brookings Institution, 1977).

4. For a discussion of the role of values in the political process, see Martin Rein, *Social Science and Public Policy* (New York: Penguin Books, 1976).

5. Examples of comprehensive treatments of the public policy process are James E. Anderson, *Public Policy-Making* (New York: Praeger Publishers, 1975); George C. Edwards III and Ira Sharkansky, *The Policy Predicament: Making and Implementing Public Policy* (San Francisco: W.H. Freeman, 1978); and Jones, *An Introduction to the Study of Public Policy.*

6. For treatments of political participation, see Roger W. Cobb and Charles D. Elder, *Participation in American Politics: The Dynamics of Agenda-Building* (Boston: Allyn and Bacon, 1972); Lester W. Milbrath and M.L. Goel, *Political Participation,* 2d ed. (Chicago: Rand McNally College Publishing Company, 1977); and Sidney Verba and Norman H. Nie, *Participation in America: Political Democracy and Social Equality* (New York: Harper and Row, 1972).

7. Charles O. Jones, *Clean Air: The Policies and Politics of Pollution Control* (Pittsburgh, Penn.: University of Pittsburgh Press, 1975).

8. Robert Michels, *Political Parties: A Sociological Study of the Oligarchical Tendencies of Modern Democracy* (New York: Collier, 1962).

9. Jones, *Clean Air.*

10. For discussions of centralized policy planning and making, see Hanna J. Cortner, "Formulating and Implementing Energy Policy: The Inadequacy of the State Response," *Policy Studies Journal* 7 (Autumn 1978):24-29; and David Howard Davis, *Energy Politics,* 2d ed. (New York: St. Martin's Press, 1978), pp. 244-249.

11. H.H. Gerth and C. Wright Mills, trans. and eds., *From Max Weber: Essays in Sociology* (New York: Oxford University Press, 1946); Luther Gulick, "Notes on the Theory of Organization," in Luther Gulick and Lyndall Urwick, eds., *Papers on the Science of Administration* (New York: Institute of Public Administration, 1937), pp. 3-13; and Frederick W. Taylor, *Scientific Management* (New York: Harper and Brothers, 1911).

12. Theodore J. Lowi, *The End of Liberalism* (New York: W.W. Norton, 1969). Other discussions of delegated legislative authority are in Martha Derthick, *Uncontrollable Spending for Social Services Grants* (Washington, D.C.: The Brookings Institution, 1975), chap. 2; and Edwards and Sharkansky, *The Policy Predicament,* pp. 109-114.

13. Robert H. Salisbury, "The Analysis of Public Policy: A Search for Theories and Roles," in Austin Ranney, ed., *Political Science and Public Policy* (Chicago: Markham Publishing, 1968), p. 169.

14. General Accounting Office, *16 Air and Water Pollution Control Issues Facing the Nation* (CED-78-148B) Washington, D.C., 1978.

2 The Responsiveness of State Legislators in the Four Corner Area

Helen Ingram, Nancy Laney, and *J.R. McCain*

The American Southwest is an interior frontier, still in the process of becoming. The Four Corners states of Arizona, New Mexico, Utah, and Colorado are rich in energy resources at a time when such resources are scarce. Large formations of coal underlie northwest New Mexico, at Black Mesa on the Navajo and Hopi reservations in northeast Arizona, at the Kaiparowits Plateau in Utah, and throughout western Colorado. The highest grade oil shale deposits in the United States are located in northwest Colorado. Uranium occurs in the region in large quantities. Whether and how these resources are developed have large implications for the region's sensitive and vulnerable physical and social environment. The area is renowned for its natural beauty. Six national parks, twenty-eight national monuments, two national recreation areas, and many state parks and national forests are concentrated here.

Much of the visual attraction of the Southwest cannot be preserved in parks; it adheres in endless stretches of unfettered land, open, clear blue skies, breathtaking mountain vistas, and sparkling clean, clear air. Extensive and/or insensitive energy development may threaten these values. The Southwest is arid, and the large water use involved in energy development raises serious problems. As Utah's governor states, "In the West if you touch water you touch everything." The social vulnerability of the Four Corners states is nearly as great as the physical. The area contains large numbers of poor people, who may or may not profit by development. The region contains several indigenous cultures including Mormons and American Indians, which are important to the value of national diversity and which can be severely affected by development.

Among the institutions positioned to understand and shape future energy development and environmental and social values are state legislatures. The legislatures' strongest claim to the right to address these issues springs from the direct election of their members by those who live in the four states. More than any other governmental institution, state legislatures have the potential to reflect the preferences of voters on many of the determinative issues for the region. This chapter examines whether the attitudes of state legislators on energy and environmental issues are responsive to those of the voters. Congruence between voters' opinions and representatives' opinions is one indicator of representation. This chapter will examine how accurately the opinions expressed by voters are mirrored in the preferences of state legislators. Where the differences between

13

opinions of voters and legislators emerge, they will be explained by an analysis of the linkage mechanisms that transmit cues to legislators about voter preferences. However, as Hanna Pitkin illustrates in her book on the subject, representation is too complex to be captured by simply measuring congruence. She concludes that representation means acting in the interest of the represented. Pitkin counsels that when voters and their representatives disagree, we should look to the substance of the disagreement and determine why they disagree and which position is right.[1] The final section of the chapter will consider more broadly the meaning of representation in the context of energy and environmental policy making in the Four Corners states.

Data

The data come from a larger study of legislators and voters in the Four Corners states. A sample of fifty voters, stratified according to party registration, were selected from all registered voters in each state legislative district; questionnaires covering a number of policy issues were mailed to each voter. Repeated mailings resulted in a response rate of over 70 percent of all deliverable mail. A similar written questionnaire was given to state senators in each of the states as well as followup personal interviews. These data were collected during 1975 in Arizona and New Mexico and before the 1976 election in Colorado and Utah. Some questions were asked in only two states. Only responses from state senators are reported.

Energy Development

The responses for voters and legislators to a variety of questions (reported on later) indicate that both are generally in favor of energy development with a larger proportion of legislators than voters taking prodevelopment positions. For instance, a strong commitment exists for funding energy research and development. Table 2-1 indicates that a majority of all categories favor greater expenditures on energy research and development; senators in all states but Colorado are more generous than the voters. A high level of agreement is also displayed by Colorado and Utah voters and senators toward encouraging oil shale development, the technology of which has not yet been demonstrated economically feasible. Large unexploited oil shale fields exist in Utah and Colorado. A majority of all voters and senators are in favor of going ahead, senators responding more positively than voters. (See table 2-2.)

While it is one thing for voters and senators to support energy research and development in general and oil shale development in particular, it is something else for them to back concrete energy projects having specific costs. Our survey

Table 2-1
Voter and State Senator Opinions on Energy Research and Development Spending
(percent)

Legislature Should Spend	Arizona		New Mexico		Colorado		Utah	
	Voters (n=1,433)	*State Senators (n=23)*	*Voters (n=2,019)*	*State Senators (n=23)*	*Voters (n=1,680)*	*State Senators (n=28)*	*Voters (n=1,374)*	*State Senators (n=21)*
Less	5.0	4.3	7.7	17.4	7.0	10.7	6.2	9.5
Same	29.5	21.7	34.3	8.7	37.5	35.7	36.3	9.5
More	65.5	73.9	58.0	73.9	55.5	53.6	57.5	81.0

Table 2-2
Voter and State Senator Opinions on Encouragement of Oil-Shale Development
(percent)

	Colorado		Utah	
	Voters *(n=1,695)*	*State Senators* *(n=28)*	*Voters* *(n=1,399)*	*State Senators* *(n=21)*
Strongly agree	13.6	21.4	22.4	33.3
Agree	41.4	57.1	54.9	61.9
Not sure	29.9	7.1	11.5	0.0
Disagree	10.7	14.3	3.8	4.8
Strongly disagree	4.4	0.0	1.3	0.0

consequently asked a series of questions to reveal the degree of support for specific energy projects where values were thought to conflict. The first issue involved the construction of a large thermal-electric generating station in southern Utah, the Kaiparowits power project. Sponsored by a consortium of public utilities, the Kaiparowits generating station threatened substantial environmental and social impacts. The project generated a great deal of controversy, including a star-studded campaign by environmentalists featuring Robert Redford, who claimed the plant would seriously harm southern Utah. Utah's governor, congressional delegation, and most other officials were vocal in support; but the mayor of Salt Lake City opposed Kaiparowits. In mid-April 1976, four months before our survey, the Secretary of the Interior cancelled the project. Although a majority of Utahans agree with the construction of Kaiparowits, voter responses indicate surprising ambiguity. (See table 2-3.) Large numbers of Colorado voters and a somewhat smaller number of Utah voters indicate they are "not sure." The project was well publicized in area newspapers and other media, but it may be that some respondents were "not sure" because they were not well informed about the issue. More than one in five Utahans opposed the project, although Utah senators were overwhelmingly in favor. Even though Kaiparowits was the most publicized energy issue in the region, most Colorado voters were not sure about it, possibly because there were no clear implications for their state. More Colorado senators approved than disapproved the project; but as was the case with Colorado voters, many were not sure.

Few nuclear power plants currently exist in the Four Corners states, but the issue of nuclear power has received considerable national debate. A referendum requiring stringent safeguards for nuclear power plants was defeated in Colorado and Arizona in 1976 by a division close to that found in our survey conducted before the elections.[2] Table 2-4 shows that while a number of the voters are "not sure," most voters and senators agree that the possible benefits from a nuclear power plant far outweigh the possible hazards. The intensity of agreement differs from state to state, but the proportion of senators who agree

Table 2-3
Voter and State Senator Opinions on Construction of Kaiparowits
Power Project
(percent)

	Colorado		Utah	
	Voters *(n=1,637)*	*State Senators* *(n=10)*	*Voters* *(n=1,400)*	*State Senators* *(n=26)*
Agree	19.7	60.0	50.8	96.2
Not sure	69.4	40.0	26.0	0.0
Disagree	10.9	0.0	23.2	3.8

are fairly representative of the voters. Small percentages of opponents among voters are overrepresented in Arizona and underrepresented in Utah.

All recipes for energy development (thermal electric, nuclear electric, coal gassification, oil shale) include "add water" in their instructions. We asked voters and senators the following question in our questionnaire: "Water use is also an issue of importance in our area. Indeed, the Southwest may eventually have to set priorities among various water users. In your opinion, should each of the following users get *more,* the *same* or *less* water in the future." A list of water users was presented, including electrical energy productions. Table 2-5 displays voter and senator opinion concerning future water allocation for energy. Although only the Utah Senate has an absolute majority that prefers giving energy more water in the future, a substantial proportion of voters and senators in all four states take this position. With the exception of Arizona, more senators than voters prefer more for energy, and Utah senators express greater support toward more water for energy than their constituents. Although these responses would seem to indicate strong support for giving more water to energy, interpretation should be made with the understanding that energy, at present, uses a very small amount of water. For instance, thermal-electric power's use of water represents less than 3 percent of total depletion in any of the four states.[3] Water consumption figures would increase dramatically if energy resources were actually developed.

Adverse Consequences of Development

The foregoing data indicate that voters and, even more strongly, legislators favor energy development; however, responses to other survey questions indicate that both groups of respondents are also concerned with adverse effects of energy production. The strip mining of western coal is essential for the region's energy development; yet it has severe land-use, water-use, and environmental implica-

Table 2-4
Voter and State Senator Opinions that Nuclear Power Plant Benefits Outweigh Hazards
(percent)

	Arizona		New Mexico		Colorado		Utah	
	Voters (n=1,438)	State Senators (n=23)	Voters (n=2,038)	State Senators (n=24)	Voters (n=1,675)	State Senators (n=28)	Voters (n=1,398)	State Senators (n=21)
Strongly agree	25.6	17.4	15.1	25.0	18.6	25.0	17.1	9.5
Agree	29.8	34.8	34.6	50.0	30.7	28.6	33.1	52.4
Not sure	31.5	21.7	36.6	8.3	35.3	35.7	33.6	33.3
Disagree	8.7	13.0	8.2	12.5	9.8	3.6	13.5	0.0
Strongly disagree	4.4	13.0	5.4	4.2	5.5	7.1	2.7	4.8

Table 2-5
Voter and State Senator Opinions on Allocation of Water for Energy
(percent)

	Arizona		New Mexico		Colorado		Utah	
	Voters *(n=1,396)*	*State Senators* *(n=22)*	*Voters* *(n=1,992)*	*State Senators* *(n=22)*	*Voters* *(n=1,646)*	*State Senators* *(n=25)*	*Voters* *(n=1,348)*	*State Senators* *(n=20)*
More	42.3	31.8	33.0	40.9	35.5	36.0	43.1	75.0
Same	45.2	50.0	50.1	54.5	50.5	44.0	43.2	20.0
Less	6.3	9.1	5.1	0.0	4.5	4.0	4.9	0.0
No opinion	6.2	9.1	11.8	4.5	9.5	16.0	8.9	5.0

tions. A national strip mine reclamation act, requiring land to be returned to its approximate original condition after stripping—which involves substantial costs— had been debated in the West for several years prior to our survey. Table 2-6 shows little agreement on the issue. Many voters are "not sure." Whereas substantial percentages of voters and senators see strip mining as "not serious" or "no problem," as many or more see it as a "serious" or "very serious" problem. Only in Utah do those not concerned with the problem outnumber those who are concerned. Proportions differ slightly and fewer are "not sure," but senators feel much as the voters do about strip mining.

Boomtowns, with their accompanying shortages of services and demands on taxpayers, are a potential hazard of energy and other resource development.[4] We asked our Colorado and Utah respondents how serious a problem boomtowns were. (See table 2-7.) The data indicate that only Utah senators see potential boomtowns as a very serious hazard. A larger proportion of voters see the problem as not very serious than do those who see it as serious. Senators are as or more concerned about boomtowns than voters.

The real test of how concerned voters and senators are about adverse consequences of energy development comes when they are forced to make tradeoffs among competing values. Voters and senators in all four states were asked whether or not they agreed with the statement: "We should be willing to accept more air and water pollution in order to insure plentiful supplies of energy." The responses to the question are reported in table 2-8. A majority of all groups except the New Mexico and Utah senators do not feel that energy is worth more pollution. Senators in all states are more willing to accept increased pollution as a price for energy than are voters; but there are fewer senators in Arizona and Colorado who are more willing than unwilling. The percentages of voters who disagree with environmental sacrifices are large, even in Utah, where they are committed to such projects as Kaiparowits.

Data presented in table 2-5 indicate that voters and especially senators are willing to allocate additional water supplies to energy. This finding should not be interpreted to mean that voters and senators are in favor of making other users sacrifice. Irrigated agriculture currently uses more than 80 percent of the total water consumption in the Four Corners states. With cities, industries, Indian tribes, recreation, and other users all making claims for additional water, demand is pressing close on supply in the arid Southwest. It seems unlikely that without the construction of many additional expensive water projects development could significantly expand without cutting into the water supplies available to irrigated agriculture. Yet, when we asked our voter samples to allocate more, less, or the same amount of water to agriculture in the future, voters generally want agriculture to receive an even greater share of water. In all four states voters support agriculture more strongly than energy. The difference between percentages of voters saying more for agriculture and more for energy was 4.5 in Arizona, 27.9 in New Mexico, 23.5 in Colorado, and 24.3 in Utah.

Table 2-6
Voter and State Senator Opinions about Seriousness of Strip Mining
(percent)

	Arizona		New Mexico		Colorado		Utah	
	Voters *(n=1,447)*	*State Senators* *(n=24)*	*Voters* *(n=2,040)*	*State Senators* *(n=24)*	*Voters* *(n=1,672)*	*State Senators* *(n=28)*	*Voters* *(n=1,393)*	*State Senators* *(n=21)*
Very serious	16.0	33.3	13.4	25.0	16.3	14.3	7.3	0.0
Serious	25.1	29.2	21.2	20.8	25.8	32.1	15.8	19.0
Not sure	31.6	4.2	36.8	16.7	31.9	7.1	38.0	14.3
Not very serious	17.2	20.8	19.2	29.2	20.1	39.3	29.0	38.1
No problem	10.1	12.5	9.5	8.3	6.0	7.1	9.9	28.6

Table 2-7
Voter and State Senator Opinions on Seriousness of Boomtowns
(percent)

	Colorado		Utah	
	Voters *(n=1,674)*	*State Senators* *(n=35)*	*Voters* *(n=1,391)*	*State Senators* *(n=29)*
Very serious	6.6	10.7	5.2	9.5
Serious	17.1	53.6	15.2	42.9
Not sure	36.4	10.7	28.4	14.3
Not very serious	26.1	25.0	52.7	23.8
No problem	13.8	0.0	18.5	9.5

More water for agriculture receives considerably less support from senators than voters in the Four Corners states. Senators are more likely to want to give the same rather than more water to agriculture in the future. However only in Arizona do substantial numbers of senators, although less than half those interviewed, favor reallocating water away from agriculture so that it would receive less in the future. In comparison with the voters, senators are more generous in their allocation of supplies to energy relative to agriculture. The difference between the percentage of senators responding more water for agriculture and more water for energy was −10.1 in Arizona, 2.0 in New Mexico, 8.0 in Colorado, and −40.0 in Utah. Whereas agriculture gets more support than energy in New Mexico and Colorado, the percentage differences are much smaller among senators than among voters. In Arizona and Utah, senators are more supportive of energy than agriculture.

Taken together, the data on voters' and senators' preferences for water allocation indicate that they are for allocating more water to energy as long as irrigated agriculture does not have to sacrifice. There is little public or legislator support, except in the Arizona senate, for forcing agriculture to cut back. Senators tend to be more sympathetic than voters to energy development claims for additional water resources; but this stand is taken in the context of agriculture's continuing large share of water use.

Voters, and to a lesser extent senators, appear to be unwilling to accept many costs associated with energy development. This unwillingness to sacrifice is particularly marked when associated with energy to be exported outside the Four Corners area. We asked our respondents whether they agreed with the statement: "This state should not permit environmental damage in order to produce energy for use in other states." (See table 2-9). Decided majorities of voters in every state and a majority of senators in all states but Utah are unwilling to see their states used as energy resource colonies if it means environmental damage.

Table 2-8
Voter and State Senator Opinions Accepting More Pollution for More Energy
(percent)

| | Arizona | | New Mexico | | Colorado | | Utah | |
	Voters (n=1,439)	State Senators (n=23)	Voters (n=2,033)	State Senators (n=23)	Voters (n=1,705)	State Senators (n=28)	Voters (n=1,403)	State Senators (n=21)
Strongly agree	5.4	4.3	6.0	0.0	3.8	0.0	3.8	4.8
Agree	19.4	21.7	21.8	43.5	15.8	21.4	22.2	42.9
Not sure	13.3	17.4	17.9	4.3	13.1	10.7	15.3	23.8
Disagree	43.1	43.5	39.7	34.8	45.8	67.9	44.3	28.6
Strongly disagree	18.8	13.0	14.5	17.4	21.4	0.0	14.5	0.0

Table 2-9
Voter and State Senator Opinions against Environmental Damage for Supply of Outside State Energy Needs
(percent)

	Arizona		New Mexico		Colorado		Utah	
	Voters (n=1,442)	*State Senators* (n=23)	*Voters* (n=2,043)	*State Senators* (n=23)	*Voters* (n=1,692)	*State Senators* (n=28)	*Voters* (n=1,397)	*State Senators* (n=21)
Strongly agree	31.2	26.1	34.5	26.1	27.4	17.9	22.8	4.8
Agree	37.9	47.8	36.5	34.8	36.6	32.1	37.1	23.8
Not sure	14.4	8.7	14.4	0.0	16.7	21.4	17.7	4.8
Disagree	13.5	13.0	11.5	39.1	17.0	25.0	20.1	61.9
Strongly disagree	3.0	4.3	3.1	0.0	2.3	3.6	2.3	4.8

Responsiveness on Energy and Environment Issues

Hanna Pitkin suggests that where legislators are responsive, they and their constituents agree generally on issues.[5] Our data on senators' and voters' attitudes about energy development in the Four Corners states shows that, in general, both are in favor of developing the rich energy resources in the region. Both senators and voters are also concerned with some of the adverse impacts associated with energy development. When asked to weigh energy development against other values, both revealed a reluctance to accept more air and water pollution, especially if the energy produced were to be used outside the state. Within the framework of general agreement, however, there emerged some significant differences in the commitment with which positions were held. Senators tended to express stronger support than voters for promoting energy development by spending more on research and development and developing oil shale technology. Legislators favored the controversial Kaiparowits project by much larger percentages than did voters. In addition, senators were more favorable to larger allocations of water to electrical energy production, which is in competition with other users including irrigated agriculture. Both voters and senators tended to agree that some energy-related difficulties, such as the hazards of nuclear energy boomtowns, were not great enough to stop development. Both showed ambivalence about the seriousness of strip mining. However a larger proportion of senators than voters were willing to accept environmental damage, including air and water pollution, for energy supplies. The data suggest, particularly in Utah, that senators are stronger proponents of energy development than their constituents, especially when faced with associated environmental costs. The next section explores the mechanisms linking senators to their constituents to help explain why the opinions of senators diverge somewhat from constituents on energy and environmental issues.

Legislator Responsiveness and the Operation of Linkages

Norman Luttbeg conceives of the process of representation as occurring through "linkages" that political leaders have with the wants, needs, and demands of the public. Such linkages include legislator-citizen belief sharing, role playing, and interest groups.[6] Kenneth Godwin and W. Bruce Shepard have argued that linkage mechanisms should not be considered as direct determinants of public policy but rather as mediating, modifying variables that more or less accurately facilitate the translation of public preferences into legislative actions.[7] The operation of linkages can be impeded under some circumstances and on some issues; and information legislators receive about citizen preferences can be distorted. The differences we have found between citizens' and legislators' opinions on energy and environmental issues may be due to the way linkages operate on these issues.

Responsiveness of legislators to constituents is sometimes built in through belief sharing. Legislators do not take cues from some external medium that informs them about constituency opinion; they simply know what it is. Legislator and constituent alike hold the same opinion because of common socialization experiences, exposure to the same news media, and like reasoning processes. Warren Miller and Donald Stokes explained their findings that congressmen agreed more closely with constituents on civil rights issues than on social welfare or foreign policy because the highly salient, emotionally charged, polarized issue allowed congressmen to perceive constituency opinion more accurately.[8] It follows that belief sharing as a linkage mechanism is likely to work less well on issues that are not highly salient. It also seems reasonable that legislators are less likely to share voters' opinions about issues when they do not agree with voters about the importance of the issue. When legislators evaluate the priority of an issue as an agenda item differently than do voters, it is more likely that legislators will also differ from voters in their opinion of how the issue should be handled.[9] It may be that the salience of energy and environmental issues and the different priorities given to them by legislators and voters affects the responsiveness of legislators through belief sharing.

We asked each of our voters and state senators to list in an open-ended format the three most important problems facing their individual states. Responses were coded and classified into seventeen broad issues. The various issues were then ranked for our two samples based on the proportion of respondents mentioning each issue. Table 2-10 shows the rankings of energy and natural resources and the environment among seventeen issue areas given some priority by voters and legislators. Table 2-10 indicates some real difference in the salience of the two issues as well as differences between what voters and senators believe are important problems. Natural resources and the environment are top priority problems for voters in three states, while senators in all four states give these problems only a moderate ranking. Voters mentioned energy as an

Table 2-10
Agenda Rankings of Energy and Natural Resources and the Environment among Seventeen Issues

| | Rank on Agenda | | | | | | | |
| | Arizona | | New Mexico | | Colorado | | Utah | |
	Voters	State Senators	Voters	State Senators	Voters	State Senators	Voters	State Senators
Energy	14	14	11	3.5a	9	4.5	11	1.5
Natural resources & environment	3	9	6	5.5	1	6.5	2	8.5

a.5 rankings result from pairs.

important issue much less often than natural resources and the environment. In contrast, senators mention energy as an important problem more often than environment and natural resources in all states but Arizona. These data indicate that impediments exist to simple belief sharing as a linkage between voters and legislators on these issues. There is not a common perception that these issues are highly salient; and senators' different evaluations of the importance of issues may well lead legislators to hold substantive opinions different from those of their constituents.

Political parties may serve as linkage mechanisms between voters and legislators on issues. When differences among voters on issues coincide with differences in their party identification, legislators can know constituents' opinions on issues by learning their party loyalties. Further, widely held preferences among the rank and file are likely to generate political activity that will put pressure on legislators who are party members to act in accord with the party stand. However party cannot perform this linkage function effectively when issues do not divide voters along party lines. Indeed if legislators see issues in partisan terms while their constituents do not, party as a linkage mechanism may somewhat mislead legislators about voter attitudes. Therefore, a reasonable test of the working of party as a linkage in the Four Corners states is the extent to which Republican and Democratic voters' and senators' opinions on energy and environmental issues divide along party lines.

Table 2-11 shows correlations between voters' and senators' opinions on selected energy and environmental issues. It indicates that voters at large do not link their opinions on energy and environmental issues with their association to political parties. Concern about the environment and the weight given environmental quality in a tradeoff with energy development would seem to transcend voters' partisan beliefs. Thus, cleavages between energy-oriented and environmentalist attitudes among Four Corners voters cut along a dimension other than party.

Much of the political science literature suggests that elites are much more likely than the mass to see issues in partisan and ideological terms.[10] Indeed, table 2-11 shows senators in Arizona and Colorado dividing along partisan lines on some energy and environmental issues; however the relationship is scattered and not uniformly robust. The relationship of partisanship to attitudes all but disappears when we examine New Mexico and Utah. Evidently the extent to which energy and environmental issues are important to state legislators is situational. Where parties are important to state legislatures as they are in Arizona and Colorado, senators differ with each other on these issues according to party membership. However, where party is weak as in New Mexico (which is a one-party state) or as in Utah (where voters do not register according to party and parties play a small role in decisions), senators do not associate party with the stands they take on energy and environmental issues.

Our data suggest that there are serious blocks in the linkage of political

Table 2-11
Correlations (Tau *b* and Tau *c*) between State Senator and Voter Attitudes on Issues and Party

| | Arizona | | New Mexico | | Colorado | | Utah | |
Issue	Voters	State Senators	Voters	State Senators	Voters	State Senators	Voters	State Senators
Seriousness of strip mining	.18	.59	.04	.15	.10	.54	.06	.05
Oil shale production					.07	.30	−.02	.17
Pollution for energy	.06	.61	−.04	.24	.05	.21	−.01	−.08
Nuclear benefits outweigh hazards	.16	.41	.07	.15	.15	.46	.11	.22
Damage for outside energy	.06	.16	.05	.35	.10	.55	.03	−.03

party impeding the flow of accurate cues to legislators about energy and environmental preferences of constituents. In no state do voters see these issues in partisan terms, and partisanship plays a role only in the Arizona and Colorado senates. Even in these two states where partisanship is relevant, senators seem to be reacting to the partisanship of their legislative system rather than to preferences of constituents. It is even possible that senators' partisan allegiances may make them less sensitive to voter preferences, since voters see energy and the environment in other than partisan terms.

Some researchers have identified role as an important linkage between representatives and their constituents.[11] When legislators see themselves as trustees they are likely to follow what they think is right in making up their minds on issues. When legislators see themselves as delegates, they are motivated to seek out and follow constituency wishes even if they may personally disagree. Investigators have generally found little or no relation between what role legislators say they prefer and what action they take.[12] However little attention has been given to the possibility that legislators may play different roles in different issue areas.

Legislators are much more likely to follow their own opinion when they feel strongly about an issue. When legislators have a strong sense of what is the right thing to do—based on their experiences or expertise—they are likely to act on their convictions whatever the stand of their districts.[13] In our interviews with senators we asked what they would do if they favored a hypothetical bill but their constituency seemed against it. Most senators were not willing to give a blanket response but instead explained that it would depend on the issue and the circumstances. Expertise was the most frequently cited reason given by senators for following their own opinion on an issue. They preferred to follow their own opinion when they had more information on the issue than their constituents and were better able to judge the merits of the particular bill. It would follow then that the more numerous the legislators who believe they are experts in energy and environment, the greater the obstacles to playing the delegate role.

Senators interviewed in our survey were asked to name the areas in which they felt they were experts or had some expertise. Over 90 percent of the senators in Arizona, Colorado, and Utah were willing to claim expertise in at least one subject area. Of the senators in New Mexico, 75 percent were willing to do so. The general subjects of energy and the environment, exclusive of water and natural resources not mentioned in the specific context of energy or natural resources, were mentioned only thirteen times. Six legislators claimed to have expertise in energy. It would not seem, therefore, that few legislators were insensitive to external cues because their expert knowledge dictated their positions on these issues. Clearly, Four Corners state legislators are open to outside influences.

Interest groups are another possible linkage mechanism between legislators and constituents. Groups are likely to be especially influential on issues of lesser salience when legislators lack intuitive, belief-sharing knowledge of constituent attitudes, when partisanship is not strongly relevant to decisions at hand, and when legislators lack special expertise. Groups are apt to be most active on issues over which their members maintain cohesion or have some agreement.[14] Ted Lowi predicts that interest group politics is likely to dominate regulatory policy making.[15] Government intervention in energy development to protect environmental quality is likely to be regulatory. For these reasons the operation of interest groups as a linkage between voters and legislators on energy and environmental issues may be important.

Our questionnaire provided voters with a list of groups including environmentalists as well as development-oriented ones such as mining companies, railroads, utilities, banks and business, and land developers. We asked voters "which of these groups, if any, do you associate with, identify with, or feel close to?" We then correlated identity with environmental or developmental groups and attitudes toward some of the energy and environmental issues in our survey. The results are presented in table 2-12. Whereas there is considerable variation in how divisive different issues are between the two groups, many of the correlations are quite robust. Voters divide much more sharply along interest group lines than they do along party lines, as evidenced by the much lower correlations in table 2-11. Logic suggests that such differences of opinion would generate lively group conflict with competitive lobbying of legislators.

As a number of authors have suggested, interest groups may be quite inaccurate translators of public opinion. The differences between environmental and developmental groups and the divisions that exist among all voters at large, on some issues, may affect the accuracy of the cues that interest group opinion alone may give to state legislators. Environmental and developmental interest groups may transmit to legislators wide differences of opinion that do not really exist among voters at large. Insofar as legislators depend on the views of members of conflicting interest groups to portray voter opinion, they may not get an accurate picture. For example, environmental and developmental groups divide much more sharply on the issue of the Kaiparowits power plant construction and, in Colorado, on oil shale development than do voters at large.

Table 2-12
Correlations (Tau c) between Identity with Environment or Development Groups and Attitudes on Issues

Issue	Arizona	New Mexico	Colorado	Utah
Seriousness of strip mining	.35	.57	.50	.42
Oil shale encouraged			.52	.29
More pollution for energy	.22	.47	.19	.33
Nuclear benefits outweigh hazards	.37	.31	.26	.28
Damage for energy in other states	.17	.19	.32	.34
Kaiparowits built			.45	.57

Environmental and developmental interest groups as linkage mechanisms between voters and legislators may cause translation errors for additional reasons, many of which are difficult to explore with our survey data. Group leaders may poorly reflect the opinions of rank-and-file members. Some groups may have resources, including money and expertise, that give them influence out of proportion to the strength their point of view commands in public opinion.

Access to legislators is an important determinant of group influence; it is possible for some groups to have better access than they might deserve if only the support of their views in public opinion were taken into account. Legislators may be more willing to listen to and be influenced by groups that they agree with. The general attitude of state senators toward the environment and environmentalists was tapped in two ways in our surveys. The interviewer was asked to characterize each senator's general reaction to the terms "environmental quality" and "environmentalists" after the entire interview was over. Senators were also categorized according to the general solution they personally would favor for the problem of economic development versus environmental quality. The results are displayed in table 2-13.

The data presented in table 2-13 are consistent with our findings that senators tend to be more development-oriented than voters. That Arizona's senators are more and Utah senators far less sympathetic to environmentalists could have been anticipated. The reader may recollect that Arizona senators tended to be more concerned about the hazards of nuclear energy and less willing to give more water to energy than their constituents. They were also more likely to see strip mining as more serious than the senators of any other state. Through their responses to nearly all questions, Utah senators revealed themselves to favor development strongly.

The mediating, modifying effect of belief sharing, political parties, role playing and particularly interest-group linkages reviewed in this section of the chapter have helped explain why Four Corners state senators are somewhat more favorable than their constituents to energy development. It must be emphasized, however, that the differences we found between voters and senators were not large. Further, responsiveness as Pitkin defined it has meaning beyond simple congruence of opinion between voters and legislators.

Table 2-13
Arizona and New Mexico State Senator Attitudes toward Environmentalists
(percent)

Attitude	Arizona (n=27)	New Mexico (n=28)	Colorado (n=36)	Utah (n=26)
Generally positive	55.6	22.2	35.7	11.5
Generally neutral	18.5	47.2	28.6	42.3
Generally negative	25.9	30.6	35.7	46.2

Responsiveness and Leadership

Whether a representative acts in the interest of the represented is Pitkin's criterion of representation. In the final analysis, the opinion of the voters probably must be taken as the most accurate reflection of the public interest and the most conclusive test of representation. However, in the short run there may be a distinction between what is in the interests of voters and what they say they want.[16] Our data indicate that voters have conflicting values about energy and the environment and are not aware of or reconciled to the tradeoffs that may be necessary. On the one hand, voters wish to proceed with oil shale development that may be an environmentally costly technology; on the other hand, they are not willing to accept more air and water pollution as the price of plentiful supplies of energy. Voters wish to give more water to energy and yet strongly believe that agriculture should maintain or increase its lion's share of scarce water resources. At a time when the nation is looking to the West for energy supplies to offset Arab oil imports, the position of Four Corners voters that environmental damage should not be allowed in developing energy sources for other states may be unrealistic.

The patterns of congruence between legislators' and voters' opinions need to be interpreted in the context of the issues in question. Whereas the ultimate test of legislative responsiveness may be congruence with voters, legislators may now and again believe that they see voters' interests better than the voters themselves and that, given time, events, and information, voters will come to have a more refined perception of their own interests. When legislators differ from voters on our survey questions they often express somewhat more consistent and perhaps more realistic views than the voters do of what may be feasible in energy development and environmental quality in the West.

The failure of legislators to mirror with complete accuracy voter opinion on energy and environmental issues cannot be taken as ipso facto unresponsiveness. It may mean only that legislators are engaged in a leadership function encouraging voters to reevaluate issues. Our analysis of the operation of linkages raises some important questions for how well legislators may perform this leadership function. The small number of legislators who claimed expertise in the energy and environmental fields combined with the dominance of interest groups in transmitting cues in these issue areas do not indicate that legislators are exercising policy leadership. Four Corners state legislators may lack the personal understanding and command of energy and environment issues necessary to make judgments that are truly responsive to the interests of the represented. Such policy leadership evolves from a commitment to affect the issues and a reliance on balanced sources of information in deciding which policies to pursue.

Summary

This chapter has examined the responsiveness of Four Corners state senators on energy and environmental issues. The major findings deal with the attitudes of state senators and voters toward energy and environmental issues, differences between voter and official opinions, and the responsiveness of state senators to their constituencies.

State senator attitudes generally reflect those of the voters in favoring energy development while being concerned with environmental costs. Senators, especially in some states, are more favorable than voters toward energy development and more willing to make environmental sacrifices.

The differences that do exist between legislator and voter opinions can be explained by the operation of linkage mechanisms. Voter and legislator belief sharing on energy and environmental issues may not translate citizen preferences accurately, because these issues are not highly salient for both groups and there is not close agreement on priorities. Political parties may not be operative transmitters of accurate cues about energy and environmental issues, because voter opinions on these issues do not divide along party lines. Also, the number of legislators with expertise in energy and the environment adopting a "trustee" role is small.

Since voter opinion does not divide along party lines, interest groups may serve an important linkage function on these issues, because voter opinions divide along the lines of the groups with which they identify. However, interest groups may translate citizen attitudes to legislators with some important errors.

Responsiveness goes beyond simple congruence between voter and senator opinions. The voters' conflicting desires for energy development and environmental quality will be difficult for government to resolve. Responsiveness in a broader sense will require leadership in formulating policies in the interests of the represented and in encouraging voters to hold more realistic and consistent opinions. How well legislators perform the leadership function is also related to the linkage mechanisms and cues to which legislators are receptive. Lack of expertise on energy and the environment among legislators and attentiveness to interest group cues—especially if biased toward some particular interest—may not be conducive to broad responsiveness to citizen interests.

Notes

1. Hanna Pitkin, *The Concept of Representation* (Berkeley and Los Angeles, Calif.: University of California Press, 1967), pp. 109, 214.

2. The pronuclear position in Colorado received 70.9 percent of the vote, and our survey data indicated that 76.3 percent of respondents (recoded to omit "not sures") felt the possible benefits outweigh the hazards. In Arizona, the corresponding percentages were 70.1 and 80.8.

3. U.S. Department of the Interior, *Westwide Study Report On Critical Water Problems Facing the Eleven Western States,* Washington, D.C., April 1975, table II-31, p. 47.

4. B.C. Ives, W.D. Schulze, D.S. Brookshire, "Boomtown Impacts of Energy Development in the Lake Powell Region," *Lake Powell Research Project*

Bulletin No. 28 (Los Angeles: University of California at Los Angeles, Institute of Geophysics and Planetary Physics, 1976).

5. Pitkin, *Concept of Representation*, p. 165.

6. Norman Luttbeg, ed., *Public Opinion and Public Policy: Model of Political Linkage* (Homewood, Ill.: Dorsey Press, 1974), p. 4.

7. Kenneth Godwin and W. Bruce Shepard, "Political Process and Public Expenditures: A Re-examination Based on Theories of Representative Government," *American Political Review* 70 (December 1976):1129.

8. Warren E. Miller and Donald Stokes, "Constituency Influence on Congress," *The American Political Science Review* 57 (1963):51.

9. Susan B. Hansen argues a correlary proposition that when citizens and leaders tend to agree that a certain issue is (or is not) salient, the correlation between political factors and citizen-leader agreement on that issue should be zero. See "Linkage Models, Issues, and Community Politics," *American Politics Quarterly* 6 (January 1978):7.

10. Sidney Verba and Norman Nie, *Participation in America: Political Democracy and Social Equality* (New York: Harper and Row, 1972); Philip Converse, "The Nature of Belief Systems in the Mass Public," in David Apter, ed., *Ideology and Discontent* (Glencoe, Ill.: Free Press, 1964), pp. 206-256, reprinted in Luttbeg, *Public Opinion and Public Policy*, p. 314.

11. John C. Wahlke et al., *The Legislative System* (New York: John Wiley and Sons, 1962).

12. Ronald D. Hedlund, "Legislative Socialization and Role Orientation: A Study of the Iowa Legislature" (Ph.D. diss., University of Iowa, 1967); Ronald D. Hedlund and H. Paul Friesema, "Representatives' Perceptions of Constituency Opinion," *Journal of Politics* 34 (August 1972):730-752; H. Paul Friesema and Ronald D. Hedlund, "The Reality of Representational Roles," in Luttbeg, *Public Opinions and Public Policy*, pp. 413-417; Malcolm E. Jewell, "Attitudinal Determinants of Legislative Behavior: The Utility of Role Analysis," in Allan Kornberg and Lloyd D. Musolf, eds., *Legislatures in Developmental Perspective* (Durham, N.C.: Duke University Press, 1970), pp. 460-461.

13. Leroy Rieselbach, "Congressional Responsiveness: An Approach to Some Speculation" (Paper prepared for delivery to the Western Political Science Association, Phoenix, Ariz., March 31-April 7, 1971), p. 13.

14. David B. Truman, *The Governmental Process: Political Interests and Public Opinion* (New York: Alfred Knopf, 1955), p. 159.

15. Theodore J. Lowi, "American Business, Public Policy, Case Studies and Political Theory," *World Politics* 16 (July 1964):688.

16. Our argument here is compatible with that of Heinz Eulau and Paul D. Karps, who suggest that responsiveness is more complex than can be captured by simple measures of congruence. See "The Puzzle of Representation: Specifying Components of Responsiveness," *Legislative Studies Quarterly* 11 (August 1977).

3

Energy Reorganization Legislation in Illinois: Agency and Clientele Influence

Albert J. Nelson, Kenneth E. Mitchell, and *Leon S. Cohen*

Introduction

This chapter explores the political conflict surrounding attempts to reorganize energy-related functions in Illinois. The General Assembly, surprisingly, initiated the first substantive responses to the current state debate concerning energy development and conservation in Governor James Thompson's administration. As might be expected, the reorganization of state agencies was bound to affect a large number of disparate private interests associated with their services. In this potentially explosive environment, the legislature, which is also divided into different vested interests, sought to change the ongoing power relationships. The negotiation surrounding reorganization was not visible to the public and generally seemed low-key. This public view of the issue was misleading—the conflict among vested interests, agencies, and legislators was extremely intense and caused reorganization to fail.

Historical Context

In 1976 and 1977, the Illinois Energy Resource Commission (IERC), a legislative body created in 1974 whose primary concern was coal development, conceived a comprehensive plan to reorganize energy-related functions in Illinois. This was not an entirely new idea, since other political figures had considered some change in government structure necessary in this field. In 1975, Governor Dan Walker proposed the creation of an Illinois Energy Agency. His proposal would have removed the Division of Energy (DOE) from the Department of Business and Economic Development. The new agency would have operated independently with broad authority. However, the plan met with legislative hostility and was defeated in both 1975 and 1976.

An earlier version of this chapter was presented at the 1978 Annual Meeting of the Midwest Political Science Association, Chicago, Illinois, April 20-22 and is part of an enlarged monograph supported and published by the Illinois Legislative Studies Center, Sangamon State University, Springfield, Illinois.

While the IERC was formulating its proposal in 1976, the future governor-elect, James Thompson, was making extensive promises in his campaign that energy reorganization would be important in his administration. This promise of action and the action of the IERC reflected the necessity of solving organizational problems in energy management. Very simply, the administration of energy-related functions in Illinois was a decentralized web of twenty uncoordinated departments, agencies, and commissions. This structure represented a confused pattern of authority over natural resource development (particularly coal-mining and strip-mining reclamation), environmental protection, utility regulation, and energy efficiency standards in construction codes. The management of these areas was characterized by extensive duplication of effort and conflicting regulations.[1]

Reorganization typically was considered an executive problem, and the governor was expected to set policy goals for change; but Governor Thompson made no specific proposals for reorganization following his election. However the IERC did submit a reorganization plan in 1977. This initial plan envisioned the consolidation of the Department of Conservation, the Department of Mines and Minerals, the Environmental Protection Agency, and several divisions of other agencies into a new Department of Natural Resources.[2] The explicit goal was the coordination of state energy administration in the interest of efficiency. Waste, conflicting regulations, and duplication of effort were to be replaced by a cost-benefit approach. The proposed new department was to maximize the efficient delivery of services to clients while minimizing costs. The manageability of energy-related matters would ideally improve because clear divisions of responsibility and the latest management techniques would make working units within the department accountable for the quality of services delivered. Other evidence of a search for efficiency was also evident.[3]

An additional rationale for such massive reorganization was the desirability of coordinating energy and environmental policy. A public policy-making body—the Energy, Environment and Natural Resources Commission—was recommended in the plan with authority to promulgate all rules and regulations in the area. Separation from political control was the major reason for suggesting its creation. The proposal consequently called for the abolishment of the General Assembly's Energy Resources Commission, and this was in itself a relatively serious item of debate. As one legislator indicated, "A lot of legislators are on legislative commissions and have a vested interest in serving on them. For this reason, any reorganization of legislative commissions in the General Assembly will be extremely difficult."[4]

The plan was drafted into a legislative package, introduced, and referred to the House Select Committee on State Government Organization. There it was summarily dismissed because, as one legislator later explained in floor debate:

Some of us thought [it] was somewhat of a grand plan to create a super agency. On the Select Committee on Government Reorganization we suggested that this was too much at this time. It would be too much for any time [although] there should be a cabinet level department on energy, but at the same time we should not create a new bureaucracy.[5]

One committee member also commented during a hearing that it "essentially abolishes state government and starts all over." This statement reflected the complexity of existing routines in state government: the clients of departments and agencies as well as the administrative units themselves were being threatened. It was clear that such a sweeping reshuffling of power was far too drastic; however the plan did stimulate the development of a second proposal by the House Select Committee.

The counterproposal shifted from a comprehensive to an incremental plan to deal with energy and the environment. The new proposal called for the creation of a Department of Mines and Energy by consolidating only two agencies: the Department of Mines and Minerals (DMM) and the Division of Energy in the Department of Business and Economic Development (DOE/DBED).

This reorganization proposal represented a policy initiative of a clearly incremental nature. Each addition to the final legislative package was segmentally attached following extensive negotiation with the groups affected. This type of "disjointed incrementalism" provided a fertile environment in which agencies and clients (private interest groups) dominated policy choices and eventually defeated the proposal.[6]

Theory: Policy Initiation and the Power Setting

An analysis of a reorganization seeking to centralize the regulation of energy functions must ascertain its potential effects on public and private decision makers. One must recognize that structural change challenges the existing access of private groups to the political arena. The structure of these relationships represents a power setting, which can, in many policy conflicts, control policy initiation.

Policy initiation is a key stage in government decision making, because dominant public and private actors can control the content of government's agenda. Obviously, actors dominating this phase of policy making will seek to formulate policy alternatives acceptable to their own interests in solving public problems.[7] This can be done best if conflict is "privatized"—that is, the negotiation is largely restricted to a power setting including interested legislators, agencies, and their clients.[8]

Focusing on an agency's power setting provides an extremely useful model for examining relationships that control agenda setting. This setting includes a number of important actors: a sovereign (a chief executive or governor), functional and allocational rivals, beneficiaries and sufferers, regulatees, suppliers, and allies.[9] This concept is parallel to Freeman's political "subsystem" or Seidman's "iron triangle" of relationships among an agency, its clients, and legislators. This power setting performs an important role in controlling the government agenda as it affects the member actors' interests.[10]

This framework assumes that there is a near symbiotic relationship between an agency and its clients, particularly where regulatory policy is concerned.[11] This relationship is often identified with a more mature agency. As an agency grows older, it finds that its original allies may lose interest in its function. When this occurs the agency must turn to the regulated to maintain its functional domain and resource allocations. Regulated actors become clients—allies and beneficiaries of agency policy—and will provide crucial support in the agency's conflicts.

The structure of energy organization under these circumstances continues to function as a model of inertia. An agency's services may be wasteful and duplicating, but its support system insures continued operation.

An attempt to establish new lines of authority for state agencies must deal with this power setting. This investigation is essential, since organizational change and the addition of statutory authority to regulate energy-related functions does threaten existing political relationships. This power setting represents strong mutual supports among, for example, legislators with a vested interest in coal development policy; the DMM, which regulated this policy; and the agency's clients, the Coal Operators Association (COA) and the United Mine Workers (UMW). Legislators representing a district dominated by coal interests would probably seek a committee membership in which they could serve these interests. Similarly, a "captive" DMM would seek to provide services to its clients rather than actually trying to regulate them. A good example of DMM services would be to deemphasize action insuring that strip-mining reclamation meets other than client interests. The DMM would also provide legislators with coal-related information while clients could provide a similar service to the agency and legislators, not to mention the electoral muscle they could provide in the legislators' districts.

This triangle is extremely difficult to break or change when legislators with a vested interest in coal development dominate a committee influencing coal development policy. The crucial feature of this political structure is that the agency and its clients have access to it that other groups may not have.[12]

When one views the power setting this way the enormity of the reorganization attempt becomes clear. The problem in Illinois—twenty uncoordinated departments, agencies, and commissions performing duplicating functions—indicates that any structural change will affect a large number of triangles. However one must not assume that all would be alienated by reorganization.

Some subsystems might support the effort, since their agency budgets and authority may increase; others will oppose reorganization because their budgets and authority will decline or be lost. The incremental proposal, unlike the IERC's comprehensive initiative, did not threaten vast change; but the attempt to grant more statutory authority, or shift authority, to increase regulation was still pronounced. These threats led to a final watered-down version of the incremental plan and eventually to its defeat.

Methodology

The use of participant observation requiring involvement in reorganization negotiations was very important to this case study. It was the best method of analysis, since the conflict was privatized. One of the coauthors performed what must be considered the role of a "complete participant."[13] He was entirely involved in writing energy legislation and participated in negotiations among legislators, agency representatives, and private interest groups. During this period his perceptions were recorded daily; and in the best tradition of participant observation, they were fully supplemented by an analysis of events by other participants, by related documents, by floor debates in the legislature, and by roll-call votes.[14] While it is often possible to provide statistical evidence that large interest groups can affect legislative behavior, participant observation represents an attempt to enrich conceptual understanding. One can use the participant's observations to test theoretical assumptions about the behavior of clients and agencies concerning the reorganization proposal.[15] In essence, this case study attempts to provide qualitative information about the positions of different participants, which would otherwise not be available.

Analysis

Our analysis focuses on the two state agencies most affected by the second reorganization proposal: the Department of Mines and Minerals (DMM) and the Division of Energy in the Department of Business and Economic Development (DOE/DBED). These units will be analyzed in terms of their stage in a life cycle, power setting, and client relationships.

The two agencies took very different positions toward the reorganization proposal. The working-unit personnel in DOE/DBED were very favorable toward it. However, administrative personnel in the department with authority over the division were strongly opposed, since the adoption of the proposal would mean the loss of an important segment of the department. The position of DMM toward the proposal can best be characterized as cautious: neither strongly supportive nor strongly opposed. The eventual shifting of DMM toward a mildly negative position was an important factor in the final defeat of the legislation.

By that point in the process, DMM viewed the addition of general energy functions not as an opportunity for greater authority but as a dilution of its more central functions of mining regulation and coal development. The basis of the different positions of the two units should become clearer as this analysis progresses.

Life Cycle

The location of the two agencies within the life-cycle framework clearly distinguishes them. DMM is an old unit, established substantially in its current form in 1919; this would lead all to expect that it had been captured by its clientele by this stage of its life cycle. DOE/DBED, a young agency created in 1974, would be expected to be in a mission-oriented phase. These hypotheses based on life-cycle theories hold up in this case. While the younger DOE/DBED was more eager to concentrate on environmental issues and alternative sources of energy, DMM maintained virtually exclusive interest in coal development.

Differing decision-making processes and relationships to clients also seem to be related to agency age differences. DMM was much more likely to base decisions on a careful analysis of the support of their client groups, such as the United Mine Workers and the Coal Operators Association. Because these two groups opposed each other on many occasions, the department consistently attempted to create a balance between them in its policies, supporting both equally. This support was reciprocated by the two client groups when attacks were made on the department during reorganization efforts.

DOE/DBED, on the other hand, seemed much less concerned about the reaction of constituent groups. For example, the division crusaded for energy conservation programs without basing its position on industry's needs and interests. Although the division is a part of the department, which by its title would be expected to favor business viewpoints and maintain its industry constituency, the department itself was also quite young. It was established in 1965 and had not formed strong industry ties in its short history. It is unclear whether the department itself, let alone the division, had reached what Anthony Downs terms the "initial survival threshold": where the agency is "large enough to render useful services, and old enough to have established routinized relationships with its major clients."[16] Serious attempts were made by members of the legislature in 1977 to deny funding for major programs in tourism and minority enterprises under the department. These attempts were unsuccessful because of extensive personal lobbying by the department's director, but they do indicate something of the precariousness of the department's existence. Again, these trends tend to confirm the law of increasing conservatism. Perhaps as DBED and DOE/DBED grow older, if they are able to survive this initial period, they will establish firmer relations with a broad group of constituents.

Their positions on policy issues may change in the process. Evidence of movement in this direction is that current policy positions of the department are increasingly and avidly probusiness.

Relations to the Chief Executive

Analyzing different relationships to the chief executive is particularly interesting in this case study. Although the governor's impact on actual agency operations at the work level is probably minimal, his influence on major policy decisions can be substantial when issues become publicly salient.[17] One of the traditional functions of the governor is to resolve conflicts between the various agencies under his jurisdiction when normal interaction between them fails to achieve agreement. This may be the case in the energy reorganization attempt; the governor was forced to take a position on the reorganization proposal when conflict both between DMM and DOE/DBED and within DBED emerged.

The governor's role is more complex on closer examination however. Since DMM is a cabinet-level department, it is closer to the authority of the governor, and he could conceivably exercise a greater impact on its operation. The director of the department is also appointed by the governor and serves in his cabinet, which creates a personal channel of communication between them. However the distance between DOE/DBED and the governor is much greater. When conflicts arise the division is directly responsible to administrative personnel within the department. The DBED director also has a more tenuous relationship with the governor, since the agency is less well established. This means that much of the interaction between DBED and the governor goes through the governor's office; that is, it is filtered by staff and advisors serving directly as aides to the governor.

This tenuous relationship is illustrated well by incidents occurring shortly after the shape of the second reorganization proposal developed. DOE personnel, including the division head, supported the proposal, since it would have extended their energy authority in the state generally, even though it would move the division to another department. Their loyalty was to their division and the substance of greater energy-directed activity rather than to DBED. The reaction of the DBED director and other ranking administrative officials was very negative, since the adoption of the proposal would have meant loss of a significant division. The director instructed DOE personnel not to comment on the proposal at all and certainly not to aid it in any way. They ignored instructions. He then discussed the proposal with members of the governor's staff and discovered that they were generally favorable to the proposal. Although this surprised the department director, it did not surprise DOE personnel, since they had already carried on such discussions rather extensively. In fact, members of the governor's staff were working closely with the House Select Committee on State Government Organization pushing the proposal.

Thompson's response was an apparently calculated nonresponse: he decided not to intervene on the director's behalf and allowed his staff's mild support to continue.

In contrast to this maneuvering, DMM personnel did not contact the governor directly or work actively with his staff. Perhaps they felt no need to—that their position was strong enough. However, they did work with the House Select Committee toward revisions in the proposal. Their strong clientele relationships protected them from needing gubernatorial support.

A tenuous relationship with the chief executive can have both positive and negative effects from an agency's perspective. It may limit an agency's accountability to the governor, allowing it to pursue its own goals and programs without interference or direction; however, it also may limit the agency's ability to gain support in crucial situations, as this example illustrates. The effective use of strong support from the chief executive is illustrated by J. Leiper Freeman's study of the federal Bureau of Indian Affairs.[18] The bureau chief was able to gain support directly from President Roosevelt in congressional hearings because of his personal political work for him. In our case, however, it appears that gubernatorial support was not decisive.

Rivals

Other agency power relationships appear more important in explaining this reorganization proposal than relations to the governor. The relationship to rivals seems to be very significant in determining the growth and success of an agency and is particularly relevant in this case. Downs delineates two types of rivals: functional and allocational. Functional rivals are those "other agencies whose social functions are competitive with those of the bureau itself"; allocational rivals are "other agencies who compete with it for resources, regardless of their functional relationships with it."[19] In a very broad sense all state agencies can be considered allocational rivals of each other; they all compete for favorable funding decisions by the Bureau of the Budget, the governor, and the legislature. Agencies receiving appropriations out of earmarked and federal funds specifically designated for their operations are largely exempted from this type of competition; but the possibility exists that the legislature could change the earmarking provisions, reexposing them to allocational competition.

Federal funding of agency functions often reduces allocational tension, since it typically receives only cursory review by the legislature and executive authorities. In many cases state officials (executive as well as legislative) consider federal funds "free" and thus do not examine their allocation. Furthermore, the detailed provisions for compliance to receive such funds limits the competition between agencies for specific monies. DOE/DBED has increasingly been supported by federal money and thus escapes most allocational rivalry. The actual shift to federal funds in fiscal year 1978 and the anticipated shift for fiscal year 1979 are dramatic within this division. This largely has been the result of federal funding under the Energy Conservation and Production Act of 1975 and the Energy Policy and Conservation Act of 1976. The shift of funding from the General Revenue Fund to the more restricted Public Utilities Fund also contributes to diminished allocational rivalry.[20]

The funding pattern of DMM presents a totally different picture. Only a very small portion of the department's operational budget is provided from federal sources, leading to allocational rivalry over virtually the entire budget. This is heightened by the fact that the major part of the DMM appropriation comes from the General Revenue Fund, the most intensely competitive of all state funds. The rapid rise in funding for the DOE/DBED indicates an aggressive, young agency; the stable pattern in DMM funding seems more characteristic of an older agency with a well-defined domain and routinized operations. Although DMM is theoretically more open to allocational rivalry than DOE/DBED, it is protected from severe budgetary cuts because of its close ties with important private interests developed during its long history.

The second type of rivalry is functional. Here DOE/DBED is open to severe competition. This is illustrated by the background report of the legislative IERC which indicated that as many as twenty agencies had energy-related functions (broadly defined).[21] The report used this information to indicate the need for reorganization in order to achieve efficient coordination, but it also delineated the level of competition faced by the division. Nearly all its functions are in direct competition with activities of one or more other agencies and their clienteles.

A prime example of this competition involves the efforts of DOE/DBED to initiate a program to develop energy-efficient building codes for new construction. This effort was in direct competition with the Capital Development Board, which not only has clear authority for such programs in state-owned buildings but also was attempting to broaden that mandate to include all construction in the state. It also affected the Department of Local Government Affairs which had some authority to develop suggested codes for adoption by local authorities. In the reorganization proposal, this authority would have been consolidated in the new department. This became a major source of objection by local governmental units, as will be discussed in the policy issues section. Another example of the division's functional rivalries involves the federal home winterization program. Although the division did much of the background work on the application for the federal funds and was preparing to administer the program, the governor decided to locate it in his Office of Manpower and Human Development when the funds actually became available. Again, because of closely related social functions, these agencies were able to snatch various responsibilities and resources from the division.

The DMM, on the other hand, does not face functional rivalry to any significant degree. Over its life the agency has carved out a specific domain. The only area where functional competition has occurred recently is the reclamation of mined land. When this program was first established in the mid-1960s, it was administered under the Department of Conservation, which was friendlier to the position of the environmental groups who favored it. It was transferred by legislation to DMM in 1969. During the reorganization proposal debate several unsuccessful attempts were made to shift this function back to the Department of Conservation. This was a clear case of functional rivalry, and DMM was able to maintain its authority. Part of the rationale DMM used in this controversy was that the function was intimately related to its other activities; it thus argued that the integration of new functions into existing ones is useful in achieving goals and reducing interagency rivalry.

Agency rivalries are important in explaining the greater power of DMM over the division. Because the latter faces much greater functional rivalry, it seems unable to gain as much power. The new influx of federal funding to DOE/DBED, however, may change the situation.

Allies, Beneficiaries, Sufferers, and Regulatees

The groups referred to by Downs as allies, beneficiaries, sufferers, and regulatees may usefully be collapsed and considered under the general category of constituent/clientele relations. We will generalize here about the basic differences between the two agencies under consideration with respect to these relations. DOE/DBED, because of its comparative youth and mission orientation, has failed to gain reliable and strong allies or beneficiaries. Although the division looks to some environmental groups for positions on various issues, such as the Illinois Environmental Council, it actually receives insufficient support for most of its functions.

Actors in a regulatee or sufferer position with DOE/DBED include the industry and business groups that would be affected by strong conservation measures, the utilities that feel threatened by the division's advocacy of solar and other alternative energy sources, and local governmental units that would lose authority to the division's energy-efficient building-code program. This formidable group of opponents forces the division either to move toward more moderate positions or to seek more support from latent consumer and environmental groups that might back energy conservation and alternate energy programs. A potentially strong ally might be found in agricultural organizations if the division adopted a position favoring automotive fuel mixtures of gasoline and alcohol made from agricultural by-products. Such support is speculative at this point however.

The DMM, on the other hand, has succeeded in gaining impressive support from both sides of the coal industry. The United Mine Workers and the Coal

Operators Association can both be viewed as strong and well-organized allies of the department. Both benefit by having an independent body to deal with the difficult issues of mine safety and regulation. The utilities are also strong allies of the department, since the department helps maintain continuous and adequate supplies of coal needed to run coal-fired electrical generating plants. The political base of this constituency in the legislature is impressive. Since the coal industry dominates the economies of large sections of southern Illinois, it has enormous power over legislators from that region. Obviously, legislators must be sensitive to such pressure.

Suppliers

The supplier of resources is primarily the General Assembly. Although the governor and federal authorities may at times supply funds independently of the legislature, it is particularly relevant to this study that decisions usually must come through it. Statutory authority for agency functions as well as funding typically must go through the General Assembly, which may grant or deny requests for specific programs as well as appropriations for existing ones. Additionally, the governor may exercise some independent control through his personal authority and state constitutional provision for reorganization by executive order. In fact, DOE/DBED was established by the governor without any authorizing legislation. But the General Assembly still exercises extensive control through both of these channels.

Thus, agencies must constantly attempt to build and maintain support for their activities in the legislature. This takes many forms, including responding to legislative requests on behalf of constituents and activating clientele groups to contact legislators. The main intent is to gain support for vital authority and allocational decisions. Again, DMM has been consistently better able to garner such support than DOE/DBED. The department has a strong, organized constituency dispersed through southern and central Illinois providing legislative support. Illinois coal deposits have taken on even more value because of the energy crisis and the federal government's policy to support increased coal utilization. DMM controls, through its constituent relations, a resource that the state must support for the increased revenues it will obtain and the energy it will need to heat the governor's mansion and General Assembly chambers.

Policy Issues

The policy issues handled in the negotiations between agencies, legislators, and clients were raised in unique ways by the reorganization proposal. These issues and their discussion will illustrate the way in which policy questions may be affected by reorganization. In addition, the outcomes of the negotiations provide a focus to evaluate the interplay of the different actors in the power setting.

The policy debate in Illinois reflects a more general conflict over the development and increased exploitation of energy resources vis á vis their conservation.[22] The issue of developing various natural energy resources in the state is very broad and complex. The dominant approach thus far has been toward more extensive development, particularly of coal. Both coal miners and mine operators have an interest in extending the amount of mining activity, since this is viewed as resulting in more jobs and more profits. These interests are well organized with established channels of access to policy makers. These relationships are reflected strongly in the attitudes taken by DMM and legislators, particularly from southern Illinois. Here again the interdependence of private groups and public agencies is clear.

The opposite perspective on this issue is represented by DOE/DBED. Reflecting the attitudes of environmental and consumer groups, the division emphasizes the conservation of energy over more development of energy resources. However these interests have been largely latent and unorganized. Although it has a mandate to help develop coal research projects and does devote some effort in this direction, the division emphasizes conservation, partially in response to the availability of federal funding for this function. Consistent with this focus on conservation is an emphasis on developing alternate energy sources, such as solar energy. This is a matter of emphasis rather than a matter of excluding considerations of resource development, but it does indicate a basic difference in policy orientations.

This difference in basic orientation between DMM and DOE/DBED reflects their different constituencies and contributed to the difficulty in consolidating the two units into one department. Although both are vitally concerned with energy issues in a broad sense, they take virtually opposite positions on extending the development of energy resources. Much of the division's reluctance to emphasize continued development of resources such as coal seems to stem from environmental considerations. Because of its alliance with various environmental groups, the division is especially conscious of the environmental damage that is being done by unregulated strip mining and other practices. Another impetus in this direction, perhaps a major one for the division, is the federal policy of providing money to states for energy conservation. The division, to obtain the greatest amount of federal funding, structures its programs in a manner consistent with the federal guidelines.

The original reorganization plan proposed by the legislative IERC was built on the philosophy that energy and environmental considerations should be dealt with together. Evidence of development versus conservation pressure is clear here. Since the commission is dominated by legislators and public representatives favoring continued development of energy resources, the idea of combining energy (development) and environmental (conservation) considerations was probably meant to insure dominance of developmental over conservation interests. Although this is a broad generalization, it is reflected in fact. A major function of the commission is the promotion and approval of funding for coal development projects such as coal gassification and liquification projects. The interests represented on the commission are primarily legislators from southern Illinois, who favor development of coal, legislators from suburban Chicago, who strongly favor nuclear development, private interests representing energy distributors, and other energy development industries. The focus of the commission, particularly its strong emphasis on coal development, has consistently been toward resource utilization. This may explain some of the long-standing antagonism between DOE/DBED and the Energy Resources Commission.

The issue can be stated in terms of continued economic growth through development of energy resources versus limited economic growth emphasizing large-scale energy conservation. From this perspective, it would be expected that business and industry would strongly favor continued development of energy resources, and environmental and consumer groups would favor conservation. Although many of the environmental groups do not seem to have clearly articulated the implications of energy conservation for economic growth, these positions are logically consonant. Stated this way, the precarious position of the division becomes clearer; located administratively under a department designed to cater to business interests, the division was emphasizing a position logically opposed to the interests of its administrative superior. The division could do this by independently drawing on the strength of environmental and consumer groups and by relying on federal funds. However these groups are generally not as well organized or as strong as business groups, and it will be difficult for the division to maintain its current position. On the other hand, no such tension exists within DMM. Perhaps, as reflected by the age of the agency, a balance between its various constituencies has developed, and the department can safely take a relatively strong developmental position.

Specific Policy Positions

A variety of specific policy conflicts were raised by the reorganization proposal. This case study will analyze only three: emergency energy planning, building code standards, and the reclamation of strip-mining lands. The first of these, emergency energy planning, has been a major policy issue since the 1973 oil embargo. It was largely as a response to this crisis that DOE was formed. Although the division was instrumental in allocating fuel during emergencies, it lacked statutory authority to undertake the kind of detailed planning necessary to meet them. Even without specific authority, however, the division had conducted several planning studies.

This issue was raised during consideration of the second reorganization proposal, since it would have given explicit authority to the new Department of Mines and Energy to develop and implement contingency plans to meet energy emergencies. The Illinois Petroleum Council and other energy distributing and industry groups were very concerned about this provision, viewing it as an excessive regulating power that would give the department authority to implement mandatory fuel allocations. Through Senate influence, the provision was changed in the first conference committee report to give authority to develop plans, not to implement them. However even this proved unacceptable to senators sensitive to industry pressure. The second conference committee weakened the provision further by only allowing the department to develop the plan and requiring it to submit the plan to the legislature for approval. Legislative-executive tension and industry pressure combined to shape the final form of this provision. Allowing a state agency to develop and implement mandatory allocation plans to meet energy emergencies will continue to be a key issue in energy policy debates. Federal preemption and planning without authority are the current policies by default.

The issue of energy-efficient building code standards was another key policy issue raised during the proposal's consideration. DOE felt that authority for development and enforcement of mandatory standards was essential for an effective energy conservation program and to insure continued federal funding for its conservation efforts. However the separate bill introduced by the division to give it authority in this area failed. The House Select Committee on State Government Organization included a weaker provision, which would have granted the new department the authority only to propose energy-efficiency standards for buildings for consideration by local governments. The division worked extensively with the committee to modify this provision, but the essential weakening remained. This became a major issue mobilizing local government groups and especially the City of Chicago, where building codes are particularly important in protecting the trade unions. The bloc of Senate votes controlled by Chicago interests succeeded in further weakening the language of the provision.

The final specific policy issue, reclamation of strip-mined land, reflects a basic conflict between mining and environmental interests over the rigorous enforcement of reclamation standards. Environmental interests, particularly the Illinois Environmental Council, were initially successful in convincing the House Select Committee on State Government Organization to shift this function to the Department of Conservation, where enforcement would be more rigorous. House floor debates over this issue indicate rather strenuous oratorical attempts to define how strip-mining reclamation is enforced. An environmentalist representative stated:

> I think that (strip-mining) would work better if we had . . . the Land Reclamation Council out from under the . . . Department that regulates mining. It's as somebody said around here quite often, it may be kind of like letting (the) fox guard the chicken house. I'm not sure but what for better environment and better control over the reclamation of strip mines . . . (that) . . . the conservation people could do and would do a better job.[23]

The response was predictable in defense of how reclamation was being carried out by DMM. One merely defines reclamation to be "mining":

> Mr. Speaker, . . . you're talking about mining. When you talk about reclamation, you talk about mining. I don't think it's a case of the fox guarding the chicken coop or anything like that. Let's be reasonable about this. When you talk about mining land, you're talking about the Department of Mines and Minerals. When you talk about reclamation of mined land, the two things are tied together completely. I don't think you can separate them into two different departments. I think you would lose a great deal of effectiveness, a great deal of expertise. It would just be foolish to have these two departments working at odds to each other.[24]

The select committee had agreed informally with environmental interests; but the influence of clients, the UMW and COA, led to a different solution on the floor of the General Assembly, where the floor vote went against environmental interests. This vote is a compelling example of the effect of private power on public policy.

The success of an agency in protecting its budgetary allocation and functional domain is strongly related to its political standing. This standing is enhanced by a number of factors, one of which is the esoteric quality of the agency's bureaucratic skills as they relate to state needs. If the skills of an agency are not particularly esoteric, then it becomes important for the agency to maintain a positive image with the public and be able to cultivate client and legislative support for its goals. The size of an agency's client group, the distribution of the group's membership among legislative districts, and its cohesion remain crucial to agency goals.[25]

In the case of energy reorganization, the conflict was privatized; therefore the cultivation of clients was more crucial than that of the public at large. This was particularly true when one views the success of DOE and DMM. The preceding short analysis of different policy issues indicates that DMM had strong, dispersed, cohesive supporters in the UMW and COA. DOE's supporters were not as cohesive or influential; but its sufferers were far better organized and influential in determining the content, and finally the demise, of the legislature's incremental proposal.

The vote in the House of Representatives on Amendment Six of Senate Bill 1142 concerning strip-mining reclamation was instructive. As stated above, the UMW and COA were strongly interested in the functional domain of DMM, particularly where strip-mining reclamation was concerned. Amendment Six was an attempt to remove this function from DMM and transfer it to the Department of Conservation, a move supported by environmentalists and opposed by the UMW and COA. On the whole, one could expect that legislators with a large number of well-organized coal operators and mine workers in their districts would be opposed to the amendment. This was essentially the case when the House of Representatives narrowly defeated Amendment Six. The vote was sixty-one to sixty-nine with one representative voting present and forty-six members absent.

Conclusion

The reorganization of energy agencies in Illinois reflects the importance of state government's close legislative, agency, and client relationships when political conflict is privatized. The substance of energy reorganization, particularly when it tends to be regulatory, represents a challenge to clients and agencies. Any reorganization proposal could affect the future of an agency if its functional domain is seriously altered. If alterations occur, the budgetary allocation an agency receives might be more seriously questioned by the executive's Bureau of the Budget and the General Assembly's appropriation committees. The demise, or contraction, of an agency's budget and mandate affects its clients and indirectly its legislative adherents. The effect is to narrow the client's access to political arenas where it is able to control, to some extent, political debates concerning its interests.

In the regulatory politics implicit in energy reorganization, agencies and their clients seek to control access to the political arena and limit the scope of conflict to insure an outcome adjusted to their interests. To do so, legislative adherents are strongly lobbied by a combined client and agency effort to prevent any contraction of influence.

This was the major effect of energy reorganization bargaining. As an example, when environmentalists challenged DMM's strip-mining reclamation function, the UMW and COA provided the muscle needed to defeat the amendment in the General Assembly. The defeat of the final measure, following a gubernatorial amendatory veto, was because a large number of clients, legislative adherents, and agencies were concerned about the potential influence of the proposed Department of Mines and Energy.

It is interesting that the proponents of both conservation and development strategies generally withdrew their support. An environmentalist would be uncertain how energy could be conserved, or the environment protected, if the new organization was made captive of a powerful development-oriented group. The development-oriented group would have similar fears—how would the new organization affect their interests? The crucial factor for this group was its uncertainty about the proposed department's future behavior; being uncertain, it opted for the status quo.

There was also a serious question about the effectiveness of the incremental proposal. Why support a reorganization proposal that did not really tackle the immense problems of coordination and waste? The answer was simple—the measure deserved to be defeated. Whatever support the proposal obtained was related to Republican support of the Republican governor's amendatory veto and Democratic opposition.

The conditions surrounding energy reorganization in Illinois were detrimental to the enactment of both comprehensive and incremental proposals. Several factors made enactment unlikely. First, one must recognize the enormity and complexity of the task. Analysts of public policy must ascertain how much information was available to legislators and whether their professional staffs were capable of providing them with neutral sources of information. These matters are crucial given the technological problems related to building codes, nuclear-plant siting, utility rates, and strip-mining reclamation. If information does not exist on these problems, and there are insufficient professional staff workers to aid legislators, legislation will probably fail to satisfy legislative values of economy and efficiency. If legislators depend on captive agency and client information, policy choices will be severely limited, as this case indicates.

If the task is complex, the conflict engendered by reorganization is even more intense. A privatized conflict is often dominated by those interest groups with access to the political arena, who, perhaps, have even captured the agency that must regulate them in the public interest. Finally, the governor failed to take a strong stand, although his campaign promised an improved, efficient state government through some reorganization. As the state's chief administrator he is the logical force to provide impetus to reorganization; and perhaps most important, his statewide constituency is not limited to groups or people within particular legislative districts. He is in a strategic position to marshal widespread political support; but Thompson's unusual 2-year term in office caused him to be less initiative-oriented in 1977 and 1978.

If one is to bring about the reorganization of energy agencies, or of state government as a whole, one must consider at least two factors as crucial. First, the governor must play an active role; and second, the scope of the conflict must be expanded to offset the influence of clients, agencies, and legislative adherents who generally dominate policy formation and adoption. Finally, information must be made available to policy makers so that they may pursue more rational choices.

Notes

1. Clyde Kurlander, "The Illinois Energy Resources Commission and the Creation of a Coordinated Energy Policy," *Chicago Daily Law Bulletin,* 9 November 1976; *Illinois Energy Reorganization Options,* Illinois Energy Resources Commission, October 1976, and *Illinois Energy Reorganization Proposal,* Illinois Energy Resources Commission, March 1977 pointed these problems out and proposed comprehensive reform.

2. Ibid; see IERC analyses of 1976 and 1977.

3. Robert J. Batson, "Reorganization of the Executive Branch of Government," in Leon S. Cohen, ed., *Issues in Illinois Policy,* Springfield, Ill.: Illinois Legislative Studies Center Monograph, 1974. *Orderly Government,* Illinois Task Force on Governmental Reorganization, November 3, 1976, represents a private task-force report submitted on behalf of gubernatorial candidates during the 1976 election.

4. Channel 20 News Report, May 3, 1978.

5. *Illinois General Assembly Floor Debates,* June 25, 1977, pp. 176-177.

6. Charles E. Lindbloom, "The Science of Muddling Through," *Public Administration Review* 19 (Spring 1959):79-88; David Braybrooke and Charles E. Lindbloom, *A Strategy of Decision* (New York: Free Press, 1963).

7. James E. Anderson, *Public Policy-Making* (New York: Praeger, 1975), pp. 55-70; Roger W. Cobb and Charles D. Elder, *Participation in American Politics: The Dynamics of Agenda-Building* (Baltimore: Johns Hopkins Press, 1972); David Easton, *A System Analysis of Political Life* (New York: John Wiley and Sons, 1965), pp. 86-99; Charles O. Jones, *An Introduction to the Study of Public Policy* (North Scituate, Mass.: Duxbury Press, 1977), pp. 25-46.

8. E.E. Schattschneider, *The Semi-Sovereign People* (New York: Holt, Rinehart, Winston, 1960).

9. Anthony Downs, *Inside Bureaucracy* (Boston: Little, Brown, 1967), pp. 44-47.

10. J. Leiper Freeman, *The Political Process* (New York: Random House, 1965); Harold Seidman, *Politics, Position and Power* (New York: Oxford University Press, 1976); Francis E. Rourke, *Bureaucracy, Politics and Public Policy* (Boston: Little, Brown, 1976).

11. Joseph LaPalombara, *Interest Groups in Italian Politics* (Princeton, N.J.: Princeton University Press, 1965).

12. Marver H. Bernstein, *Regulating Business by Independent Commission* (Princeton, N.J.: Princeton University Press, 1955); Freeman, *Political Process;* LaPalombara, *Interest Groups;* Rourke, *Bureaucracy, Politics;* Seidman, *Politics, Position and Power;* Downs, *Inside Bureaucracy,* pp. 5-23.

13. Norman K. Denzin, *The Research Act* (Chicago: Aldine, 1970), pp. 185-218; Raymond L. Gold, "Roles in Sociological Field Observations," *Social Forces* 36 (March 1958):217-223.

14. Ibid., p. 186.

15. Howard S. Becker, "Problems of Inference and Proof in Participant Observation," in George J. McCall and J.L. Simmons, eds., *Issues in Participant Observation* (Reading, Mass.: Addison-Wesley, 1969), pp. 245-257. Denzin, *Research Act,* pp. 197-198; Alfred R. Lindesmith *Addiction and Opiates* (Chicago: Aldine, 1968).

16. Downs, *Inside Bureaucracy,* p. 9.

17. Martha W. Weinberg, *Managing the State* (Cambridge, Mass.: M.I.T. Press, 1977).

18. Freeman, *Political Process.*

19. Downs, *Inside Bureaucracy,* p. 10.

20. For the division's funding history, see: Illinois Bureau of the Budget: *Budget Appendix, Fiscal Year 1979,* pp. 67, 127; *Budget Appendix, Fiscal Year 1978,* pp. 58, 126; *Budget Appendix, Fiscal Year 1977,* pp. 121, 182; *Budget Appendix, Fiscal Year 1976,* p. 122; and *Budget Appendix, Fiscal Year 1975,* p. 140.

21. Illinois Energy Resources Commission, *Illinois Energy Reorganization Options.*

22. A good discussion of continued development and limited growth may be found in Walter H. Heller, "Coming to Terms with Economic Growth, and the Environment," Sam H. Schurr, ed., *Energy, Economic Growth, and the Environment* (Baltimore: Johns Hopkins Press, 1973), pp. 3-29; Barry Commoner, "The Environmental Cost of Economic Growth," in Sam H. Schurr, ed., *Energy, Economic Growth, and the Environment,* pp. 30-65; and Herman Daly, ed., *Toward a Steady-State Economy* (San Francisco: W.H. Freeman, 1973).

23. *Illinois General Assembly Floor Debates,* June 24, 1977, p. 248.

24. Ibid., p. 249.

25. Rourke, *Bureaucracy, Politics,* pp. 42-106.

4

Public Participation in Water Quality Planning

Jonathan Czarnecki and Sheldon Kamieniecki

The most ambitious effort ever undertaken by the federal government to clean up the nation's waterways began with the passage of the Federal Water Pollution Control Act Amendments by Congress in October 1972. The 1977 revised version of the Act establishes a national goal of zero discharge in navigable waterways to be reached by 1987.[1] Section 208 of both the 1972 and 1977 acts establishes a number of comprehensive procedures to encourage regional planning for future water quality management in areas of the country that have experienced serious water quality problems.[2] The procedures set forth in Section 208 are designed to consider the many interrelated factors which contribute to poor water quality.

To try to insure that public opinion is considered in water quality planning and management the U.S. Congress requires public participation in Section 208 planning. Section 101(e) of the Federal Water Pollution Control Act Amendments states:

> Public participation in the development, revision and enforcement of any regulation standard, effluent limitation, plan, or program established by the Administrator or any State under this Act shall be provided for, encouraged and assisted by the Administrator and the States. The Administrator, in cooperation with the States, shall develop and publish regulations specifying minimum guidelines for public participation in such processes.[3]

As required, the Environmental Protection Agency has set guidelines for citizen participation in Section 208 water quality planning. It is hard to determine what kinds of participatory strategies are needed to elicit a wide range of citizen input. Some recommend that natural-resource and water quality planners use traditional mechanisms, such as task forces, workshops, public hearings, citizen advisory committees, and others, to obtain broad public involvement.[4] Others, however, believe that policy makers need to rely on survey research, in addition to traditional participatory strategies, to elicit more representative public opinion.[5]

The authors would like to thank Mr. Steven Cohen and Professors Marilyn Hoskin, Lester Milbrath, Paul Sabatier, and Michael Steinman for their comments and suggestions. We are also grateful for aid supplied by the staffs of the Environmental Studies Center and the Survey Research Center at the State University of New York at Buffalo in gathering the data.

How many citizens ought to participate also is a difficult question. If only a handful of citizens participate, planners may formulate an inaccurate picture of the population's views. If too many people actively participate, however, little may be done. D. Stephen Cupps points out the perils posed by the involvement of too many active citizens' groups. He argues that there is no guarantee that if many people participate effective programs will be produced.[6] In contrast, Robert Aleshire concludes there are more advantages than disadvantages to increasing public input as a result of his cost-benefit analysis of citizen participation in planning.[7]

The general pattern across the country is that relatively few citizens have become involved in the Section 208 water quality planning effort. To understand how to increase public involvement we first need to know why people are willing to become involved in water quality planning. Research on political participation in the past has primarily focused on non-issue-specific activities such as voting or protesting. Few have attempted to examine citizen involvement within specific issue areas. Susan Hansen believes: "The problem for political researchers is to develop a theory specifying the model of linkage relevant to a particular issue area and unit of analysis."[8] Walter Rosenbaum concurs and adds: "Formulating an agenda of reforms may well be premature in light of the major theoretical problems we have observed in participation literature."[9] He feels there needs to be "a very careful, explicit, and searching reappraisal of the underlying assumptions of participation literature."[10]

This chapter uses Sidney Verba and Norman Nie's approach in *Participation in America* to explain public involvement in water quality planning.[11] In their work they present a "standard socio-economic model of participation" whereby people of upper socioeconomic status come to participate more through the development of a general set of civic orientations. Using data collected prior to the development of a Section 208 water quality plan in western New York, socioeconomic status is used as a base line to explain people's willingness to participate in water quality policy making. A variety of other forces that modify the effects of socioeconomic status, such as people's beliefs, attitudes, and perceptions relating to water quality, are examined. The implication this inquiry has for achieving increased broad public involvement in water quality planning is presented at the conclusion of the chapter.

The Data Base

To add a new dimension of citizen input into regional water quality planning, the Environmental Studies Center commissioned the Survey Research Center of the State University of New York at Buffalo to sample randomly and interview over 1,000 citizens (1,021 were actually interviewed, reflecting a 68 percent response rate) residing in Erie and Niagara Counties of western New York. The

Survey Research Center had a recently constructed sampling frame from which to draw the broad public sample. The survey instrument was carefully designed by the Environmental Studies Center in cooperation with the regional water quality planning staff.[12] The field work was completed in the summer months of 1976.

Two hundred and thirty-three leaders (a 96 percent response rate) were interviewed by the Center's project staff with a similar questionnaire. The major criterion for including a leader in the sample was whether the leader might be expected to play a role in the development, acceptance, or implementation of the final water quality plan. The leader sample is comprised of elected officials (such as the two county executives, county legislators, city and village mayors, town supervisors, and others), appointed administrators and officials representing New York's state, county, city, town, and village governments, steering committee members for the planning project, regional and local planning board members, Water Quality and Citizen Advisory Committee members, Section 208 project staff and consultants, developers, environmental leaders, industrial leaders, agricultural leaders, and active citizens. A "snowball" selection procedure was employed to insure that no leaders had been overlooked.[13]

Constructing a Theoretical Framework of Citizen Participation

The socioeconomic model of political participation has been successfully used by political researchers in examining participation behavior. Yet anomalies remain concerning the model's predictive and explanatory power. Verba and Nie, for example, find that one mode of participation, "particularized contacting," fits the model very poorly.[14] Particularized contacts are those participatory acts that are citizen-initiated at nonstandardized times, for purposes relevant to those of the initiator or his immediate social-psychological referent group.[15] It is important to devise additional explanations to increase understanding of diverse modes of participatory behavior, such as particularized contacting, which occurs in water quality planning.

Recent research on particularized contacting has revealed that people's awareness and perception of the need for governmental services can better explain participation than the conceptual approach used by Verba and Nie.[16] Other participation research has emphasized the importance of the issue environment as an explanation of participation behavior.[17] Alternatively, the rational-choice school of voting and public participation theorizes that people participate according to their subjectively perceived self-interest.[18] Perhaps people's perceptions of environmental quality, in addition to other factors, can better explain their willingness to become involved in environmental policy making.

It is helpful to turn to psychological theory and research to gain a deeper understanding of environmental perception. Environmental perception is roughly an analogous term for the psychological "field."[19] The field is the life space of the individual; it consists of the personality and the environment that the person cognizes. There has been some psychological research on perception and, more recently, on perception of the environment as an explanation of behavior. There is no agreed on theory of perception and behavior; however, there are threads that provide some hints of a theory linking perception with behavior. First, perceptions provide the person's source of reality; perceptions can, therefore, be construed as information. Second, perceptions act as guides for individual behavior; the person must have information to relate to the environment. Third, psychological perception processes provide individuals with an information-ordering process. In this process, incoming information from the environment is sorted and catalogued according to internal rules. Fourth, perceptions and behavior do not seem to be linked in a simple recursive causal pattern. The relationship seems more transactional. The important point to note is that perception as knowledge does not mean knowledge defined by objective standards; perception means knowledge defined by the person's own standards. In this view, the only knowledge is that which the person knows from his perception.

Perceptions of water quality may be important for understanding why people intend to participate in public policy making involving water quality (in this case Section 208 water quality planning). The next question is how these perceptions relate to attitudes and beliefs concerning water quality.

Once a person perceives some information, attitudes and beliefs are brought to bear on that information. A person's attitudes evaluate the emotive content of the information; a person's beliefs assess the credibility of the information. Knowing this a researcher can structure questions to emphasize the attributes of the particular psychological factor he wishes to measure. Perception measurement emphasizes information about a situation; attitude measurement emphasizes affect; and belief measurement focuses on credibility.

Consider the recursive situation where attitudes, beliefs, and perceptions are independent variables, and willingness to participate in water quality planning is the dependent variable. Perceptions of water quality may be a trigger for citizen involvement. Without knowledge of water quality, behavior within this issue domain is unlikely. The trigger is pulled when information about water quality reaches the person. How the information is processed depends on the person's attitudes and beliefs relating to water quality. One may perceive information but discredit it because it does not mesh with what one believes to be true or because it is in conflict with one's feelings. Perceptions can sometimes overcome prejudicial attitudes and beliefs and influence behavior. This may be more likely to happen when perceived information is distressing information.[20] We can hypothesize that if a person perceives the quality of the water to be poor he is more likely to act.

In addition to socioeconomic status and several demographic variables, the ensuing investigation suggests that attitudes, beliefs, and perceptions concerning water quality are important intervening, psychological variables for explaining intent to participate in water quality planning. Figure 4-1 describes our view of the relationships among these factors. Because of the complex nature of the interrelationships among the variables within the model, a path analysis will not be conducted. Instead, a multiple-regression analysis will be used to explain and predict variation in intent to participate in water quality planning.

The Power of the Analysis

There are two conditions that affect the power of the analysis. First, the full range of political attitudes used in previous studies (such as in Verba and Nie's work) is not available in this study. Instead, attitudinal indicators concerning water quality and water quality planning are used. This makes conceptual sense, since the issue of interest to this inquiry is water quality planning.

The second condition affecting the analysis is the fact that level of active involvement in water quality planning is not measured in the study; rather participation intent is the dependent construct. At the time of the survey regional water quality planning was a very new concept; there were few other planning efforts preceding the Section 208 water quality planning endeavor, locally or nationwide. Moreover, the public participation mandate in the Act itself [Section 101(e)] was unique in water quality planning. Thus people probably have not developed clear patterns of participation behavior in water quality policy making. In addition, from a policy maker's standpoint, it is often more useful to have an idea of what the public intends to do than to know past participation. Because we do not present measures of actual behavior, we must interpret the findings cautiously. Michael Steinman, facing a similar dilemma in his study of Mexican-American orientations to health care services, says, "Although there may be a gap between inclinations and behavior, it need not preclude making tentative conclusions calling for further research."[21]

Socioeconomic Status and Demographic Variables

This analysis uses five socioeconomic and demographic measures. Household income, job prestige score, and educational attainment are combined into one measure of socioeconomic status.[22] Research by Verba and Nie and Lester Milbrath and M.L. Goel suggests that those of high socioeconomic status are more likely to become psychologically involved in politics; these same people tend to possess the necessary skills and intellectual capacity for active involvement in political affairs.[23] Drawing from this research, it is hypothesized that the higher one's socioeconomic status the more willing one will be to participate in efforts to improve water quality.

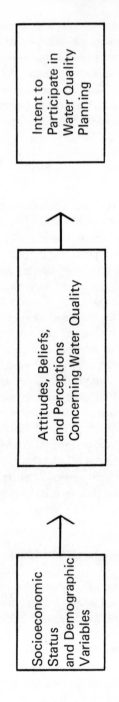

Figure 4-1. Factors in Participation in Water Quality Planning.

A second variable examined in this portion of the study is age. It has been found that participation increases steadily with age until it reaches a peak in the middle years and then gradually declines with old age.[24] The relation between age and participation is probably best explained by position in the life cycle. People are more likely to participate after they have become established in a job, a home, and start to raise a family. Young unmarried citizens tend to feel apathetic and are unlikely to become deeply involved in politics.[25] Thus it is expected that as citizens reach middle age they will be more inclined to participate in water quality planning.

Generally speaking, people who join groups tend to be extroverted and find it easier to interact with people. Perhaps they also feel a great deal of civic pride and wish to improve the quality of life of the community. These citizens may think that improved water quality will contribute to the overall well-being of their community. It is hypothesized that the more organizations people belong to the more willing they are to participate in water quality policy making.

Another demographic variable that is thought to be related to intent to participate in water quality planning is the type of community in which people live. Verba and Nie believe that variation in levels of participation can be explained by the size of the community and the extent to which it is well defined and autonomous.[26] They feel that the more the community is well defined and autonomous, the greater the likelihood citizens will know the ropes of local politics, know whom to contact, and participate. We felt there might be a relationship between what they call the "boundedness" of the community in which people reside and intent to participate in water quality planning. In other words, perhaps the more bounded a community is the more inclined its residents will be to participate in efforts to improve water quality.[27]

Attitudes, Beliefs, and Perceptions

Perceptions of water quality are measured in four ways. The first two measures are comprised of respondents' ratings of the water quality in lakes Erie and Ontario (and the Niagara River), and a rating of the inland lakes and streams on a ten-step ladder. People were told that the bottom rung represents "filthy" water and the top rung represents "clean" water.[28] The third measure determines the extent to which people are aware of the causes of poor water quality. This measure is a composite scale ranging from "not aware of the causes of poor water quality" to "very aware of the causes of poor water quality." The fourth measure taps citizens' perceptions of the size of water quality problems affecting them. This measure also is a composite scale ranging from "very small or no water quality problems affecting the respondent" to "very many, large water quality problems affecting the respondent." The four measures are significantly interrelated; the Pearson product-moment correlations range from .12 to .35, significant at the .01 level.

Interest in water recreation is one of several measures of attitudes and beliefs concerning water quality used in this study. People who are interested in water recreation probably realize that to enjoy water recreation fully there must be clean water. These same individuals also may know that a major goal of Section 208 planning is to improve water quality. Since water recreation enthusiasts have something to gain from water quality planning, they probably are more likely to become involved. Using respondents' reported level of interest in each of nine water-related activities, a scale of interest in water recreation was constructed. The values of the scale range from "not interested in water recreation" to "very interested in water recreation."

In a self-administered portion of the survey people were asked how pleased they were with forty-four broadly defined environmental conditions. Five of these conditions relate to water quality. They are: (1) public water systems around here, (2) facilities for sewage disposal around here, (3) beauty of the shoreline on lakes and streams around here, (4) quality of water for fishing in Erie and Niagara Counties, and (5) quality of water for swimming in Erie and Niagara Counties. These items are combined into a composite index representing levels of satisfaction with water quality. This index is used in the analysis.

In the same section of the instrument respondents were also asked how important it would be to improve each condition (if the condition was of poor quality) to bring overall quality to their lives. Using people's responses to the five conditions relating to water quality, a composite index representing levels of importance for improving water quality is used. This measure provides us with some notion of the level of saliency of water quality problems.

One expects that if people hold beliefs supportive of water quality planning they will be more inclined to participate in this issue area. A measure of the degree to which people support water quality planning is therefore included in the analysis. The measure is an index of the number of beliefs supportive of water quality planning people hold. The items used to develop the index are: (1) how much extra taxes (if any) respondents are willing to pay to achieve specific levels of water quality, (2) how much governmental regulation respondents are willing to accept to achieve specific levels of water quality, (3) whether people think it is better to turn over the area's water quality problems to a regional governmental body or allow local government to make its own decisions on these questions, and (4) whether citizens think an effort to improve water quality in their community would cause people to lose their jobs, create more jobs, or have no effect. The values of the index range from "no beliefs supportive of water quality planning" to "all beliefs supportive of water quality planning."

Presumably, people who believe the public should be involved in environmental planning will be more likely to participate in planning than those who feel the public should not be involved. Respondents were asked the following question: "Is it important for the public to be involved in developing environmental plans or is it better to leave planning to those who have special training?" Responses to this question are used in this inquiry.

Intent to Participate in Water Quality Planning

In the survey conducted by the Environmental Studies Center, citizens were given a list of some ways people can become involved in water quality planning. Respondents were asked what they were really likely to do, not what they might like to do. Included in the list of possible modes of public involvement were: (1) getting informed about the Section 208 plan, (2) joining a group that gets involved, (3) working on a water quality committee, (4) attending public hearings, (5) expressing views to planners or officials, and (6) contacting a public official to support or oppose the plan. Using people's responses to these six items, a composite scale ranging from "no possibility of participation in any mode" to "great possibility of participation in all modes" was constructed and used as the dependent variable in the analysis (see chapter appendix).

Multivariate Analysis

Thirteen independent variables are included in a multiple-regression analysis to explain and predict people's level of intent to participate in water quality planning.[29] The independent variables are grouped into two blocks in the regression: socioeconomic and demographic factors, and psychological factors. Multicolinearity does not appear to be a major problem. The highest intercorrelation between the thirteen variables is $r = .49$ while most other intercorrelations are below $r = .20$.

The results of the regression analysis are revealed in table 4-1.[30] Interest in water recreation exhibits the greatest independent impact on intent to participate in water quality planning ($B = .244$, significant at the .01 level). It also explains 4 percent of the variance in the dependent variable. In other words, the more interested people are in water recreation, the more they are willing to participate in water quality policy making. Note that perception of water quality problems also exerts a significant independent impact on intention to participate ($B = .157$, significant at the .01 level). The perception of water quality problems explains almost 3 percent of the variance in intention to participate. Thus the more that people perceive water quality problems affecting them, the more they will intend to participate in water quality planning. Other psychological variables that significantly predict variation in the dependent variable, although to a lesser

Table 4-1
Participation-Intent Scale Regressed on All Independent Variables

Independent Variables	Percent Explained Variance	Unstandardized Regression Slope b	Standard Error of b	Standardized Regression Slope b
Step 1. Socioeconomic status and demographic variables				
Organizational membership	.0399	.345	.071	.158[a]
Community type	.0087	.687	.196	.102[a]
Soecioeconomic status	.0000	−.053	.073	−.024
Age	.0164	.006	.009	.022
Step 2. Psychological variables				
Importance of water quality	.0327	.746	.249	.089[a]
Beliefs index	.0128	.229	.149	.046
Perceived water quality–inland streams	.0045	−.033	.076	−.014
Public involvement in planning	.0112	.962	.288	.096[a]
Perception of water problems	.0279	1.230	.244	.157[a]
Interest in water recreation	.0419	.308	.042	.244[a]
Awareness of causes	.0046	.059	.028	.064[b]
Pleasingness of water quality	.0011	−.369	.238	−.053
Perceived water quality–Great Lakes	.0009	.102	.092	.038
Total percent explained variance	20 percent			

Note: Regression is two-stage; socioeconomic and demographic variables are entered first. Y intercept = 1.53; N = 1,021.
[a]Significant at the .01 level.
[b]Significant at the .05 level.

extent, are support for public involvement in environmental planning, importance of improving water quality, and awareness of the causes of poor water quality.

Generally speaking, the socioeconomic and demographic variables do not explain and predict intent to participate in water quality planning as well as the psychological variables do. Together, socioeconomic and demographic variables explain approximately 6.5 percent of the variance (the psychological variables explain about 13.5 percent of the variance in comparison) in the dependent variable. Increased membership in organizations and residency in more bounded communities significantly influence the extent to which people are inclined to participate in water quality policy making. Curiously, according to table 4-1, age and socioeconomic status are poor predictors of intent to participate. Perhaps their predictive power is channeled through the block of psychological variables. A further investigation revealed that when the psychological variables are excluded from the regression, the influence of age and socioeconomic status increases significantly.

The results of a correlational analysis proved to be even more revealing. Members of high socioeconomic status groups and younger people are more likely to intend to participate in water quality planning. Moreover, higher socioeconomic status and youth are positively related to greater interest in water recreation, support for public involvement in environmental planning, beliefs supportive of water quality planning, and displeasure with water quality. Further regression and correlation analyses therefore suggest that there is a causal flow from age and socioeconomic status through attitudes, beliefs, and perceptions relating to water quality to intent to participate in water quality policy making.[31]

Discussion

As mentioned earlier, past political participation research has found a positive relationship between age and participation; as people grow older (until extreme old age) they are more likely to participate. Yet we find a negative relationship existing between age and intention to participate in water quality planning. One possible (but not probable) explanation for this discrepancy is the different focus of the dependent variable—intention rather than behavior. Another explanation may be the nature of the water quality issue. The current generation of younger people has grown up in an era when environmental issues and problems are considered extremely important. Media coverage of environmental problems are more frequent than before. Many high school science classes give considerable attention to the environment. In addition, increasing numbers of young people are choosing recreation that brings them into contact with their natural environment (for example, camping). Water recreation, particularly swimming and water skiing, is especially attractive to young people. Through exposure and experience the younger generation seems to have placed environmental problems high on its list of issue priorities and is willing to become involved in efforts to improve environmental quality.

We did find that increased membership in organizations and residence in more bounded communities significantly increased people's willingness to become involved in water quality policy making. It could be that organizational membership and the type of community people live in are surrogate measures for other psychological factors—level of community pride and loyalty. One would think that citizens who tend to join groups and live in bounded communities are very community oriented. These civic minded people probably feel a great deal of community pride and loyalty and wish to see their region flourish. Perhaps they perceive that, among other things, improving the quality of the area's water will help accomplish this and therefore are willing to participate in water quality planning.[32]

The most important finding of this inquiry is the extent to which attitudes, beliefs, and perceptions relating to water quality explain and predict intent to participate in water quality planning. Psychological variables account for almost two-thirds of the explained variance. When everything is held constant, interest in water recreation, perception of water quality problems, support for public involvement in environmental planning, importance of improving water quality, and awareness of the causes of poor water quality exert a significant influence over intent to participate in this issue sphere. Interest in water recreation, the strongest predictive variable, explains 4 percent of the variation in the dependent variable. This suggests that water recreation enthusiasts place a high value on clean water and are therefore inclined to participate in efforts to improve water quality.

There is one overall observation from the findings of the regression analysis. Although the conceptual approach used in the analysis is similar to Verba and Nie's analysis of political participation, different conclusions are reached. Whereas Verba and Nie find the standard model of socioeconomic status to be a major factor in explaining several modes of participation, we find it has little influence over intent to participate in water quality planning. Instead, psychological variables play a dominant role in explaining and predicting intention to participate in this issue area. One possible explanation for this discrepancy is the focus of the dependent variable: intention rather than behavior. Perhaps the difference can be explained by the addition of psychological variables related to water quality planning—the specific issue studied here. Verba and Nie did not try to link individual issue beliefs with participation in a specific issue domain. This alone suggests the need for a reevaluation of traditional theories of participation that rely heavily on socioeconomic status to explain behavior. For analysis of special situations researchers should tailor their studies to the characteristics of the political situation being investigated. The analysis of the water quality issue indicates that such a strategy might prove fruitful.

Conclusion

We have examined the extent to which traditional theories of political participation can explain and predict intention to participate in water quality planning. The results of the analysis indicate that the standard model of socioeconomic status, effectively used by Verba and Nie to explain political participation, adds little to our understanding of why people are willing to participate in water quality policy making. Knowing a person's age also does not tell us whether a person is inclined to participate. Increased membership in organizations and residence in more bounded communities does exert a significant influence over willingness to participate. Yet, in general, psychological factors relating to water quality are more important than socioeconomic and demographic variables.

Theory played a major role in determining the direction of our causal flow and the inclusion of specific independent variables in the regression analysis. Recognizing the fact that intent to participate in water quality management is an attitude itself, one could argue that the independent, psychological variables are too close to the dependent variable. Naturally, we would have preferred to use a measure of behavior. Although intent to participate is an attitude, we believe that it is formed after the attitudes, beliefs, and perceptions relating to water quality are formed. Just as our dependent variable is a step away from behavior, it is also a step away from the psychological states relating to water quality that appear in the analysis.

One could also argue that explaining 20 percent of the variance in intent to participate in water quality management with thirteen variables is not very impressive. We believe that some researchers using regression analysis err in crowding in as many independent variables as possible to raise the percentage of explained variance. They must think their research is more successful and their theory more compelling if they include and eliminate independent variables solely to add to the total percentage of explained variance. This disregard of theory makes interpretation of results very difficult if not impossible. We believe that a regression model's worth should rest on its theoretical content as well as its empirical results. Our model contains independent variables that we think are theoretically important. We initiated our analysis with seventeen variables but eliminated those that we considered theoretically less important and that explained little variance (see note 29). We eliminated others because they measured the same concepts as those placed in the final regression model. Those variables that are theoretically important but explain little variance in the dependent variable—socioeconomic status is the best example—remain in the equation. We believe our regression model is parsimonious empirically and theoretically.

One reason why political participation programs in environmental planning have had a mixed record of successes and failures is because there is little understanding of why people become involved. Political scientists cannot explain participation in specific issue domains very well with their general frameworks. Community coordinators hired by environmental planning projects generally define the public as interest groups and orient programs to placate these groups. It is our hope that the findings of this study not only will spur additional research in this area but also will help decision makers to formulate a list of reforms for increasing public involvement in planning.

Yet this may not be enough to produce meaningful citizen involvement to achieve that goal. Federal, state, and local agencies must be willing to expand efforts to increase public participation. Presently, many agencies are reluctant to open their decision making process to public scrutiny and involve citizens meaningfully. Daniel Mazmanian and Jeanne Nienaber suggest that agencies are hesitant to increase public involvement because they have a tendency to be resistant to change.[33] Perhaps bureaucrats fear that increased public participation will lead to an increase in decision making time and will weaken their power base. Agencies that have invested the time and money to involve the public, such as the Army Corps of Engineers, have become discouraged because of the poor results and the lack of consensus such efforts have produced.[34] (This points out the need for increased understanding of why people participate in specific issue areas.) The "rational" course for bureaucrats to take, therefore, is to conduct "eyewash" participation programs. With respect to this tokenism in water quality planning we make two points. First, this kind of evasion violates the letter of the law (PL 92-217). Second, such action runs the danger of disillusioning the public about meaningful democracy. This is why water quality leaders must open more channels for public input and learn to be more patient with future participation programs seeking to incorporate the views of an uninterested but affected broad public.

Appendix 4A
Participation in Water
Quality Planning: Items
and Scale Construction

The question asked of respondents was:

On this card we have developed some ways that people can get involved in water quality planning. How likely is it that you would participate in each of these ways? Please estimate what you are *really likely* to do, not simply what you *might* like to do.

The frequency patterns of the responses are contained in table 4A-1.

The items were added together (without weighting) to form a scale. The items were found to be strongly unidimensional, and they exhibited strong external consistency. The frequencies are presented in table 4A-2.

Table 4A-1
Frequency Patterns of Questionnaire Responses

Participation Mode	Not at All	Slight Possibility	Moderate Possibility	Strong Possibility	Totals
Informed about plan	164 (16)	292 (29)	300 (30)	258 (26)	1014 (101)[a]
Join in group	463 (46)	318 (31)	169 (18)	63 (6)	1013 (101)[a]
Work on water quality committee	574 (57)	258 (26)	93 (9)	87 (9)	1012 (101)[a]
Attend public hearings	398 (39)	298 (29)	193 (19)	127 (13)	1016 (100)
Express views to planners	368 (36)	265 (26)	210 (21)	174 (17)	1017 (100)
Contact public officials	310 (31)	240 (24)	220 (22)	247 (24)	1017 (101)[a]

Note: Figures in parentheses are percentages.
[a]Rounding error.

Table 4A-2
Questionnaire Response Frequencies

| | Response | |
Range	Number	Percentage
No possibility of participation in any mode		
1.	99	9.9
2.	66	6.6
3.	60	6.0
4.	77	7.7
5.	66	6.6
6.	67	6.6
7.	71	7.0
8.	72	7.2
9.	67	6.6
10.	62	6.2
11.	73	7.3
12.	46	4.6
13.	41	4.1
14.	36	3.6
15.	23	2.3
16.	19	1.9
17.	17	1.7
18.	14	1.4
19.	27	2.7
Great possibility of participation in all modes		
Total	1003	100

Notes

1. Public Law 92-500 was amended in 1977 by Public Law 92-217. The sections that this chapter deals with were not substantively affected.

2. Public Law 92-500: pp. 24-28.

3. Ibid., p. 2.

4. Kris Kauffman and Alice Shorett, "A Perspective on Public Involvement in Water Management Decision Making," *Public Administration Review* 37 (September/October 1977):467-471; John Hendee et al., "Methods for Acquiring Public Input," in John Pierce and Harvey Doerksen, eds., *Water Politics and Public Involvement* (Ann Arbor, Mich.: Ann Arbor Science, 1976), pp. 125-144; Timothy O'Riordan, "Policy Making and Environmental Management: Some Thoughts on Processes and Research Issues," *Natural Resources Journal* 16 (January 1976):55-72; and John O'Riordan, "The Public Involvement Program in the Okanagan Basin Study," *Natural Resources Journal* 16 (January 1976):177-196. For an excellent review of actual efforts to increase citizen participation in water quality policy making see: Gregory A. Daneke, "Public

Involvement in Natural Resource Development: A Review of Water Resource Planning," *Environmental Affairs* 6 (Winter 1977):11-31.

5. Kenneth Webb and Harry Hatry, *Obtaining Citizen Feedback: The Application of Citizen Surveys to Local Governments* (Washington, D.C.: The Urban Institute, 1973); John Jackson and William Shades, "Citizen Participation, Democratic Representation, and Survey Research," *Urban Affairs Quarterly* 9 (September 1973):57-89; and Tim Ryles and John Hutchinson, "The Use of Surveys as Citizen Participation Mechanisms," *Georgia Political Science Association Journal* 2 (Fall 1974):3-16.

6. D. Stephen Cupps, "Emerging Problems of Citizen Participation," *Public Administration Review* 37 (September/October 1977):478-487.

7. Robert Aleshire, "Planning and Citizen Participation: Costs, Benefits and Approaches," *Urban Affairs Quarterly* 6 (June 1970):369-393.

8. Susan Hansen, "Linkage Models, Issues, and Community Politics," *American Politics Quarterly* 6 (January 1978):6.

9. Walter Rosenbaum, "The Paradoxes of Public Participation," *Administration and Society* 8 (November 1976):378.

10. Ibid., p. 378.

11. Sidney Verba and Norman Nie, *Participation in America: Social Equality and Political Democracy* (New York: Harper and Row, 1971).

12. Although the following analysis will mainly include survey items related to water quality and the Section 208 water quality planning process, only one-fifth of the questionnaire addressed this specific issue. The remainder of the survey was devoted to a variety of other environmental concerns.

13. Leaders already included in the sample were asked to give the names of three to five persons from the Niagara Frontier Region whom they believed were key people for the following things: developing a water quality plan, judging the acceptability of a plan, and implementing a plan. Elected officials also were asked on whom they most relied for advice in making decisions about water quality problems. Persons nominated by three or more leaders were included in the leader sample. Ninety-eight percent of those nominated already had been selected by position.

14. Verba and Nie, *Participation in America*, pp. 135-136.

15. Ibid., pp. 64-70.

16. Bryan Jones et al., "Bureaucratic Response to Citizen Initiated Contacts: Environmental Enforcement in Detroit," *American Political Science Review* 71 (March 1977):148-165. Unfortunately, they had no data on civic orientations.

17. People interested in this literature may begin with the appropriate section in Richard Niemi and Herbert Weisberg, eds. *Controversies in American Voting Behavior* (San Francisco: W.H. Freeman, 1977).

18. William Riker and Peter Ordeshook, "A Theory of the Calculus of Voting," *American Political Science Review* 62 (March 1968):25-42; and

Anthony Downs, *An Economic Theory of Democracy* (New York: Harper and Row, 1957).

19. Kurt Lewin, *Field Theory in the Social Sciences* (New York: Harper Torchbooks, 1951), pp. 238-239.

20. In a survey of public perception of water quality problems in the Atlanta metropolitan area Hines and Willeke have found a strong relationship between perception of the water quality problem and propensity to write a legislator. In other words, the more serious people considered the water quality problem, the more likely they were to say that they would write a legislator. See William Hines and Gene Willeke, "Public Perceptions of Water Quality in a Metropolitan Area," *Water Resources Bulletin* 10 (August 1974):745-755.

21. Michael Steinman, "Low Income and Minority Group Participation in Administrative Processes: Mexican American Orientations to Health Care Services," *Urban Affairs Quarterly* 11 (June 1976):523-544.

22. Income, job prestige, and education were standardized and then summed, creating a simple additive index with equal weight given to each variable. Although Verba and Nie use occupation and not job prestige to measure respondents' socioeconomic status, we do not think there is a significant difference between the two measures.

23. Verba and Nie, *Participation in America,* chap. 8, and Lester Milbrath and M.L. Goel, *Political Participation: How and Why Do People Get Involved in Politics,* 2d ed. (Chicago, Rand McNally, 1977), pp. 90-96.

24. Milbrath and Goel, *Political Participation,* p. 114.

25. Ibid., p. 115.

26. Verba and Nie, *Participation in America,* p. 243.

27. Community type is measured in a manner similar to Verba and Nie's "boundedness" index (see Verba and Nie, *Participation in America,* pp. 237-247). The community type variable in this study has the following values: (1) rural areas, (2) suburbs, (3) core urban areas, and (4) rural villages.

28. To avoid response set the two questions were introduced in different sections of the survey.

29. Originally, seventeen variables were included in the regression analysis. Four variables were found to be less theoretically important and explained little variance, and they were dropped from the final regression analysis. The four variables were: (1) the distance people live from water, (2) level of satisfaction with the "level of pride people around here have toward their community," (3) whether we should "keep our freedom to do what we want or should we do what is planned as best for the community," and (4) "should the community set rules for the use of property or should people be free to do what they want with their own property."

30. The type of regression analysis is stepwise regression. For each variable missing, data were recoded to equal the mean. An analysis of the characteristics of the subsample having missing data revealed little bias.

31. Further evidence of this can be found in Jonathan Czarnecki, "Participation Intent in Water Quality Planning: Survey Evidence" (Ph.D. diss., State University of New York at Buffalo, forthcoming); and Sheldon Kamieniecki and Steven Cohen, "Patterns of Water Recreation Activity on the Niagara Frontier," *Environmental Studies Center Occasional Papers Series,* no. 6 (Buffalo, N.Y.: State University of New York at Buffalo, 1977).

32. Further analyses along these lines revealed rather small but significant relationships between organizational membership and type of community, and level of satisfaction with the "level of pride people around here have toward their community," whether we should "keep our freedom to do what we want or should we do what is planned as best for the community," and "should the community set rules for the use of property or should people be free to do what they want with their own property." These three variables are correlated with intention to participate in water quality planning, but the correlations are small.

33. Daniel Mazmanian and Jeanne Nienaber, "Prospects for Public Participation in Federal Agencies: The Case of the Army Corps of Engineers," in Pierce and Doerksen, *Water Politics,* pp. 225-247.

34. Daniel Mazmanian, "Participatory Democracy in a Federal Agency," in Pierce and Doerksen, *Water Politics,* pp. 201-247.

5 Environmental Decision Making in the Lower Courts: The Reserve Mining Case

Norman J. Vig

Introduction: Courts and the Environment

Several years ago Professor Joseph Sax presented an eloquent and persuasive case for greater reliance on the courts in environmental decision making. In *Defending the Environment,*[1] Sax argued that the judiciary provides a far more objective, sensitive forum for protection of environmental interests than do administrative agencies charged with implementation of environmental policies. Whereas such agencies are subject to intense pressures from regulated parties and politicians to accommodate specific interests—what Sax called the "nibbling phenomenon"—judges, he argued, are relatively free of such pressures and are experienced in the art of balancing diverse rights and values, including those of citizen plaintiffs who have no other access to the power structure. Thus, the courts could better defend broader public interests such as environmental quality. Sax advocated adoption of state environmental rights acts making every citizen a "private attorney general."

At the same time, however, much of the political science literature on judicial behavior casts doubt on the political neutrality and objectivity of the courts. Local courts especially are viewed as an integral link in the political system, standing at the intersection of the judicial hierarchy and local politics. In a classic study of urban trial courts, Kenneth Dolbeare wrote of "their total integration with the local political system"[2] and noted their propensity to uphold the community status quo, particularly in matters involving individual property rights. He concluded with a pessimistic assessment of their contribution to urban policy development:

> The impact of the courts in this regard is disproportionate to the relatively small number of policy areas in which they operate and the relatively few cases they actually decide; when it comes to public action to meet urban needs, present or future, the courts acquire special and major influence in the policy-making process—almost all of which is in the direction of doing things exactly as they have been done in the past.[3]

Although other scholars have emphasized variations in judicial processes, role perceptions, and partisanship in different states,[4] or deviations among lower courts in implementing higher court decisions,[5] lower court judges are rarely seen as either innovative or free from the constraints of local political culture.

Whichever image is correct, the courts have clearly come to play a critical role in environmental policy making in the 1970s. Environmental law has exploded into a major field of litigation in the wake of federal and state legislation enacted since 1969. This legislation typically has been ambiguous and speculative, with broad delegation of regulatory authority to administrative agencies and officials. Hence the courts have been massively engaged in statutory construction and judicial review of administrative actions in the implementation process. In doing so they have undoubtedly shaped the outcome of many environmental policies. Yet numerous questions have been raised about specific decisions and about the adequacy of the courts generally in this realm. Most importantly, legal commentators and judges themselves have expressed doubts concerning judicial capabilities for resolving the complex scientific and technical issues that arise in environmental litigation. At least one well-known practitioner, Chief Judge Bazelon of the District of Columbia Court of Appeals, has argued that "substantive review of mathematical and scientific evidence by technically illiterate judges is dangerously unreliable."[6] Another federal judge recently lamented that "perhaps no other field of public regulation requires such a complex balancing of so many subtle relationships."[7] Others have suggested the need for scientific assistance or even special "science courts" to resolve technical disputes.[8] At a minimum, then, both the legal and the behavioral literature suggest caution in assigning defense of newly defined public interests such as environmental protection to the courts, especially local courts.

Focus

This chapter explores the role of the lower courts in an emerging field of jurisprudence, namely the development and application of new legal doctrines or "decision rules" for regulating uncertain risks of future harm. Although judicial innovation in this area has received considerable legal attention,[9] commentaries have thus far focused exclusively on the role of the federal courts. This study extends the analysis to state and local court decisions made persuant to federal judgments in *United States* v. *Reserve Mining,* one of the longest and costliest environmental disputes to date. In particular, we are concerned with the extent to which lower courts are following the lead of the federal courts in developing new approaches to risk assessment or use of risk-benefit analysis in resolving controversies over uncertain environmental hazards.

Most carcinogenic substances and other toxic materials pose long-range threats to public health and ecological systems that are still poorly understood by the scientific community.[10] The effects of exposure may not be evident for 15 to 40 years and such basic desiderata as response thresholds and dose-response linkages to chronic illness among different population groups may be totally unknown. Yet chronic, low-level exposures could have catastrophic impacts on both man and the environment in the future, making delay in adoption of precautionary controls increasingly risky. Hence Congress and the courts have recently begun to define new standards for regulating toxic substances and hazardous wastes—standards that go far beyond any previous regulation.[11] Since it is ultimately the courts that determine whether to prohibit particular substances or enjoin specific activities, the evolution of judicial doctrines and attitudes toward uncertain risks of future harm is vitally important.

It is further posited here that the lower courts are a critical link in the development of judicial safeguards against such environmental hazards. Environmental regulation involves an intricate sharing of powers among federal, state, and local authorities. Most federal pollution controls are directly administered by state agencies; these agencies and local governments also enforce a host of other regulations concerning land use, waste disposal, energy development, natural resources, transportation, health, industry, and agriculture. Although environmental litigation under federal law normally originates in the federal courts, action by state and local courts is often necessary to implement higher court decisions or to supplement federal regulation at some stage of implementation. While nuclear power plants are licensed by the Nuclear Regulatory Commission under careful scrutiny by the federal courts, location of other industrial and energy facilities is a state responsibility governed by state law; consequently the siting of hazardous facilities is most likely to end up in state court. In short, state and local courts may be the first (or last!) line of defense in numerous environmental disputes involving population exposure to hazardous sources.

The *Reserve Mining* case provides a good example of the problems inherent in judicial policy innovation and implementation regarding environmental risks of this kind. Decisions in the *Reserve* case require the company to invest some $300 million by 1980 for on-land disposal facilities to handle its daily discharge of 67,000 tons of taconite tailings. The federal district court decision in 1974 (later modified by the Eighth Circuit Court of Appeals) terminating discharge into Lake Superior is widely viewed as a benchmark in the evolution of judicial risk assessment. It has been the subject of extensive legal commentary.[12] Indeed, federal court decisions in *Reserve* have recently been cited as a model for resolving other technically complex disputes involving potentially catastrophic risks such as those surrounding nuclear power plant safety.[13] It is suggested here that lower court judgments on siting the disposal basin at "milepost 7" near Silver Bay, Minnesota raise considerable doubt about the precedential value of *Reserve* and the status of judicial risk assessment generally.

It is fully recognized that a single case study cannot provide definitive conclusions regarding lower-court behavior, particularly because judicial roles as well as statutory provisions vary greatly among the states. However, the choice among rules for decision making in environmental risk assessment cases appears to be limited, and *Reserve Mining* is representative of a broad range of cases with the following characteristics:

1. A high level of scientific and technical uncertainty over the nature and probabilities of future risks of harm.
2. Potential health or environmental consequences of such magnitude that even low probabilities of occurrence might justify precautionary regulation.
3. Strong community pressures or local political interests opposed to curtailment or loss of economic and social benefits provided by the potential risk agent.
4. Wide disagreement among experts representing different parties over the economic and technical feasibility of risk abatement options.
5. Conflicts among state laws and between state and federal policies regarding standards and procedures for review of administrative decisions on environmental risk taking.
6. A consequent need for judicial policy making in balancing largely indeterminate risks to society (including future generations) against more tangible (although often unquantifiable) costs and benefits of risk reduction to present community groups.

In the following section we present a brief summary of the *Reserve Mining* case and an overview of its legal and political significance. Then follows a discussion of the emergence of risk-benefit standards of proof in the federal courts and the problem of environmental balancing. We then examine the conflicting decisions of state environmental agencies and state courts on siting the Reserve disposal basin at Milepost 7. Finally, we offer in conclusion several hypotheses regarding environmental judgments by lower courts in cases such as those outlined.

The *Reserve Mining* Case

On July 7, 1978, the corporate owners of the Reserve Mining Company announced their intention to continue operations in Minnesota despite anticipated costs of $370 million for plant improvements and construction of the disposal facility at Milepost 7 by April 15, 1980.[14] Thus culminated the decade-long battle of state and federal governments and environmentalists to force Reserve to stop the discharge of its taconite tailings into Lake Superior. Had it not been for the intervention of the state courts, however, it is possible that Armco and Republic Steel would have closed their Reserve subsidiary by 1978, for state environmental agencies had denied permits for construction of the tailings basin at Milepost 7. Throughout the litigation company attorneys had insisted that Reserve would leave Minnesota if permission were not granted for this site.[15]

We cannot summarize the entire Reserve controversy here. A brief chronology of events is included in table 5-1. State officials had strongly encouraged the development of taconite mining in the 1940s and 1950s as a means of reviving the Mesabi Iron Range economy following exhaustion of most high-grade ore deposits. State permits were granted in 1947 for construction of Reserve's

Table 5-1
Reserve Mining Case: Chronology of Key Events

Date		Event
1947		Reserve Mining granted permits by state agencies to build taconite beneficiating plant at Silver Bay, Minnesota
1955		Beginning of plant operations
1968		Taconite Study Group (Stoddard Report)
1969	May	Federal-state enforcement conference convened
	December	First state suit filed against Reserve Mining in district court
1970	December	State district court finds for Reserve Mining
1972	February	U.S. Justice Department files suit in federal district court
1973	August	Federal trial begins
1974	April 20	Judge Lord enjoins all further discharge of Reserve Mining tailings into Lake Superior. Reserve found guilty of violating various state and federal air and water pollution laws and ordered to cease operations
	April 22	8th Circuit Court of Appeals stays injunction pending full hearing
	November	Reserve makes first application for tailings basin at Milepost 7 site
1975	March 14	Court of appeals issues full opinion on merits: Reserve Mining found guilty of air and water pollution violations, with tailings in lake presenting a potential risk to public health; Reserve Mining ordered to begin installation of air pollution equipment and seek permits from State of Minnesota for on-land disposal; company and state given 1 year to reach agreement on site; if no agreement reached, Reserve Mining to have 1 additional year to find solution or close down; Reserve Mining to have reasonable time to complete facilities if permits granted.
1976	July 1	Minnesota Pollution Control Agency and Department of Natural Resources accept hearing officer's report and deny permits for Milepost 7 site in favor of Milepost 20.
1977	January 28	State district court upholds Reserve Mining and finds state agency decisions unreasonable and arbitrary
		State agencies appeal to state supreme court
	April 8	State supreme court affirms district decision and orders state agencies to issue permits for Milepost 7 with certain conditions
		Reserve appeals permit conditions defined by Pollution Control agency
	October	State district court upholds Reserve Mining on claims that permit conditions are more stringent than allowed under supreme court decision
1978	April	State supreme court reverses district court and orders Reserve Mining to comply with permit conditions
	July	Reserve Mining announces intention to continue operations in Minnesota

"beneficiating" or pelletizing plant at Silver Bay on the shore of Lake Superior, and the plant began operating in 1955. The town of Silver Bay was largely built by the company and came to house some 3,000 employees and their families. It was not until 1968 that federal officials in the Interior Department and state officials in the Pollution Control Agency began to manifest concern over pollution of the lake as they began developing water quality standards under the Federal Water Pollution Control Act.

For analytical perspective the Reserve litigation may be divided into four stages: (1) initial state and federal litigation over pollution of Lake Superior *per se*, beginning with federal-state enforcement conferences in 1969 and continuing into state and federal suits under water pollution standards up to mid-1973; (2) the major federal district court trial and circuit court appeal of 1973-1975, during which attention shifted dramatically to the potential risks to public health posed by the asbestos-like fibers in Reserve's tailings, which entered the drinking water supply of North Shore communities. This culminated in the court of appeals mandate of March 14, 1975, requiring Reserve to reach agreement with Minnesota on an on-land disposal site within two years or shut down; (3) state administrative proceedings and state court decisions on the suitability of Milepost 7 and other sites for this facility, leading to the state supreme court decision of April 8, 1977, reversing state agency denial of Reserve's permit application for Milepost 7; and (4) final litigation between Reserve and state agencies over specific permit conditions, ending in a second supreme court decision upholding agency permits in April, 1978. This study focuses primarily on the third phase in light of the federal court decisions of the second stage.

Legal scholars have concentrated much attention on the introduction of a risk-benefit standard of proof by Judge Miles Lord in the district court decision and its subsequent adoption (in modified form) by the Eighth Circuit Court. Judge Skelly Wright of the D.C. Federal Circuit subsequently elaborated this standard in *Ethyl Corporation* v. *EPA* in which federal regulation of lead additives in gasoline was upheld despite uncertainties in the chain of effects on public health.[16] Federal regulations on asbestos, vinyl chloride, pesticides, and other potentially carcinogenic substances have been sustained on similar grounds, as have restrictions on atmospheric ozone depletion and nuclear power plant licensing. It had been argued for some time that the traditional "imminent injury" test for court injunctions was no longer adequate for control of long-term, uncertain risks at the lower exposure levels presented by many new technologies; but it was not until the *Reserve* and *Ethyl* cases that the federal courts clearly espoused an alternative risk-benefit standard for enjoining such threats.

The political significance of *Reserve Mining* is apparent. The abatement costs may be the largest ever imposed on a single industrial firm; litigation costs alone have been estimated at well over $20 million. The Reserve Mining Company accounts for some 12 percent of all iron ore production in the United

States, a significant factor in the national economy. As an employer of 3,200 workers in its Babbitt mine and Silver Bay plant, the company is clearly a major economic force in northeastern Minnesota. The economic and social costs of shutdown were thus obvious and inevitably became a divisive political issue. Reserve's repeated threats to leave Minnesota put enormous pressure on state and local officials and courts throughout the litigation. On the other hand, Minnesota has strong environmental constituencies and vigorous state agencies for pollution control and resource management.[17] The governor, Wendell Anderson, and leading Democratic-Farmer-Labor-Party politicians in the state legislature clearly favored conversion to on-land disposal but preferred to leave controversy to the agencies and courts, since the issue split party members along regional lines. Indeed, the *Reserve* case was one in a long series of disputes pitting liberal environmental organizations and state agencies in the Twin Cities metro area against more conservative mining, lumbering, and recreational interests in the northeastern region.

With the exception of environmental organizations (such as the Save Lake Superior Association) and the city governments of Duluth and Superior whose water supplies were most seriously threatened, most local groups supported Reserve at various stages of litigation. Among intervenors on behalf of Reserve in the federal court appeal were the mining towns of Babbitt, Silver Bay, and Beaver Bay, the Range League of Municipalities and Civic Associations, the Northeastern Minnesota Development Association, the Duluth Chamber of Commerce, Lake and St. Louis Counties, and last but not least, the United Steelworkers of America, AFL-CIO. The union and some other groups favored on-land disposal but were adamantly opposed to closure of the plant and, consequently, to any alternative to the Milepost 7 site. The company-union alliance and overwhelming civic opposition to Judge Lord's injunction could not but weigh heavily in the deliberations of local judges who ultimately decided these matters.

Risk Assessment and Environmental Balancing

The courts have always had to assess risks or the probabilities of harm in seeking to balance equities or conveniences in common law cases. However, judicial principles generally required a high degree of certainty to prohibit action: evidence of "imminent injury" or "irreparable damage" as the direct conse-quence of the contested action. The burden of proof was on the plaintiff to demonstrate almost certain damage in a cause-effect sequence. Insofar as medical or other scientific analysis might help to define probabilities, such evidence must reflect a clear consensus of experts called to testify. Mere scientific theories or studies contested by other scientific authorities were unlikely to be permissible as evidence.

The problems of such an approach to environmental hazards are obvious. Many causal linkages in our ecological systems and biophysical processes are simply unknown. The mechanisms by which carcinogenic, mutagenic, and teratogenic responses are triggered by various substances are not yet known, although the incidence of many such responses are measurable. Moreover long latency periods limit the validity of current assessments of risk. Scientific uncertainty and conflict surround most projected environmental threats, making expert agreement impossible. In short, we are dealing with uncertain or unknown risks of future harm.

The federal courts have responded by seeking new legal formulae for acting against uncertain threats of potentially great consequence. One formula, first enunciated by Judge Wright in a dissent on the first *Ethyl* decision, and subsequently cited by the circuit court in *Reserve Mining,* involves a redefinition of risk as a reciprocal function of both probability of occurrence and magnitude of the harm threatened.[18] Thus risks of very low probability may nevertheless be regulated if the anticipated consequences are sufficiently grave (for example, if large populations are exposed or if there is potential for a catastrophic accident). However this is not an automatic conclusion. As the Ethyl majority later recognized in *Carolina Environmental Study Group* v. *United States,* a case involving review of nuclear power plant licensing:

> There is a point at which the probability of an occurrence may be so low as to render it almost totally unworthy of consideration. Neither we, nor the A.E.C. on this record, would treat lightly the horrible consequences of a Class 9 [catastrophic] accident. Recognition of the minimal probability of such an event is not equatable with nonrecognition of its consequences.[19]

This qualification is a logical necessity, since there is some mathematical probability of virtually every alleged occurrence. Thus the courts must decide if the probability is more than minimal before assessing the overall risk of harm as a function both of this probability and the potential severity of consequences.

The problem with this formulation is that the probabilities may not be known in any precise or mathematical sense. In cases such as *Reserve* involving potential carcinogenesis the precise incidence of exposure, the threshold level of response (assuming there is one), and cumulative dose-response linkages may all be unknown. As the Eighth Circuit Court stated in postponing Judge Lord's closure order at the end of the federal district trial: "the discharges by Reserve can be characterized only as presenting an unquantifiable risk, i.e., a health risk which either may be negligible or may be significant, but with any significance as yet based on unknowns."[20] The appellate court then went on to ask "what manner of judicial cognizance may be taken of the unknown," and concluded that

We do not think that a bare risk of the unknown can amount to proof in this case. Plaintiffs have failed to prove that a demonstrable health hazard exists. This failure, we hasten to add, is not reflective of any weakness which it is within their power to cure, but rather, given the current state of medical and scientific knowledge, plaintiff's case is based only on medical hypothesis and is simply beyond proof.[21]

However, after completing its review of the case on its merits a year later, the circuit court majority reached a different conclusion:

In assessing probabilities in this case, it cannot be said that the probability of harm is more likely than not. Moreover, the level of probability does not readily convert into a prediction of consequences. On this record it cannot be forecast that the rates of cancer will increase from drinking Lake Superior water or breathing Silver Bay air. The best that can be said is that the existence of this asbestos containment in air and water gives rise to a reasonable medical concern for the public health. The public's exposure to asbestos fibers in air and water creates some health risk. Such a contaminant should be removed.22

In effect, the court ruled that an unknown risk of future harm was judicially cognizable and enjoinable if some evidence existed for "reasonable medical concern" for public health. Hence there are grounds for regulation even when "minimal probability" cannot be established.

With this said, judicial assessment of risks cannot be realistically separated from consideration of social costs and benefits. Although measurement of risk is ideally an objective, scientific process as distinguished from the determination of safety,[23] in legal practice the two are both part of a subjective balancing process. Cost-risk-benefit analysis is not an objective science in any case.[24] In judicial decision making (as in other spheres of politics) the evaluation of economic and social costs is likely to affect the assessment of risk and vice versa. This is not to say that risk assessment is purely arbitrary or "political" however; as in scientific research, the process of reasoning employed must ultimately stand the test of superior peer review.

Chief Justice Burger enunciated the balancing principle most generally when sitting as a circuit judge in *Aberdeen & Rockfish R. Co.* v. *SCRAP* (1972):

Our society and its governmental instrumentalities, having been less than alert to the needs of our environment for generations, have now taken protective steps. These developments, however praiseworthy, should not lead courts to exercise equitable powers loosely or casually whenever a claim of "environmental damage" is asserted. The world must go on and new environmental legislation must be carefully meshed with more traditional patterns of federal regulation. The decisional process for judges is one of balancing, and it is often a most difficult task.[25]

In its initial *Reserve* decision, the Eighth Circuit noted this dictum and stated that the issues "dissolve into a single equitable judgment: balancing the health and environmental demands of society at large against the economic well-being of those parties and local communities immediately affected."[26] Judge Lord had taken a definite stand on this balance:

> The Court has been constantly reminded that a curtailment in the discharge may result in a severe economic blow to the people of Silver Bay, Babbit and others who depend on Reserve directly or indirectly for their livelihood. Certainly unemployment in itself can result in an unhealthy situation. At the same time, however, the Court must consider the people downstream from the discharge. Under no circumstances will the Court allow the people of Duluth to be continuously and indefinitely exposed to a known human carcinogen in order that the people in Silver Bay can continue working in their jobs.[27]

In response, the circuit court chastised Judge Lord for resolving "all doubts in favor of health safety" and characterized his decision as "a legislative policy judgment, not a judicial one."[28] In its final decision of 1975, the court reiterated that "in fashioning relief in a case such as this involving a possibility of future harm, a court should strike a proper balance between the benefits conferred and the hazards created by Reserve's facility."[29] The court went on to state: "A court is not powerless to act in these circumstances. But an immediate injunction cannot be justified in striking a balance between unpredictable health effects and the clearly predictable social and economic consequences that would follow the plant closing."[30] Thus, while acting to enjoin the potential health hazard on "reasonable medical concern," the court applied the balancing test to fashioning a remedy. Since the health risk was indeterminate but the economic and social costs were immediate, Reserve must be given "a reasonable opportunity and a reasonable time period" to convert to on-land disposal. The Court of Appeals thus called for Reserve and the State of Minnesota to reach early agreement on a disposal site that was both economically feasible and environmentally acceptable.

This approach to risk assessment has recently been endorsed by Joel Yellin in a superb analysis of alternative legal formulae or decision rules applicable to cases involving potentially catastrophic consequences.[31] He argues that judges must in practice decide whether probabilities or consequences are to predominate in estimating societal risks; and he suggests that in cases such as *Reserve* the gravity of possible consequences should be taken as sufficient to trigger remedial action. The balancing of probabilities, costs, and benefits should therefore be deferred to the secondary stage of fashioning a remedy, giving due weight to economic factors and other social values. The presumption is, as in the Eight Circuit opinion, that a remedy can be found that both preserves economic benefits and reduces potential risks to acceptable levels, for example, through safeguards in the siting and operation of the potentially hazardous facilities. As indicated, however, decisions on these matters are likely to fall in the province of state and local agencies and courts which may employ quite different approaches to risk assessment. We may take the siting of Reserve's facilities as an example.

The Milepost 7 Controversy

In Minnesota permits for mining operations are required from the Department of Natural Resources (DNR) and Pollution Control Agency (PCA). These agencies are governed both by their own enabling statutes and by general laws on administrative procedure and environmental policy. In this context provisions of the Minnesota Environmental Policy Act (MEPA) of 1973 became especially important, particularly chapter 116D.04, subdivision 6, which states:

> No state action significantly affecting the quality of the environment shall be allowed, nor shall any permit for natural resources management and development be granted, where such action or permit has caused or is likely to cause pollution, impairment, or destruction of the air, water, land or other natural resources located within the state, so long as there is a *feasible and prudent alternative* consistent with the *reasonable* requirements of the public health, safety, and welfare and the state's *paramount concern* for the protection of its air, water, land and other natural resources from pollution, impairment, or destruction. *Economic considerations alone shall not justify such conduct.* [Emphasis added.]

This law, modeled in part after the National Environmental Policy Act of 1969 (NEPA), requires environmental impact analysis including consideration of alternatives but goes beyond NEPA in its substantive provisions regarding permits; indeed, subdivision 6 would appear to tilt the balance in favor of environmental considerations.[32]

DNR and PCA jointly commissioned environmental impact statements on Milepost 7 and other sites and appointed a hearing examiner (Wayne Olson) to conduct formal hearings and make recommendations on Reserve's Milepost 7 application. These hearings lasted nearly 11 months and generated some 18,000 pages of testimony plus thousands of pages of exhibits. At their conclusion, the hearing officer recommended against Milepost 7 as the least desirable of the five sites investigated and determined Milepost 20 to be a "feasible and prudent alternative." After initial hesitation, PCA joined DNR in accepting this recommendation on July 1, 1976, thus setting the stage for Reserve's appeal in state court. On January 28, 1977, a three-judge panel of the Minnesota Sixth Judicial District Court (Duluth) ruled that denial of the permits by DNR and PCA was "unlawful and unreasonable," a judgment later affirmed by the State Supreme Court.

Administrative Decisions

The hearing examiner and state agencies based their decisions on environmental impact assessments and other evidence that Milepost 20 constituted a feasible and prudent alternative. Although all five sites were compared on numerous criteria including impacts on water quality, wildlife, and land use, the rejection of Milepost 7 was justified principally on two critical issues: the consequences of potential dam failure and impact of air pollution.

The first issue related to the safety of the enormous dams necessary to contain the tailings in settling ponds at Milepost 7. The largest of these dams, to be constructed of coarse tailings, would be nearly 3 miles long and 180 feet high, one of the fifteen or twenty largest dams in the country. Although the dam consultants hired by both the state and Reserve testified that such tailings dams could be safely built on the site, the hearing officer concluded that careful design and construction could not entirely eliminate the risk of dam failure. "Despite all efforts to avoid it, dams designed to be safe do fail because of accidents, errors, oversights and other causes."[33] He therefore reasoned that the consequences of dam failure at Milepost 7 must be compared to those of such potential failures at other sites. At Milepost 7 a major failure would be catastrophic since it would send a steep wall of water cascading down the embankment to Lake Superior, removing everything in its path (including several houses). Aside from loss of life and property, such a disaster would vitiate the entire project by permanently contaminating the lake as well. Hence, if given a choice between a dam site located above a populated area and another site at which the consequences of a dam failure would be much less severe, prudence dictated choice of the latter. Since Milepost 20 was in an uninhabited forest zone, in more level terrain, and beyond the coastal watershed, the hearing officer found it preferable to Milepost 7.

The second issue was even more difficult, one that plagued courts and agencies through all phases of the litigation. Epidemiological surveys had clearly established a link between inhalation of asbestos fibers and the incidence of cancer and other disease in occupational settings. In the *Reserve* trial it was first necessary to establish that fibers in Reserve discharges were identical to those of amosite asbestos known to cause disease. It was then necessary to measure the number of fibers in the air and water around Silver Bay, an exceedingly difficult task given the extremely minute size of these particles (five microns or less in length). Accurate fiber counts could not be established during the federal trial and different estimates continued to be presented and contested during the Milepost 7 hearings. Beyond this, the effects of exposure remained uncertain: for example, whether any threshold existed for the onset of adverse health effects; what the dose-response relationships and latency period were; and whether ingesting (as opposed to inhaling) asbestos fibers had any health effects at all. Nevertheless, the federal district and circuit courts had reached several basic conclusions justifying their decisions:

1. Fibers found in Reserve's discharge are asbestiform needle-like fibers with properties identical or similar to amosite asbestos, a known human carcinogen.
2. Fibers of less than five microns in length cannot be considered less dangerous to health than fibers of greater than five microns of length.
3. Reserve's discharges into the air and water give rise to a potential threat to the public health.
4. The threat to public health from air emissions is more significant than that from the water discharge.
5. There is no known safe exposure or threshold limit to asbestiform fibers.[34]

Within this framework, controversy over the Milepost 7 site centered on the potential adverse health effects to people in the Silver Bay area from air pollution generated by the new disposal facility.

Specifically, this question turned on projections about the amount of fugitive dust to be generated in the vicinity by construction and operation of the tailings basin. Conflicting projections (based on different assumptions and methodologies) were presented by state and Reserve witnesses, while the parameters changed as Reserve agreed to various alterations for mitigating dust escape from the ponds and dams. New techniques of climatological dispersion modeling were employed for projecting this flow with widely varying results. In the end, the hearing officer concluded that most of the projections were conservative and that if Milepost 7 were implemented, the level of fibers in the Silver Bay area would be at least as high as that found to present a potential health hazard by the federal courts. Since the Court of Appeals had ordered immediate abatement of air pollution and since an alternative site farther from centers of human population was available at Milepost 20, the officer found Milepost 7 unacceptable on air quality criteria. Indeed, he determined that Milepost 7 was the worst of the five alternatives on these grounds as well as on dam safety. (The examiner also found Milepost 7 the least desirable of all sites in terms of water quality impacts and land-use planning, although it did have some advantage over Milepost 20 on potential energy consumption.)

The agencies, then, based their decisions on a comparative assessment of risks that they believed were mandated by the Minnesota Environmental Policy Act. In terms of Yellin's analysis of decision rules, they regarded potential consequences as determinative in their consideration of alternative sites as in the earlier federal decision to halt discharge into Lake Superior. As mission-oriented environmental agencies it is not surprising that they perceived their role as one of minimizing environmental risks by choosing the least dangerous alternative. In light of our earlier discussion, however, two questions arise concerning this approach to risk-benefit assessment. First, did the agencies establish a minimum significance threshold of potential danger at any site (or, alternatively, did "reasonable medical concern" justify consideration of alternatives at this stage)? Second, regardless of this, did the agencies give sufficient weight to economic and social factors in considering "feasible" and "prudent" alternatives "consistent with the reasonable requirements of the public health, safety, and welfare" as well as the state's "paramount concern" for the environment (that is, did the agencies engage in the kind of balancing required by law)? Reserve contested both of these points as well as the factual findings and conclusions of the hearing officer in its appeal to the state district court. Before examining the local court's response let us reflect briefly on the court's role in the process.

Judicial Decisions

Few judicial bodies are overtly political. Partisan and personal value preferences are normally moderated by legal training, socialization, established role perceptions, and nonpartisan methods of recruitment. In Minnesota, judges are required to have professional qualifications and are elected by nonpartisan ballot for six-year terms. Although interim appointments are frequently made by the governor between general elections, judicial elections are rarely contested and are regarded by most as genuinely nonpartisan.[35] On the other hand, local judges have frequently served in other political offices before selection and may have well-established ties to social and economic interests or community (if not party) elites. Moreover, if they are life-long residents of the district, they are likely to embody community values and resist changes that arouse intense local opposition or community conflict. For example, judicial impact studies have demonstrated that lower courts in other states have strongly resisted Supreme Court decisions that contravene local mores regarding civil rights, religion in schools, and criminal procedure. Although there are no comparable studies of environmental litigation, we might expect similar patterns of judicial accommodation when local interests feel strongly threatened by higher-level decisions concerning risk assessment.

It must also be recognized that local courts may have wide latitude in applying federal and state precedents and in construing precedents and state legislation. While subject to reversal by higher appellate courts (in Minnesota only the state Supreme Court), the great majority of local court decisions are final. Moreover, the power of judicial review is flexible, often permitting extensive local court intervention in state administrative decision making. The scope and standard for judicial review of agency actions is typically ambiguous or subject to conflicting statutes.[36] In the *Reserve* case, much of the legal argument turned on whether the local court should apply a narrow "arbitrary and capricious" test in reviewing the Milepost 7 decisions or whether, as Reserve argued, the court should adopt a broader "rule of reason" in reconsidering the overall rationality of the decision. Federal and state precedents were cited on both sides (notably U.S. Supreme Court dicta from the leading federal case, *Citizens to Preserve Overton Park, Inc.* v. *Volpe*); and the local court in this instance opted to reopen the case, take new testimony of its own, and probe the reasonableness of the entire permit decision. This "searching judicial scrutiny" was justified on grounds that the hearing officer's findings "involving policy determinations, risk analysis and predictions based on the frontiers of scientific knowledge" required especially thorough review.[37]

There is some evidence that higher state courts are less likely to overturn environmental agency decisions than those of most other state agencies.[38] Insofar as state appellate courts have broader constituencies than local courts, they might be more insulated from direct economic and social pressures and more inclined to support state regulatory authority. However, patterns vary considerably among states, and relatively few cases have yet been decided. In Minnesota, the Supreme Court has upheld discretionary regulatory decisions of environmental agencies in two other recent cases, both involving strong citizen opposition to planned transmission line routes.[39] The *Reserve* case, on the other hand, was a major state and federal issue placing the state court at the center of intergovernmental decision making and corporate political pressures. It is noteworthy that Reserve Mining reiterated its intention to leave Minnesota in the event of a contrary decision in its final oral argument before the Supreme Court, a threat taken as credible by the entire bench. In zero-sum situations such as this, cost-risk-benefit analysis becomes extremely difficult. But let us examine the arguments of the district and state courts.

The district court found agency cost-risk-benefit assessment deficient in three major respects: (1) on dam safety, the hearing examiner's report concerned "imaginary or speculative possibilities" or "remote contingencies"; (2) in regard to ambient air quality, the agencies failed to establish that projected fiber counts around Milepost 7 reached a "medically significant level"; and (3) in considering alternatives and balancing risks and costs, the agencies paid insufficient attention to economic factors. We will consider each of these in turn.

Remote Contingencies. The district court found the hearing officer and agencies unreasonable in demanding "absolute safety" in dam construction. The five dam experts who testified at the trial unanimously agreed that the Milepost 7 dams would be "safe beyond human doubt." "By definition," the court stated, "a *safe* dam cannot fail."[40] Hence "the speculative catastrophic results from a failure could not occur," and the hearing examiner was improperly concerned with remote contingencies. Risk can never be eliminated absolutely, the court argued; to think otherwise would mean that "no project would be permitted, and the wheels of industry and progress would grind to a halt."[41] It was therefore unnecessary to consider the comparative consequences of dam failure.

In upholding the lower court on this point, the Minnesota Supreme Court argued that absolute safety is impossible and that environmental statutes do not contemplate such certainty. The court cited the minimum threshold of risk standard from *Carolina Environmental Study Group,* as well as another nuclear power plant case (*North Anna Environmental Coalition* v. *U.S. Nuclear Regula-tory Commission*), in which absolutely risk-free siting was rejected in favor of "adequate protection to the health and safety of the public."[42] Since a minimum threshold of risk was not met, the court reasoned, the law requiring consideration of feasible and prudent alternatives could not apply. In the author's judgment there is clearly precedent for this position in the federal case law cited and in the state Environmental Policy Act, which forbids action which "has caused or is likely to cause pollution, impairment, or destruction of . . . natural resources. . . ." On the other hand, the agencies were not con-cerned with absolute safety but with minimizing risks, a strategy that also appears justified in the state law.

Medically Significant Level. The question of air pollution was even more difficult. Whereas the consulting experts agreed unanimously on dam safety, state and Reserve witnesses differed sharply over projected asbestos fiber counts at Milepost 7 and other sites. At the federal trial a court-appointed witness had testified that, given existing methods of counting, the margin of error was enormous—a factor of nine in either direction or nearly two orders of magnitude overall. Given this constraint, and the absence of any known safe level of exposure to asbestos dust, the circuit court adopted a surrogate standard: it ordered Reserve to reduce the fiber count in the ambient air around its facilities "below a medically significant level," which was defined as the level found in the city of St. Paul (where no adverse health effects had been observed). The federal court accepted initial estimates (subject to ninefold error) of 62,600 fibers per cubic meter at Silver Bay compared to about 7,000 fibers per cubic meter in the control city of St. Paul.

The issue of fiber counting was enormously complicated by two further factors in the later stages of litigation: the need to project fiber counts resulting from construction and operation of the tailings basin in the future, and the offsetting effects of mitigating measures agreed to by Reserve near the very end of the administrative hearings. Suffice it to say that projected fiber counts (using different assumptions and methodologies) varied wildly. Reserve experts, for example, projected a level of 7,826-13,680 fibers per cubic meter, well within later estimates of ambient fibers at St. Paul. This compared to state predictions of 132,000 per cubic meter at Silver Bay if Milepost 7 were used (or 32,000 if Milepost 20 were adopted). Sierra Club witnesses, on the other hand, rejected both state and Reserve methodologies and projected fiber levels at Silver Bay ranging from 620,800 to 1,891,500. The second set of uncertainties involved projecting the offsetting effects of Reserve's abatement measures at the existing Silver Bay plant and mitigating design changes at Milepost 7. Reserve claimed, and the air quality staff of PCA agreed, that fiber emissions from Reserve's beneficiating plant within Silver Bay could be reduced by up to 97 percent under negotiated stipulation agreements. The district court calculated that this factor alone would reduce the combined impact of Silver Bay and Milepost 7 operations by 75 percent regardless of mitigative measures at Milepost 7. Considering design changes at Milepost 7 accepted by Reserve in the last stages of the administrative hearings (notably to submerge most coarse as well as fine tailings under water), the court found no substantial evidence that fiber counts at Silver Bay would approach a "medically significant level." Hence, as in dam safety, no consideration of alternative sites was necessitated.

Was this conclusion justified? The state agencies, while in agreement that fiber levels could be greatly reduced if appropriate control technologies were in fact implemented by Reserve, nevertheless argued that since precise fiber counts were impossible and no known threshold of safe exposure existed, prudence required selection of any feasible alternative site more remote from population centers (relative exposure being largely a function of distance). The state Supreme Court rejected this "less is better than more" logic on two counts: if the tailings dump were to present a health hazard, it would not be fair to shift the burden from residents of Silver Bay to other communities (for example, users of Superior National Forest in the vicinity of Milepost 20); and second, "No medically significant level of dust has been determined and no standards for emission have been established."[43] In regard to the latter point, the Supreme Court noted that no accurate fiber count had yet been made for St. Paul and that all estimates for Silver Bay remained well below occupational standards for asbestos.

What the Supreme Court admitted at this point is that the issue of public health had not been resolved. Given the medical uncertainties over exposure effects noted by the federal courts and the continuing inaccuracies of measurement and prediction admitted by all parties in the state proceedings, the court could not in fact say whether a medically significant risk would exist or not. Nor could the circuit court's surrogate standard be implemented if accurate fiber count comparisons could not be made. Moreover the federal courts had ruled the occupational standards irrelevant to environmental air pollution. Nevertheless, the Supreme Court ruled that "no risk has been proved by substantial evidence." In essence, the state courts demanded a higher standard of proof than had the federal courts in removing the tailings from the lake in the first place. Although asbestos fibers were known to cause cancer and other diseases when inhaled (as opposed to ingested), the burden of proof was shifted from "reasonable medical concern" to "substantial evidence" of a "medically significant level" as the tailings were transferred from water to land and air.

Economic Feasibility. In these circumstances, choice of a site presenting lesser risk to population centers was certainly desirable. But was it also prudent financially? The difference in cost between Mileposts 7 and 20 was estimated by the state at $80 million and by Reserve at $140 million. Both Judge Lord and the state hearing examiner had found either alternative within Reserve's financial resources despite the company's argument that Milepost 20 was economically unfeasible. The federal Court of Appeals had clearly weighted this argument heavily in chastising Judge Lord for resolving all doubts in favor of health safety. Similarly, the state district court devoted considerable discussion to the social and economic consequences of closure and condemned the agencies for failure to take them seriously. The basic principle espoused by the local court was that "economic factors must be given at least equal consideration in making environmental decisions."[44] Hence the substantial additional cost to Reserve of going to Milepost 20 and the economic, social, and psychological impact of potential closure on the people of Silver Bay must be considered in striking a balance. Given the indeterminate risks at Milepost 7 and the evident willingness of Reserve employees to bear them, the district court found an overwhelming balance in favor of Reserve's application.

The nature of the balancing process mandated by even the best environmental statutes is unclear. The provisions of the Minnesota Environmental Policy Act emphasize both the state's "paramount concern" for its natural resources as well as "reasonable" requirements of public health, safety, and welfare. While economic considerations alone cannot justify pollution, impairment or destruction of natural resources, such considerations are clearly not irrelevant either. Another passage in the law directs agencies to "ensure that environmental amenities and values, whether quantified or not, will be given at least equal consideration in decision making along with economic and technical considerations."[45] In this context, the law can be read to require equal consideration of environmental and economic parameters; but this hardly clarifies its use as a guide to decision making. The Minnesota Supreme Court attempted to explain the balancing process as follows:

> We have previously indicated that state agencies and courts are required by statute to consider both the economic impact and the environmental impact in rendering decisions dealing with environmental matters. . . . As we construe the statutes, . . . if there were substantial evidence that Reserve's proposed tailings site at Mile Post 7 would have significantly adverse medical effects on the residents of Silver Bay, no further consideration would be given to the economic consequences of a total shutdown and the site would be rejected. We are not free to barter the health of residents of Silver Bay for their economic security, even if that were their intention, which it is not. It is only where the likelihood of danger to the public is remote and speculative that economic impacts which are devastating and certain may be weighed in the balance in arriving at an environmentally sound decision.[46]

This formulation appears far more congruent with the intent of the law than the district court's blunt demand for "at least equal consideration of economic factors." However it rests in this instance on a presumption of "remote and speculative danger," although, as indicated earlier, the degree of risk could not be accurately determined by the courts.

The courts are understandably reluctant to shoulder the consequences of economic dislocation in the absence of clear legislative direction. Yet, given the nature of environmental issues and statutes, the burden of making such decisions will increasingly fall on the courts. Since the marginal costs and benefits of most environmental hazards cannot be accurately measured, no fine-tuned balancing is likely to prove possible in making such decisions. Hence, when economic costs are tangible, quantifiable, and substantial, but risks and benefits are uncertain and unquantified, the latter are unlikely to prevail in the balancing process.

Summary and Conclusions

Two conclusions emerge from the *Reserve* case study. First, the development of decision rules for judicial risk assessment is both critical and highly problematical given the uncertainties of present environmental hazards. Second, the lower courts are unlikely to take the lead in constructing judicial safeguards against future environmental risks. Let us consider each of these points briefly.

Judicial Risk Assessment

Although the federal courts have begun to formulate risk-benefit standards for controlling long-term uncertain hazards, no single formulation has emerged for relating probabilities of occurrence to the severity of consequences in estimating overall risk of harm. The courts have alternatively considered probability or consequences as the determining standard, with profound implications for the outcome. When probabilities are taken as the determining factor, a threshold of "minimal probability" (or, conversely, "remote contingency") or "minimal significance" (for example, a "medically significant level" of exposure) must be crossed for judicial remedy, regardless of the severity of potential consequences. But if potential severity of consequences is determinative, precautionary action may be justified even though probabilities of occurrence are unknown (for example, on the basis of "reasonable medical concern"). In the *Reserve* case, the latter precautionary standard was formulated and applied by Judge Lord, whereas the lower courts clearly emphasized the minimal probabilities of health impacts.

The third parameter—that of balancing risks against social and economic costs and benefits—may be even more important in the overall judicial outcome. The Eighth Circuit Court made it clear that, however risks were determined, economic and social realities must be considered in fashioning a remedy. Under Minnesota law, however, economic factors could not override environmental protection; hence it was the duty of state officials, no less than the federal judges, to seek an appropriate balance in the siting process. It is instructive that the state agencies and local courts arrived at opposite conclusions in this context. The environmental agencies perceived their role as one of minimizing risks to public health and natural resources by selection of the least consequential alternative. Local judges, by contrast, viewed the controversy in terms of their traditional rule of reason, by which substantial evidence of probable harm was deemed necessary for imposing economic and social costs on the community. If the agencies, like Judge Lord, could be faulted for resolving doubts in favor of public health and safety, the local district court resolved all environmental uncertainties in favor of maximum economic and social benefits. Although the Minnesota Supreme Court attempted to avoid both pitfalls by considering assessment of health risks a precondition for economic balancing, it too was unwilling to lower the barriers to regulation of uncertain consequences.

The *Reserve* case thus suggests that formidable problems face the courts (and other agencies of government) in developing consistent decision rules for evaluating uncertain environmental risks. We hypothesize that judges face two fundamental and interdependent choices in making risk-benefit decisions: a choice as to definition of risk—that is, whether risk is to be conceptualized in probabilities or consequences, with the implications noted, and second a balancing choice, or value judgment, as to the relative significance of socio-economic costs and benefits as against environmental or health risks, however determined. Either of these decisions may in practice influence the other and determine the overall outcome. We illustrate these relationships by combining the two types of choices in a single matrix. (See figure 5-1.) This yields four possible types of decision making. In type I decisions, risk may be evaluated in terms of unacceptable environmental consequences, with these consequences considered more significant than any economic or social consequences that might result from eliminating them. In effect, the projected severity of harm is the determinative factor in this type of decision; that is, any socioeconomic consequences are considered secondary or irrelevant. This pattern characterizes Judge Lord's decisions in the federal district trial and state agency decisions over Milepost 7.

Type II and III decisions are more complex, since the components of the decisions pull in opposite directions. In case II, the court accepts a definition of risk in terms of intolerable environmental consequences; but it also attempts to maximize socioeconomic benefits to the community by seeking a remedy that permits continuation of the activity under mitigating controls. This type of decision (which characterizes much federal regulation) is possible in the earlier phases of control when abatement strategies are feasible; but it may only provide temporary relief if pollution is shifted from one medium to another (for example, from water to land) or cannot be reduced sufficiently to allay environmental concerns. The decisions of the Eighth Circuit Court fall in this category. In type III decisions, the probability of adverse environmental or health effects is determinative in risk assessment; but elimination of such effects is considered more important than any socioeconomic costs or benefits in the balancing process. Hence, if a minimum threshold of significance is crossed,

	Balancing	Principal Benefits
	Environmental/ Health	Economic/ Social
Consequences	I	II
Probabilities	III	IV

Risk Definition (row label at left, spanning lower section)

Figure 5-1. Decision-Making Matrix.

protection of the environment and health is a precondition for tradeoffs to preserve economic benefits. The opinion of the Minnesota Supreme Court espouses this doctrine regarding Milepost 7, although it is questionable if the evidence on potential health risks supported it.

In type IV decisions, on the other hand, the balance is clearly drawn in favor of maximizing socioeconomic benefits, unless the probabilities of environmental or health impairment definitely require tradeoffs (the state district court's position). In this case, as in type I, one of the basic choices is likely to determine the other, in both cases influencing the standard of proof and willingness to enjoin a potential threat of future harm.

The sequence of judicial decisions in *Reserve Mining* are summarized in table 5-2. Thus the *Reserve* case does not provide a single model for environmental decision making, but rather illustrates a full range of choices among decision rules for judicial risk assessment. Yellin's analysis supports pattern II as a general approach to other complex issues involving potentially catastrophic consequences (for example, nuclear power plant licensing). This study suggests, however, that issues of similar gravity arise in siting hazardous facilities, requiring comparable risk assessment at state and local levels. When the potential consequences of proposed actions remain highly uncertain, as in this case, the decision model adopted by the lower courts may have a decisive influence on the final evaluation of alternatives.

Decisions of the Lower Courts

The *Reserve* example suggests the following tentative hypotheses regarding lower-court behavior in risk assessment cases:

Table 5-2
Sequence of Judicial Decisions in the *Reserve* Case

Court	Decision Type
Federal District Court	I
Federal Circuit Court	II
State District Court	IV
State Supreme Court	III

1. State and local courts are likely to define risk in terms of probability thresholds rather than in terms of the severity of possible consequences.

2. Probability definitions of risk are more compatible with traditional judicial standards of proof than are consequential definitions; since the lower courts are less innovative in approaching new problems than the federal courts, they are less likely to lower traditional standards of evidence.

3. When probabilities are unknown or uncertain, local courts are least likely to consider them significant because they do not meet traditional substantial evidence tests.

s   4. Lower courts are likely to place greater weight than higher courts on economic and social costs and benefits in environmental balancing.

5. Local courts are most responsive to social and economic pressures and therefore least likely to give priority to environmental values when risks are uncertain.

6. State courts are likely to weigh environmental benefits more heavily than local courts but are less likely than federal courts to enjoin uncertain risks.

These propositions, which may appear self-evident to many political scientists, require testing in a broad range of cases involving risks of future harm. It may be that, where community opinion is divided or strongly opposed to proposed developments, the courts may adopt a quite different approach to projected risks. This case suggests, however, that strong tendencies may exist to make what we have defined as type IV decisions which maximize short-term economic benefits. Whereas no single model of decision making may be appropriate in all circumstances, we would argue that type I and type III decisions may be necessary in many instances of long-term hazards to society.

There is clearly no magic formula for eliminating uncertain risks. The federal decisions discussed earlier are a significant beginning, as is the Toxic Substances Control Act of 1976 and other recent legislation. We need to recognize that precautionary action may now be necessary at all levels of government lest one uncertain risk be traded for another. In the *Reserve* case it was presumed by the federal Court of Appeals that an acceptable on-land dump could be found and that any such site was preferable to continued disposal in Lake Superior, which the court condemned as a "monumental environmental mistake." But in shifting pollution from water, to land, to air we must be aware of redistributing risks, costs, and benefits and take precautions to insure that the new balance is genuinely acceptable. When risks are unquantifiable, uncertain, or unknown, this requires extremely careful judgments at all levels of government. Local courts and agencies are often at the forefront of environmental decision making and they must follow the tentative leads of the federal courts in safeguarding the future.

Notes

1. Joseph L. Sax, *Defending the Environment: A Strategy for Citizen Action* (New York: Knopf, 1971), especially chaps. 2-4.

2. Kenneth M. Dolbeare, *Trial Courts in Urban Politics: State Court Policy Impact and Functions in a Local Political System* (New York: John Wiley & Sons, 1967), p. 123. Reprinted with permission.

3. Ibid., p. 128. Reprinted with permission.

4. Henry R. Glick, *Supreme Courts in State Politics* (New York: Basic Books, 1971); Henry R. Glick and Kenneth N. Vines, *State Court Systems* (Englewood Cliffs, N.J.: Prentice-Hall, 1973).

5. See Stephen L. Wasby, *The Impact of the United States Supreme Court: Some Perspectives* (Homewood, Ill.: Dorsey Press, 1970); Theodore L. Becker and Malcolm M. Feeley, *The Impact of Supreme Court Decisions,* 2d ed. (New York: Oxford University Press, 1973); and for a recent review, Lawrence Baum, "Lower-Court Response to Supreme Court Decisions: Reconsidering a Negative Picture," *The Justice System Journal* 3 (Spring 1978):208-219.

6. Quoted in James L. Oakes, "The Judicial Role in Environmental Law," *New York University Law Review* 52 (June 1977):498.

7. Ibid., p. 502.

8. See Harold Leventhal, "Environmental Decisionmaking and the Role of the Courts," *University of Pennsylvania Law Review* 122 (January 1974):546-554; Arthur Kantrowitz, "Controlling Technology Democratically," *American Scientist* 63 (September-October 1975):505-509; R.J. Roberts and J.L. Sullivan, "The Role of the Technological Expert in Complex Environmental Litigation," *The Canadian Bar Review* 54 (March 1976):65-104.

9. See especially Marcia R. Gelpe and A. Dan Tarlock, "The Uses of Scientific Information in Environmental Decisionmaking," *Southern California Law Review* 48 (November 1974):371-427; Bowden V. Brown, "Projected Environmental Harm: Judicial Acceptance of a Concept of Uncertain Risk," *Journal of Urban Law* 53 (February 1976):497-531; Jeff Masten, "Epistemic Ambiguity and the Calculus of Risk: Ethyl Corporation v. Environmental Protection Agency," *South Dakota Law Review* 21 (Spring 1976):425-451.

10. See William W. Lowrance, *Of Acceptable Risk: Science and the Determination of Safety* (Los Altos, Calif.: William Kaufmann, 1976); Richard Kraus, "Environmental Carcinogenesis: Regulation on the Frontiers of Science," *Environmental Law* 7 (Fall 1976):83-135; T.H. Maugh II, "Chemical Carcin-

ogens: the Scientific Basis for Regulation," *Science* 201 (September 29, 1978):1200-1205, and "Chemical Carcinogens: How Dangerous Are Low Doses?" *Science* 202 (October 6, 1978):37-41.

11. See especially Kevin Gaynor, "The Toxic Substances Control Act: A Regulatory Morass," *Vanderbilt Law Review* 30 (November 1977):1149-1195; and special issue of *Ecology Law Quarterly* 7 (1978), on "Hazardous Substances in the Environment: Law and Policy."

12. Gelpe and Tarlock, "Uses of Scientific Information"; Brown, "Projected Environmental Harm"; "Note: Reserve Mining—The Standard of Proof Required to Enjoin an Environmental Hazard to the Public Health," *Minnesota Law Review* 59 (April 1975):893-926; William L. Prater, *"Reserve Mining Co. v. Environmental Protection Agency:* Scientific Uncertainty and Environmental Threats to Human Health," *Utah Law Review* 1975 (Summer 1975):581-592.

13. Joel Yellin, "Judicial Review and Nuclear Power: Assessing the Risks of Environmental Catastrophe," *The George Washington Law Review* 45 (August 1977):969-993.

14. *Minneapolis Tribune,* July 8, 1978. Not all the projected $370-400 million in costs is attributable to pollution abatement, since the company is also modernizing its plant operations. The IRS has recently allowed sale of tax-exempt bonds on $236 million for construction and equipment at Milepost 7. See *Minneapolis Tribune,* Oct. 28, 1978.

15. Opinions are deeply divided over whether Armco and Republic Steel had reliable alternative sources of iron ore and actually intended to carry out their threat to close Reserve. For a skeptical view, see, for example, the *Washington Post* editorial of July 19, 1976. The evidence suggests, however, that the courts judged the threat credible and that is the important point for this analysis.

16. Thomas Drechsler, "Public Health Endangerment and Standards of Proof: Ethyl Corp. v. EPA," *Environmental Affairs* 6, no. 2 (1977):227-247; Brown, "Projected Environmental Harm."

17. See Elizabeth H. Haskell and Victoria S. Price, *State Environmental Management: Case Studies of Nine States* (New York: Praeger, 1973), chap. 2.

18. *BNA Environment Reporter* 7 (February 25):1636 and refs. cited therein. [Note: all further legal references are to options cited in *BNA Envir. Rep.*, hereafter cited as "ERC."

19. 7 ERC 1675.

20. 6 ERC 1615.

21. Ibid.

22. 7 ERC 1636.

23. Lowrance, *Of Acceptable Risk,* pp. 75-76.

24. Ibid., pp. 79, 99-101; Amory B. Lovins, "Cost-Risk-Benefit Assessments in Energy Policy," *The George Washington Law Review* 45 (August 1977):911-943; Burke K. Zimmerman, "Risk-Benefit Analysis," *Trial* 14 (February 1978):43-47.

25. 4 ERC 1369.

26. 6 ERC 1611.

27. 6 ERC 1451.

28. 6 ERC 1616.

29. 7 ERC 1648.

30. Ibid.

31. Yellin, "Judicial Review."

32. The language in subdivision 6 was incorporated into MEPA from the Minnesota Environmental Rights Act of 1971 (Minnesota Statute 116B.04). The "feasible and prudent" clause was based on the U.S. Supreme Court opinion in *Citizens to Preserve Overton Park* v. *Volpe* (2 ERC 1250) (1971). See "Note: The Minnesota Environmental Rights Act," *Minnesota Law Review* 56 (March 1972):599-601.

33. State of Minnesota, Department of Natural Resources, *In the Matter of the Applications by Reserve Mining Company for Permits for the Mile Post 7 On-Land Tailings Disposal Plan at Silver Bay, Minnesota, Findings of Fact, Conclusions, Order* (July 1, 1976) [hereafter cited as "Hearing Report,"] finding 31. This finding was substantiated by failure of the Teton Dam in June 1976, a fact that may have influenced PCA adoption of the hearing officer's report. See the supplementary *Memorandum* dated June 29, 1976, by Wayne H. Olson, hearing officer, for further discussion on this point.

34. Ibid., finding 53.

35. Keith O. Boyum, "Minnesota Courts: Essentials of Process and Structures," in Millard L. Gieske and Edward R. Brandt, eds., *Perspectives on Minnesota Government and Politics* (Dubuque, Iowa: Kendall/Hunt Publishing, 1977), p. 263.

36. Comment, "The Environment: An Agency-Court Battle," *Natural Resources Journal* 17 (January 1977):123-137.

37. 9 ERC 1656. Compare the Eighth Circuit's very different interpretation of this language, citing with approval Judge Wright's warning that ". . . the court should [not] view itself as the equivalent of a combined Ph.D. in chemistry, biology, and statistics." (7 ERC 1626, n. 20).

38. Stephen I. Frank, "State Supreme Courts and Administrative Agencies," *State Government* 51 (Spring 1978):119-123.

39. See *No Power Line, Inc. v. Minnesota Environmental Quality Council,* 11 ERC 1001; and *People for Environmental Enlightenment and Responsibility (PEER), Inc. v. Minnesota Environmental Quality Council,* 11 ERC 1481.

40. 9 ERC 1658.

41. Ibid.

42. 10 ERC 1131.

43. 10 ERC 1140.

44. 9 ERC 1664.

45. Minnesota Statute ch. 116D.03(2)(c).

46. 10 ERC 1141.

Organizational Correlates of Utility Rates

Thomas M. Pelsoci

Recent increases in electric rates have led to a growing debate about the effectiveness of state regulatory commissions and about options for regulatory reform. The issues have not been simple, however, and consensus about the proper nature of reform has not emerged.

On the one hand, economists have generally concluded that the existing regulatory framework does not have the intended impact of stabilizing utility rates,[1] and they have tended to advocate partial deregulation and greater competition.[2]

Naderites and other neopopulists have similarly concluded that state regulatory agencies have failed to keep down rates and look after the interests of the electricity-consuming public.[3] Unlike the economists, however, they have argued for more intense government intervention to be coupled with a thorough reform of regulatory agencies. As the causes of regulatory failure were presumed to be political, populist reform measures were prescribed at the political level to "promote pervasive and direct democracy in governmental and economic affairs."[4] This ideal, it was felt, could be approximated by instituting a variety of changes from open meeting requirements and full disclosure of lobbying activities to the direct popular election of state utility commissioners.

Unlike the rather radical prescriptions of both economists and Naderites, a third and more traditional approach to reform has evaluated existing regulatory institutions as basically sound and argued that reform should have the limited objective of "fine tuning the bureaucratic machine ... to remove the knocks and sputters." In other words, regulatory deficiencies could be remedied by such incremental measures as "increasing budgets, ... adopting better procedures, filling gaps in authority, clarifying statutory mandates, and appointing better regulators."[5]

For a variety of reasons, which may be ideological in nature or represent the lack of interdisciplinary ties, debate over utility reform has tended to be contained within one or the other of these perspectives and has proceeded without integrating the economic, political, and administrative dimensions. The present study attempts to reverse this tendency by exploring how cost and demand factors, together with the commissions' administrative and political attributes, have shaped an important regulatory output—the residential price of electricity. In this fashion, the analysis shows how past experience reflects on the relative merits of alternate reform proposals and suggests the nature of constructive reform.

The Evolution of Commission Regulation

At the turn of the century, state and local governments enthusiastically promoted the development of electric utilities and provided the fledgling industry with tax concessions and a variety of subsidies. This promotional era of good feelings did not last long, however, and its demise can be traced to the industry's monopolistic tendencies at a time when popular antimonopoly sentiments were high. Subsequently, utility companies became the focal points of progressive agitation, and the fight against utility barons, excessive rates, absentee ownership, and the exportation of profits came to be an important theme of the progressive movement.[6]

To break the hold of monopolists, progressive municipal regimes acquired utility systems of their own and issued competitive franchises to private utilities.[7] The first of these approaches, the movement toward public ownership, generated a great deal of interest and came to be a core provision for reform. Its impact was limited, however, and it gradually became clear that public ownership would at best be a partial remedy against monopoly abuse. The franchise approach was also beset with problems, and its record was less encouraging still. While it created intense price competition, it had the effect of restricting firms from reaching economies of scale and was perceived as a major factor in the deterioration of service quality.[8] Given these disappointments, the notion that electric utilities are natural monopolies providing essential services and are thus affected with the public interest came to enjoy increasing acceptance, and the system of franchises was gradually displaced by direct state regulation of utility operations and rates.

State public utility commissions (PUCs) were established to carry out these regulatory programs and were charged with preventing monopolistic pricing abuses and with ensuring acceptable service levels. Generally, their memberships were appointed by the governors and enjoyed immunity from subsequent removal during their fixed term of service. In contrast to this typical mode of selection, a limited number of commissions were popularly elected bodies. Political independence, in both of these senses, together with multimembered formats, were intended to provide expertise that no single official could possess as well as safeguards against arbitrary decisions. PUCs would thus be "better equipped . . . to make sound decisions, interpret the public interest faithfully . . . and remain independent of both partisan and regulated interests."[9]

The operating practices of these independent commissions developed according to case and statutory law and not at the direction of the executive branch.[10] Statutes and judicial decisions frequently lacked precision, however, and left considerable discretionary latitude to the commissioners. Thus, PUCs tended to operate under flexible mandates and were only constrained by broad expectations to insure that their actions would not be confiscatory[11] and that the regulated prices "fairly reflected" the prevailing cost and demand conditions that individual utility firms encountered.[12]

The formal determination of these cost and demand factors, together with setting of fair and nonconfiscatory rates, involved several steps. Initially, maximum permissible profit levels or rates of return on investments would be fixed to allow utility companies to attract sufficient capital to meet anticipated future power demands. Because the capital that would thus be raised could be diverted to improper uses, commissions would next determine the rate base of each firm, that is, identify all legitimate investment needs to which this rate of return would apply. The rate base and rate of return would then be used to compute expected capital outlays; operating costs for fuel, labor, and professional services would be added to arrive at the companies' overall revenue needs for a specified period of time. The regulated retail price of electricity, or rate schedule, would be determined last by dividing estimated sales to various customer classes into the overall revenue needs.[13]

In contrast to this formal process, based on the initial determination of rates of return, there developed over time a set of informal relationships between the regulators and the regulated utilities that have generally turned on retail price levels or rate schedules. In other words, as long as firms refrained from raising retail prices, PUCs have not shown much interest in intervening to regulate rates of return and have tended to "do nothing if none of the actors in the regulatory process complained."[14] During most of the post-World War II period, neither utility firms nor customers found much to complain about, since production costs could be contained or even reduced by technological innovation and by use of economies of scale. Accordingly, power companies could increase their profitability without requesting rate increases and initiating formal hearings. At the same time, given the generally stable or decreasing price of residential electric service, commissions also lacked incentives to initiate formal rate reviews, and rate regulation came to be an increasingly underutilized process.[15]

Much of this changed in the early 1970s. At this time, fuel shortages and rapid inflation drove utility companies to seek frequent and radical price increases, and the informal arrangements of the 1960s became less and less applicable. Conversely, PUCs became more involved in formal rate-of-return reviews and came to play an increasingly active role in shaping the retail price of electricity.

Unlike past commission actions, more recent regulatory determinations came under intense attack, and allegations were frequently levelled that rate decisions were influenced as much by administrative and political factors as by cost and demand conditions. Certainly, there seems to have been ample opportunity for these extraneous factors to intrude into the regulatory process. The absence of clear legislative and judicial mandates left it to the commissions to decide whether operating costs would be estimated in a strict or liberal fashion. Similarly, the determination of rate bases could proceed in a thorough or permissive manner and shape the extent to which base levels were inflated and net profits increased. Finally, commissions could be actively involved in all phases of the process or could limit their participation to estimating revenue levels and leave the design of retail price structures to the utilities.

The extensive range of these discretionary opportunities, together with rapidly rising utility rates and the widely, although not necessarily correctly perceived, tendency to approve price increases, provided support for allegations that important extraneous factors were at work. Consequently, given PUC regulatory processes especially since the early 1970s, it seems reasonable to presume that administrative and political differences among PUCs and associated discretionary tendencies have, to some extent, affected average price levels and could account for some interstate price variations. (In 1975, these regulated prices ranged from an average of 1.5 cents per kwh in Washington State to over 5 cents per kwh in New York State.) The outcomes of commission determinations or the regulated price of electricity (P) can thus be conceptualized as shaped by cost and demand conditions as well as by the peculiar discretionary tendencies of individual PUCs; the regulated price (P) can be expressed as in equation 6.1:[16]

$$P = f_1\ (C,D) + f_2\ (RE) \tag{6.1}$$

where

  C = cost conditions faced by the regulated firm
  D = demand conditions faced by the regulated firm
  RE = regulatory effect resulting from exercise of discretionary tendencies

The Model

The impact of PUC regulation can be studied along a number of dimensions. Analysis could focus on investment trends and capital allocation decisions, the development and application of technological innovation, or the extent of rate discrimination among the various classes of electricity consumers. While each of these would constitute an interesting concern, this study investigated the extent to which PUC rate regulation has fulfilled the intentions of the original progressive reformers by preventing monopolistic pricing abuses for the most vulnerable class of utility customers, for individual households. The dependent variable was accordingly specified as the statewide average price of electricity that investor-owned utility firms were permitted to charge their residential customers; it was computed by dividing statewide utility revenues by total kilowatt-hours sold.[17] It should be noted that these statewide averages frequently masked substantial variations, especially when many utility firms, each with its own separate price structure, operated within a state. These substate variations could, of course, be interesting in their own right and provide the focus for a worthwhile analysis. As the present comparative study was concerned with the overall distinctive tendencies of state PUCs, however, statewide averages were deemed the appropriate measure of the dependent variable and were not disaggregated to the substate level.

Turning to the specification of independent variables, economists have identified several cost and demand factors that ostensibly shape the regulated price of electricity. Of these, fuel and labor costs together with the total size of the market seemed to be the more important and were incorporated in the present analysis.[18] Fuel inputs were directly accounted by the average statewide costs of producing one kwh of electricity.[19] Following C. Moore's practice, state per-capita incomes were used in the dual role of proxies for labor costs as well as for overall demand conditions.[20] Additional variables, such as the percentage of firm power produced by hydroelectric generation, firm system capacity, or measures of market density, could also have been included as cost and demand inputs. Prior studies have indicated, however, that their independent impacts were weak and these variables were therefore excluded from analysis.[21]

Turning to the administrative components of the presumed regulatory effect, commission size was postulated as one important factor shaping the exercise of regulatory discretion. Originally, the multimembered arrangements of most PUCs were justified by reference to the adjudicatory and legislative functions of regulatory bodies and the belief that "rule making functions were best performed by groups . . . whose combined judgments . . . provided barriers to arbitrary and capricious action and a source of decisions based on different points of view and experience."[22] Multimembered arrangements and associated justifications do not, however, sit well with much of modern administrative theory; and there have been various suggestions to reduce the size of memberships or to eliminate group structures altogether. This, it was argued, would reduce delays and other decisions costs. It would also upgrade the prestige and influence potential of the office and promote the recruitment of better-qualified officials.[23] As much of the controversy has proceeded on speculative or impressionistic grounds, the size of PUC memberships was included in the present analysis to explore its impact on regulatory outputs.

For related administrative reasons, reformers have repeatedly advocated increasing the size and upgrading the quality of PUC staffs. These recommendations originated from widely held impressions that permissive regulation and associated high utility rates could be traced to lack of funding, inadequate staff size, and increasing work loads.[24] As the inflationary pressures of the 1970s drove utility companies to request formal rate hearings in increasing numbers, these problems must have become all the more acute. The impact is unlikely to have been uniform however; PUCs that have expanded their staffs could be expected to cope better with spiralling work loads. At the same time, one would expect a breakdown of regulatory oversight and cost-demand-based determination of rate structures at understaffed agencies.[25] For these reasons, a staff variable was introduced into the model, and, although it did not measure educational caliber, it did provide a normalized indicator of staff capacity, that is, the number of commission employees per major utility firm in each PUC's jurisdiction.

Although these administrative concerns along the information-processing and problem-solving dimensions were generally considered important, many who were critical of existing regulatory practices were unwilling to limit their attention to administrative capacity. Instead they saw regulation in largely political terms and tended to be preoccupied with corrective strategies for agency "capture" and resultant permissive regulation.

Public ownership of utilities has long been considered one ostensible remedy against agency capture and associated rate decisions favoring corporate interests. This remedy originally developed as an indirect mechanism to simulate competitive conditions and to undermine the monopolistic power of private utilities. Once PUCs were established to provide direct utility regulation, proponents of public power systems changed tack and argued for continued public ownership by claiming that public power would provide a yardstick against which state PUCs could measure the service quality and cost claims of private corporations.[26] The presence of lower-priced public power would thus have the effect of reducing commission discretion and would tend to counteract the presumed proindustry bias of the regulators. National trends appeared to support this expectation and showed that the "lowest average monthly bills were in those states where public competition was the strongest" and where public power was thriving.[27] To investigate the extent of this "yardstick phenomenon," however, and to disentangle the effects of public ownership from other inputs into the regulatory process, a public competition variable was introduced into the model. It measured the publicly owned power systems' share of electricity sales in each state and gave numerical expression to the intensity of public/private competition in the states' utility industry.

The presence of public competition could thus limit and retard effective agency capture, but much of the political reform literature has focused on commission characteristics themselves as the more important contributing factors to the commissions' alleged proindustry orientations. Typically, the age of PUCs was assumed to be related to this propensity, and it was claimed that the passage of years would lead to a shift in emphasis "from an early identification . . . with the protection of the economically weak and unorganized against the oppression of the economically powerful . . . to the assertion of governmental responsibility for the well being of the industry."[28] Thus, increasing age would mean the loss of vigor, the weakening of the agency's will to fight corporate exploitation, and the "inevitable capture" by the regulated interests. To remedy these age-induced infirmities, fundamental reorganization and restaffing at all levels of the agency would be necessary.

A more direct route was also taken. Some reformers claimed that popular control over regulatory agencies and regulated interests could be regained by opening the commission process to public scrutiny and participation and by filling commission vacancies through direct elections. Altering the agencies' political environments in this fashion was thus expected to undermine permissive regulatory practices, lead to generally lower profits and lower electric rates.

By way of summary, the interaction of cost and demand factors with administrative and political variables—and their combined influence over the commissions' discretionary tendencies and associated price levels—can be modeled in the linear form of equation 6.2.

$$P_i = a_0 + a_1 F_i + a_2 PCI_i + a_3 CM_i + a_4 SS_i + a_5 PC_i + a_6 CA_i + a_7 MS_i \qquad (6.2)$$

where

P_i = average regulated residential electric rate for state i (cents per kwh)
F_i = composite cost of fuel required for generating one kwh of electricity (cents per kwh)
PCI_i = average state per-capita income (thousands of dollars)
CM_i = commission membership; the number of commissioners
SS_i = PUC staff size/number of utility firms operating in the state
PC_i = public competition variable; publicly owned power systems' percentage share of electricity sales in state i
CA_i = commission age; years since the establishment of the PUC or since the last major reorganization
MS_i = method of commissioner selection (elected = 1.0, appointed = 0.0)

Data from the Edison Electric Institute's *Statistical Yearbook of the Electric Utility Industry, 1976* were used to compute statewide average residential rates, the level of public competition, and the composite cost of fuel. Information about commission size, staff size, age, and method of selection were obtained from the National Association of Regulatory Commissioners' *1975 Annual Report on Utility and Carrier Regulation.* The number of major private utilities operating in each state were taken from the U.S. Federal Power Commission's *Statistics of Privately Owned Utilities, 1974.*

Before examining the relationship modeled by equation 6.2 it is instructive to consider the U.S. Federal Power Commission's (FPC) role in shaping electric retail prices. The FPC has rate-setting authority over interstate wholesale transactions, and, given the regional nature of electric interconnections, one would expect this federal agency to have played a significant (indirect) part in regulating residential rates. Such expectations do not bear up under scrutiny, however, and only a very small fraction of the national power supply has come under the FPC's price-setting authority. This limited impact may be traced to the substate character of most pooling regions and to the tendency toward power exchanges or "swapping" (instead of outright sales) when pooling occurs on an interstate level.[29] Accordingly, as S.G. Bryer has indicated, "electricity regulation has taken place primarily at the state level and the restraints imposed by the FPC have been typically supplementary in character and have generally focused on coordination rather than pricing decisions."[30] For these reasons, the FPC's pricing impact was deemed insufficient to warrant inclusion in the regulatory model.

Discussion of Results

The regulatory commissions of Nebraska, Alaska, Maryland, and the District of Columbia were excluded from analysis, and the average residential rates for the remaining forty-seven states were regressed on cost, demand, and regulatory variables.[31] The overall fit of equation 6.2, as indicated by an R^2 of .537, was good for cross-sectional data, and the comparison of standardized coefficients indicated that regulatory variables along administrative and political dimensions had a substantial influence over utility rates (table 6-1). To check for spurious statistical relationships, the seriousness of the multicollinearity problem was investigated by way of Pearson correlation coefficients among the independent variables. Using the rule of thumb that multicollinearity is "tolerable" if by pairwise comparison all r_{ij}'s are less than the multiple correlation coefficient R, the entries of table 6-2 suggested that the present analysis was "tolerably" free of this difficulty.[32] The value of R was .733, while the highest pairwise correlation coefficients were $-.449$ and .422.

Turning to the consideration of individual variables, the positive signs of the

Table 6-1
Regression Results

	Standardized Regression Coefficients	Unstandardized Regression Coefficients	Student t values
Intercept		.105	.110
Fuel cost $(F)_i$	.257	.327[a]	2.085
Per-capita income $(PCI)_i$	.346	.435[b]	2.594
Commission membership $(CM)_i$	.237	.162[a]	2.059
Normalized staff size $(SS)_i$	$-.293$	$-.0054$[a]	-2.397
Public competition $(PC)_i$	$-.298$	$-.0133$[a]	-2.207
Commission age $(CA)_i$	.181	.0093	1.551
Methods of selection $(MS)_i$	.117	.225	.833

Note: Average residential rate ($¢$/kwh) regressed on cost and demand factors and on regulatory commission characteristics: $N = 47$, $R^2 = .537$, $R = .733$, $F = 6.46$.
[a]Significant at 95 percent confidence level.
[b]Significant at 99 percent confidence level.

Table 6-2
Pearson Correlations among Independent Variables

	(1)	(2)	(3)	(4)	(5)	(6)	(7)
(1) Fuel cost	1.000						
(2) Per-capita income	.260	1.000					
(3) Commission membership	−.082	.110	1.000				
(4) Normalized staff size	.228	.190	.067	1.000			
(5) Public competition	−.318	−.344	−.190	.149	1.000		
(6) Commission age	.029	.084	.028	.155	−.040	1.000	
(7) Method of selection	−.206	−.449	.043	.139	.422	.237	1.000

Note: r values in parentheses; $N = 47$.

F_i and PC_i coefficients indicated that higher fuel costs and per-capita income levels could be associated with higher residential electric rates. Although this is the effect one would expect from rising fuel costs, the interpretation of the positive per-capita income coefficient proved to be somewhat more complicated. On the one hand, higher income levels could be expected to generate higher electricity demand and, given the promotional decreasing block scales of residential rate structures, additional consumption would tend to lower average electric rates. Per-capita income, however, could also be seen as a proxy for direct and indirect labor costs, and a rise in per-capita income would, in this sense, be expected to increase electric rates. Accordingly, the positive per-capita income coefficient indicated that the latter of these two opposing tendencies was dominant in the mid-1970s and corroborated Joskow's conclusions that the price-reducing effects of increasing demand levels were not strong enough to offset inflationary pressures on the cost side.

Turning to administrative variables, the positive sign of the commission membership coefficient was consistent with expectations that larger memberships would be associated with higher prices and, by implication, with more permissive regulatory practices. Specifically, the magnitude of the unstandardized coefficient indicated that increasing the size of commissions by one member made for a marginal increase in rates amounting to .162¢ per kwh. The finding appeared to support speculation that, *ceteris paribus*, greater size decreased the influence potential and prestige of the office; that regulatory bodies with low prestige levels would attract less distinguished and able individuals; and that subsequent PUC decision making would be more easily manipulated by regulated interests. This interpretation is particularly attractive as it can be adjusted to accommodate the exceptional cases of the innovative and leading New York and California PUCs. Both of these commissions had large memberships. They were matched by the largest staffs among the forty-seven PUCs and had unusually high staff-to-commissioner ratios (87 and 175 employees per commissioner, respectively). These high ratios were important distinguishing characteristics, since other commissions with large memberships had typically low staff-to-member ratios (Louisiana 13; Georgia 22; Massachusetts 18; Minnesota 30; Missouri 38; Montana 5; North Carolina 16; and South Carolina 19). Accordingly, if the ratios are viewed as indicators of individual commissioner's power potential as well as of official prestige, the large memberships of the California and New York commissions can be reconciled with their reputation for thorough and innovative regulatory practices.

It is interesting to note that the positive coefficient of commission size was inconsistent with expectations that large commissions would be associated with excessive regulatory delay. At a time when residential rates were generally rising, such size-induced delays would have resulted in lower average prices; yet the marginally higher prices allowed by larger commissions suggested a relatively rapid and sympathetic evaluation of utility claims. The division of primary responsibility among commissioners for different substantive areas probably accounts for this and suggests the limitations of visualizing commission deliberations as random interactions within undifferentiated groups. Instead, it would appear that division of labor and specialization have tended to counteract simple size-induced delays. It is worth reiterating, however, that the presumption of size-induced fluctuations in commission prestige was consistent with present findings.

As postulated, higher commission staff-size was found to be associated with lower residential rates and, by implication, with more thorough and less permissive regulation. The impact of this variable did not, however, appear to be very sizeable. Equation 6.3 is a quick calculation of this.

$$\frac{-.0054 \text{¢ per kwh}}{\text{employees per utility firm}} \cdot \frac{120 \text{ employees}}{4 \text{ utility firms}} = .162 \text{ ¢/kwh} \qquad (6.3)$$

Equation 6.3 indicates that, in a typical state with four major utility companies, the hiring of 120 additional employees would decrease predicted price levels by .162¢ per kwh. Staff expansion of this magnitude would represent a massive change for most PUCs, and yet the predicted price-reducing effect would be no more than that of decreasing membership by one commissioner! It would thus appear that major expansions in PUC staffs would be cost-ineffective as a reform strategy.

The public competition variable had the expected price reducing impact, and the magnitude of its regression coefficient predicted that a 10 percent increase in the level of competition would be accompanied by a .133¢ per-kwh drop in residential rates. Although this represents a sizeable difference, it is unclear whether the observed tendency resulted from the postulated yardstick effect or from the wholesale transfer of less expensive public power to private utility companies. Publicly owned power systems often receive direct and indirect government subsidies, and if lower private rates resulted from the operation of the latter mechanism, the present findings would merely indicate that hidden subsidies were transferred to private utility companies. Consequently, the three-way relationship between PUCs, private utilities, and publicly owned power systems requires further study before one can determine if the generally lower private rates in the presence of higher levels of public competition reflect hidden subsidies or the operation of some yardstick effect. Only then will it be possible to provide a reliable interpretation of the public commission coefficient and to estimate the cost effectiveness of this regulatory-reform strategy.

Commission age was found to be related to higher utility rates, but the relationship was weak. With all other specified variables held constant, the coefficient predicted a .0093¢/kwh increase for every extra year of institutional existence. Accordingly, the findings did not provide any substantial basis for postulating age-related capture by regulated interests and confirmed Meier and Plumlee's conclusion that although "the concept of capture seems to have some very limited empirical support,... there is a need to revise our usually unqualified acceptance of the life cycle model of regulatory agency behavior. Regulatory agency patterns are more flexible, varied and complex than Bernstein suggested."[33]

The last independent variable of the model, the method of commissioner selection, had the most unexpected effect on residential rates. The coefficient value indicated that this presumed regulatory corrective had a perverse effect and that the election of commissioners shifted the regression line upward by .225¢/kwh. This tendency could be traced to the generally lower educational and professional caliber of elected commissioners (see table 6-3) together with the possibility that corporate representatives found it easier to manipulate and secure favorable rate decisions from less educated officials.

Along a different line of speculation, one can also envision how the utility industry could have played an important role in the election process itself. Unlike the general public, whose interest in regulatory matters was diffuse and

Table 6-3
Highest Educational Attainments of Public Utility Commission Members
(percent)

	Elected Commissioners (N=57)	Appointed Commissioners (n=125)
Postgraduate degree	23	56
Bachelor's degree	31	18
Without bachelor's degree	45	26

Source: Computed from data in *1975 Annual Report of Utility and Carrier Regulation,* National Association of Regulatory Utility Commissioners.

lacked organized expression, the utility companies had direct and compelling interests in regulatory outcomes and possessed an impressive array of economic and organizational resources to promote the political fortunes of sympathetic candidates. Accordingly, as contests for municipal judgeships have frequently turned on the endorsement and organizational support of local bar associations, it is plausible to presume that similarly low-participation and low-information elections for state utility commissioners have been substantially influenced by utility contributions and organizational support. This would certainly be consistent with the tendency of elected commissioners to allow higher residential electric rates.

If elected commissioners were thus presumed to be particularly responsive to organized interests, it becomes necessary to comment on some recent developments and speculate about their implications for future rate decisions. The energy crisis and recent double-digit inflation have pushed utility issues to the political center stage in most states, and diffuse public discontent has been gradually translated into organized pressure against spiralling rates and permissive regulation. Thus, in 1975 (the cross-sectional focus of this study), organized activity on behalf of residential utility customers was sporadic or nonexistent. By late 1977, however, the Environmental Action Foundation was able to identify permanent utility-oriented consumer groups in 62 percent of the states with elected PUCs and in 73 percent of the appointive states. Assuming that the organizational momentum of the consumer movement is sustained, it is intriguing to speculate how PUCs will respond to this new locus of power in their political environment. One would expect commissions to take the demands of consumer organizations increasingly into account and to subject utility rate requests to greater scrutiny. Moreover, one would expect change of orientation to be most pronounced at elected commissions—that is, at agencies that are least insulated from the competing demands of organized interest groups.

The recent emergence of consumer militancy and the unavailability of relevant data do not presently permit an assessment of these changing orientations, and the investigation of this interesting phenomenon must be delayed until some future date. Attempts should be made at the first opportunity, however, to study the policy linkages suggested and to assess the mediating influence of consumer militancy on the relationship between method of commissioner selection and utility-rate decisions. It should be particularly interesting to identify organizational threshold characteristics of the consumer movement that prove sufficient to overcome the elected commissions' apparent tendency to favor regulated interests.

Concluding Remarks

Public utility commissions regulate the price of electricity in forty-nine states, exercise a pivotal influence over the corporate fortunes of the $40 billion/year electric power industry, and affect the electric bills of 56 million households.[34] Increasing awareness of the commissions' wide-ranging jurisdictions, together with recent dramatic increases in utility rates, have generated growing dissatisfaction and have led to calls for regulatory reform. Subsequently, various proposals have been aired to introduce administrative and political changes, to reduce discretionary latitude by statutory means, and to bring utility rates into line with legitimate cost and demand factors.

The findings of the present cross-sectional analysis of 1975 PUC patterns provide some insights into the potential usefulness of proposed reform strategies, especially if reform interest is centered on rate reduction. Those who are primarily interested in energy conservation, income redistribution, and so forth, might naturally object to such a narrow conception of reform. Nevertheless, if rate reduction is a legitimate objective and if past experience is a guide, the combination of small commission memberships, appointive methods of selection, and public competition would appear to constitute the most favorable regulatory environment. Contrary to common expectations, the election of commissioners would very likely be counterproductive—at least as long as consumer organizations were unable to match the political resources of utility companies.

By way of conclusion, it is proper to note the exploratory nature of the present study and to lay out the ideological implications that its findings suggest. Simply put, these call into question the economists' advocacy of competition and deregulation as the sole effective reform strategies. Instead, it appears that administrative and political factors can also have significant policy impacts and can lead to sizeable differences in regulatory outputs. However, as the case of elected and appointed commissions illustrates, the impact of these institutional variables will not necessarily be in the expected direction, nor can they be divorced and analyzed in isolation from the commissions' political environment. Accordingly, the complexity and dynamism of regulatory processes will require more comprehensive and sophisticated longitudinal treatment before the claims of Naderite and administrative reformers are sorted out and effective reform strategies are advanced.

Notes

1. G.J. Stiegler and C. Friedland, "What Can Regulators Regulate? The Case of Electricity," in W. Shepherd and T. Gies, eds., *Utility Regulation* (New York: Random House, 1967); and C. Moore, "Has Electricity Regulation Resulted in Higher Prices?" *Economic Inquiry* 13 (June 1975):207-220.

2. L.W. Weiss, "Antitrust in the Electric Power Industry," and W.T. Primeaux, "A Reexamination of the Monopoly Market Structure for Electric Utilities," in A. Phillips ed., *Promoting Competition in Regulated Markets* (Washington, D.C.: The Brookings Institution, 1975).

3. D.M. Wellborn, "Taking Stock of Regulatory Reform" (Paper presented at the 1977 Annual Meeting of the American Political Science Association, Washington, D.C., September 1-4), p. 8.

4. Ibid.

5. Ibid., p. 6.

6. E.S. Griffith, *A History of American City Government: The Progressive Years and Their Aftermath* (New York: Praeger, 1974), p. 32.

7. M. Farris, *Public Utilities Regulation, Management and Ownership* (Boston: Houghton Mifflin, 1973), p. 12.

8. Ibid.

9. M. Bernstein, "The Life Cycle of Regulatory Commissions," in S. Krislov and L. Musolf, eds., *The Politics of Regulation* (Boston: Houghton Mifflin, 1964), p. 103.

10. A.E. Finer, *The States and Electric Utility Regulation* (Lexington, Ky.: The Council of State Governments, 1977), p. 19.

11. P.L. Joskow, "Inflation and Environmental Concern: Structural Change in the Process of Public Utility Price Regulation," *Journal of Law and Economics* 17 (October 1974):297.

12. C. Moore, "Has Electricity Regulation Resulted in Higher Prices?" *Economic Inquiry* 13 (June 1975):208.

13. C.F. Phillips, *The Economics of Regulation* (Homewood, Ill.: Richard Irwin, 1969).

14. Joskow, "Inflation and Environmental Concern," p. 298.

15. Ibid., p. 312.

16. Moore, "Electricity Regulation," p. 208.

17. *Statistical Yearbook of the Electric Utility Industry* (New York: Edison Electric Institute, 1976).

18. Stiegler and Friedland, "What Can Regulators Regulate"; Moore, "Electricity Regulation"; and R. Jackson, "An Empirical Evaluation of Electric Utility Regulation" (Ph.D. diss. Boston University, 1967).

19. *Statistical Yearbook*, p. 51.

20. Moore, "Electricity Regulation," p. 210.

21. Ibid., pp. 210-211.

22. E. Redford, "The Arguments for and against the Commission System," in S, Krislov and L. Musolf, eds., *The Politics of Regulation* (Boston: Houghton Mifflin, 1964).

23. M. Bernstein, "Independent Regulatory Agencies: A Perspective on Their Reform," *The Annals of the American Academy of Political and Social Science* 400 (March 1972):19.

24. Phillips, *Economics of Regulation*, p. 385.

25. Joskow, "Inflation and Environmental Concern," p. 313.

26. Farris, *Public Utilities*, p. 268.

27. Phillips, *Economics of Regulation*, p. 551.

28. L. Jaffe, "The Effective Limits of the Administrative Process," in S. Krislov and L. Musolf, eds., *The Politics of Regulation* (Boston: Houghton Mifflin, 1964).

29. S.G. Bryer and P.W. MacAvoy, *Energy Regulation by the Federal Power Commission* (Washington, D.C.: The Brookings Institution, 1974, pp. 99-104.

30. Ibid., p. 91.

31. There were gaps in the data from Alaska, Maryland, and the District of Columbia, data and all electric power in Nebraska was publicly sold.

32. D.S. Huang, *Regression and Economic Methods* (New York: Wiley, 1970), p. 153.

33. K.J. Meier and J.P. Plumlee, "Capture and Rigidity in Regulatory Administration" (paper given at the 1977 Annual Meeting of the American Political Science Association, Washington, D.C., September 1-4).

34. *Statistical Yearbook*, pp. 39, 46.

7

Air Pollution Control Policy: The Sulfur Dioxide Emission Limitation Program in Ohio

Paul Anderson

One irrefutable fact about environmental policy is that environmental goals have not been fully met. It may, however, be too early to conclude that the strategy adopted to achieve cleaner air and water was inappropriate, poorly conceived, or badly implemented. Progress in the environmental field is being made, but some individual cases remain unresolved because of delay, resistance, or imperfect administration. The sulfur dioxide emission limitation program in Ohio is a case in point. The program has been plagued by such problems as conflict between federal and state agencies, excessive litigation, and charges of "regulatory overkill." Only recently has enforcement of sulfur dioxide emission standards begun in Ohio. Although the Ohio case is unique in some ways, it is a good example of the problems in implementing air pollution control policy.

Incremental and Nonincremental Policy Making

The policy-making process often includes bargaining and accommodation among policy makers, participation of many diverse interest groups, and modest changes in ongoing policy. It is incremental. But the federal Clean Air Act Amendments of 1970, requiring states to develop enforcement plans substantially reducing air pollution and setting strict deadlines for achieving clean air, were not typical of incremental policy making. The passage of the amendments and the implementation that followed can only be called "nonincremental."

Writing extensively on air pollution control policy, Charles O. Jones says that the Clean Air Act Amendments of 1970 were enacted to satisfy an intense public demand for strong environmental laws.[1] The policy making that produced the legislation was not one of bargaining among lawmakers and affected interests; and it did not produce a modest change in existing policy. Rather, Jones says the 1970 amendments are an example of "speculative augmentation," which he describes as occurring when policy makers, in their desire to satisfy public opinion, set goals exceeding current technological and administrative

This research was funded by the Purdue Research Foundation.

117

capacities. Policy makers hope or anticipate that these capacities will grow as the ambitious program is implemented. Such growth notwithstanding, Jones calls this next stage "implementation beyond capacity." He predicts it will be marked by confusion—as the agency experiences necessary expansion and reorganization—and by a subsequent delay in implementing overly optimistic policies.

Paul R. Schulman suggests another way of understanding nonincremental policy making however.[2] He argues that nonincremental policy making is appropriate for certain kinds of policy. Like the space program for example, these policies require a large commitment of resources and a long period of growth before goals can be achieved at a satisfactory level. They are major changes and cannot be handled well in an incremental fashion of small periodic adjustments in ongoing policy. This is because the benefits of such policies are not a question of more or less but of all or nothing. There is, then, intense effort to overcome administrative and technological problems. There is also a time lag between mandating goals and goal achievement, during which necessary public support may decline before the implementing agency has succeeded. This can put the agency in a difficult political position. Thus, the space program has suffered diminished support as citizens have become more cognizant of its cost.

Schulman chose his example of the space program well. The tangible, easily defined nature of the program's goals facilitate an understanding of nonincremental policy. The analogy to the space program may have limited utility for students of environmental issues however. Although there are important similarities, there are some real differences between the two. Environmental goals are open to multiple and competing definitions, each with its own supporting data and seemingly objective analysis. We can know where the moon is and say finally when a space vehicle has visited it. But we are less sure of how clean we want the air, given the simultaneous need to make some economic sacrifices for it.

Although the experience of the space program may not be directly applicable to environmental issues, Schulman's conclusions about it are relevant and important. Given the strength of utility and industrial interests in preserving the status quo, changing the direction of government policy to promote environmental concerns requires a more assertive, wholesale effort than is possible using an incremental mode. Furthermore, agencies implementing newer environmental initiatives caused by an outpouring of intensely felt public demands may indeed find some distance between themselves and the powerful economic entities they are supposed to regulate. This may handicap an agency in generating political support for itself and in obtaining compliance with its policies. These difficulties are exacerbated by the inexperience of environmental agencies in drafting regulations that can stand up in court.

Jones and Schulman are really talking about the same thing. The differences that exist between them are related to their empirical focuses. Speculative augmentation has worked much more effectively in the space program than in environmental issues. Because it has worked less well in the latter, it has fostered patterns of behavior and events more typical of incremental modes of political action. This underscores the political vulnerability of environmental goals and the risks involved in nonincremental policy making. This chapter describes efforts to clean Ohio's air and offers evidence to support this view.

Early History of Air Programs in Ohio

Until the federal Air Quality Act of 1967, Ohio's air pollution control program was basically a local effort with agencies responsible for setting and enforcing standards in cities such as Dayton, Cleveland, Cincinnati, Steubenville, Toledo, and Youngstown. Jn 1957, the legislature gave the director of the Department of Health authority to create an air quality monitoring network, to set up a laboratory for conducting research on Ohio air pollution, and to provide technical assistance to local pollution-control agencies. Although a separate unit for air pollution control was established in the Health Department, the emphasis remained on local efforts.[3]

As a response to the requirements of the 1967 Air Quality Act, Ohio created an Air Pollution Control Board housed in the Health Department with five members: the directors of Health and Development and representatives of municipal corporations, industry, and agriculture. The latter three members served staggered 3-year terms without compensation, making it a part-time board. The board was empowered to issue installation and operating permits for "any machine, equipment, device, apparatus or physical facility" that might pollute the air; the permits could be issued if a plant submitted a compliance schedule that would have the plant meeting the state and local emission standards in a set period of time. If the polluter could not submit a compliance schedule bringing emissions below the required limits (that is, if compliance were "impractical because of conditions beyond the control of the applicant" or "technically infeasible or economically unreasonable") he could receive a variance for a specified time period that could be renewed.

Formulation of Ambient Air Quality
Standards for Sulfur Dioxide

Under provisions of the 1967 Air Quality Act, the Secretary of the U.S. Health, Education and Welfare Department (HEW) published air quality criteria (which specified threshold levels for air pollutants) for states to use in setting ambient air quality standards in the air quality control regions within each state. The air quality control regions were designed by the federal government, and fourteen were established in Ohio. The act required the secretary of HEW to designate air quality control regions and publish air quality criteria 90 days after the act was passed. In the next 180 days, states were to hold public hearings on ambient air quality standards and then set standards for themselves; in the following 180 days, the states were to formulate implementation plans that would insure attainment of ambient standards and to submit the plans to the secretary for approval.

As part of its statutory duties, the Ohio Air Pollution Control Board had the task of setting state ambient standards in 1970. That year was one of intense environmental activism and of Earth Day. The board held hearings in various cities across the state, hearings that were raucous affairs. The Cleveland hearings drew such a large crowd that the board had to move to a larger hall to accommodate the many people, almost all of whom were demanding strict air pollution standards.

The testimony of environmentalists at these hearings was rather negative. They criticized the board's recommended standards for either not being sufficiently stringent or not having an adequate margin of safety for the protection of public health. Environmental spokesmen were numerous and strident. For example, Robert Guthridge, member of the board of directors, Trumbell County Tuberculosis and Respiratory Disease Association, said of polluting industry:

> Have these people ever stopped and thought what conditions they are creating in the world today is (*sic*) going to do something to the elderly or sick people we have in our society today, those especially suffering from thoracic disease? I don't think they do.

> Instead of worrying about the dollar, they should worry about clearning up the air because the dollar will be no use to us. We might as well burn it up.[4]

Paul Fabry, Air Pollution Program consultant to the Jefferson County Tuberculosis and Health Association, argued against the proposed Ohio regulations for not being strict enough:

> I . . . feel that air quality standard goals being considered at this statewide hearing are not consistent with the air quality criteria outlined by the Department of Health, Education and Welfare, and that they will not provide an adequate safeguard to health and property.[5]

Statements from industry were also critical and, in contrast to the statements of environmentalists, attacked the program for being too stringent and for having an unreasonable (that is, too short) compliance schedule. A key industry argument was that because knowledge of the effects of pollution and of the technological capability for controlling pollution were not well developed (in 1970), air pollution control strategies should be flexible and not contain explicit

goals and attainment dates. James R. Carman, an economist with an environmental consulting firm, stated the case well:

> Standards of air quality must be adopted in a reasoned fashion
> notwithstanding today's limited knowledge of conditions and trained
> personnel. Understanding of the impact of these conditions on our
> environment, and therefore Ohio, is embryonic. These standards
> adopted now must be considered as preliminary or temporary and
> subject to future revision as research provides additional facts of
> environmental interface and/or as new control systems, capital and
> personnel become available.[6]

Most industrial representatives spoke in general terms conveying a sense of
foreboding about economic growth slowed by expensive pollution controls.
They predicted delays in meeting attainment dates because of a lack of
low-sulfur fuel (especially low-sulfur coal) and the unreliability of control
technology.

Industrial testimony contained very little data and even gave general support
to environmental cleanup. Jack Gerlach, Toledo Edison, expressed his support:

> Toledo Edison has always been conscious of the importance of
> protecting the quality of the environment, and recognizes its responsi-
> bility to do everything in its power to preserve and improve the quality
> of the air in Northwestern Ohio in the face of increasing population and
> rapidly expanding industrial and economic growth.[7]

Yet such support was usually qualified with words like "realistic" or "reasonable" when discussion moved to pollution abatement, as seen in this polite, but
firm, request for solid evidence of the deleterious effects of pollution from
Robert A. Wiesner, Ford Motor Company:

> We concur in the concept of controlling air quality and also to the need
> for the development of air quality standards. We are sure that you
> recognize your responsibility to adopt standards which are based upon
> valid technical data and which will afford real benefit to the public
> health.[8]

In 1970, therefore, industry was leery of pollution control programs but
probably lacked the data to show convincingly that the proposed ambient
standards were as unreasonable and as stifling to Ohio's economy as they had
suggested. In a sense, their opposition was speculative.

However industrial spokesmen did have several specific points to make. One
complaint that several spokesmen mentioned concerned fuel substitution. Since,
they said, it is difficult to remove sulfur from exhaust fumes, it would be
preferable to remove the sulfur from fuel beforehand or to use a fuel that
contained low amounts of sulfur. Oil, gas, low-sulfur coal, and "washed" coal

suffice as low-sulfur fuels; but there are serious problems with conversion from one fuel to another. Boilers are designed to burn a particular type of fuel and cannot be altered easily to handle a different type.

Even if fuel switching were not complicated by boiler adaptability, there was the problem of getting low-sulfur fuel. An official of Youngstown Sheet and Tube testified that alternate fuels were not available and that low-sulfur coal was not found in Ohio mines. The high-sulfur content of Ohio coal ultimately became an exceedingly important issue in the effort to write a sulfur dioxide emission limitation program.

Was there a device that removes sulfur dioxide from emissions? Again, industry representatives were negative. The principal complaint was not that the devices (called "flue-gas desulfurization" equipment or "scrubbers") were expensive—which they were—but that they did not work. Although processes for removing sulfur dioxide from flue gas existed, industry representatives agreed that the equipment should not be installed without substantial redesign and much more testing.

Industry arguments notwithstanding, the Air Pollution Control Board adopted the strict federal secondary standard for sulfur dioxide: an annual average of 60 micrograms per cubic meter of air and a 24-hour standard of not more than 260 micrograms per cubic meter.[9] Both standards were to be met by July 1975.

Federal primary standards protect public health, and secondary standards protect public welfare, meaning vegetation and buildings. The primary federal standard was supposed to be met in 1975 and the secondary standard later. Thus, Ohio went further than the federal government later in 1970 in what was a nonincremental step in federal air pollution control policy development.

Why did the Ohio Air Pollution Control Board take this step? A former director of the state Environmental Protection Agency (EPA) could not give an explanation for the board's action, except to suggest that it did not fully understand what it was doing. A further explanation for the board's action is that it wanted to mollify an angry public. The board had held hearings all over the state and had heard testimony calling for strong action from representatives of such groups as the Ohio Council of Churches, the Ohio Tuberculosis and Health Association, the Ohio AFL-CIO, and from such individuals as Mayor Carl B. Stokes of Cleveland and Governor James A. Rhodes, who had not previously been regarded as sympathetic to the environmental movement. The three interest groups (and others) formed a coalition, called the "breathers' lobby," and it—and many others—descended on the Cleveland hearings in January. After two days of testimony, the board, overnight, adopted the strict federal secondary standard.

The board's decision to adopt the more restrictive secondary standard is an extremely important turning point. One might expect stringent standards to be opposed by Ohio industries and electric generating companies that burned coal, the combustion of which caused most of the sulfur dioxide emissions. Seventy percent of all sulfur dioxide emissions in Ohio came from coal-burning electric generating plants.[10] Also, Ohio industry was considerably above the national average in relying on coal as an energy source.[11] In fact, they resorted to the courts.

Development of Emission Limitation Regulations and Preparation of the Ohio Implementation Plan

After setting ambient air quality standards, each state was required to submit an implementation plan to the newly created U.S. Environmental Protection Agency guaranteeing attainment of federal primary standards in 3 years from when the plan was approved (and secondary standards in a "reasonable time thereafter") and containing "emission limitations, schedules, and timetables for compliance."[12] The state Air Pollution Control Board and its staff in the Department of Health worked throughout 1971 on the plan and submitted it to the U.S. EPA on January 31, 1972.

The Ohio program was still in embryonic stages in 1971. Preparation of the implementation plan was marked by a lack of time, data, and resources for making an adequate inventory of all sources of air pollution and for setting the appropriate emission control standards. Under the Clean Air Act Amendments of 1970, Ohio was required to submit its implementation plan nine months after promulgation of national primary and secondary standards, which was done April 30, 1971. Previously, states had not been pressed to meet the deadlines in the Air Quality Act, and none had met them.[13] Because of the shortness of time caused by the fast approaching deadlines included in the 1970 amendments, the preparers of Ohio's plan submitted a less-than-perfect set of regulations to the U.S. EPA.

It was not easy to move from ambient air quality standards to emission standards. First, Ohio officials developed an emission inventory containing information from "each plant in the State of Ohio, each commercial institution, each building, . . . as well as area sources such as . . . open burning, general fuel use, (and) mobile sources . . . " Next, they monitored the ambient air through the use of sampling information to ascertain the concentration of each pollutant. Finally, officials modeled hypothetical emission standards to find the precise relationship between emission limitations and the ambient air quality such that the ambient standards would be met.

Under the pressure of time, state officials chose to use the "example-region-worst-case" approach along with the "rollback" or "proportional reduction" model, as suggested by the U.S. EPA. These techniques allowed them to do the laborious tasks of conducting an emission inventory, analyzing ambient air samples, and modeling regulations for only one air quality control region in a particular priority classification (based on the severity of pollution) and then apply the resulting emission standards to all other regions similarly classified. The example region must be the dirtiest region (the worst case) in that class, enabling the emission standards to handle the most severe pollution problem in the respective priority class. This would insure attainment and maintenance of ambient standards all over the state. The Cleveland metropolitan region was selected as the priority one (the most severely polluted) example region since it was the worst case of sulfur dioxide emissions for that priority class. Cincinnati was chosen as the example region for priority two.

After selecting example regions, officials used the proportional reduction model to arrive at emission regulations. The proportional reduction model uses data on the pollutant concentration in the ambient air—without reference to source—to set emission standards. If, for example, the air quality index for sulfur dioxide is 30 percent above the desired reading, emissions should be reduced by 30 percent at each source without discriminating between sources that contribute greatly to pollution and sources that do not.

If staff of the air pollution unit had had enough time to do more sophisticated modeling, they would have used dispersion modeling. The assumption in the proportional reduction model is that the concentration of pollutants in the atmosphere is directly related to the amount of emissions; but the assumption in the dispersion model is that the concentration of pollutants is determined by a number of factors. These factors include the location of pollution sources, the distance between sources, the topography of the region, climatological conditions, wind direction and velocity, and the characteristics of the gases being emitted. Emission standards based on dispersion modeling are not directly related to emissions per se, but are source-specific. The mandated reduction is related to the actual contribution of each source to pollutant concentration in the atmosphere that is not "excessive." Excessive reduction in emissions is more than what is required to meet ambient air quality standards. Industry, not surprisingly, wished to do no more than meet the ambient standards and complained of regulatory overkill.

Creation of the Ohio Environmental
Protection Agency

The administration of air programs in Ohio drastically changed after the implementation plan was completed. Along with the federal government and many states, Ohio established a separate state agency to manage the quality of the environment. Previously, as in other states, Ohio's environmental programs had been administered by such departments as health, natural resources, agriculture, and development, and by part-time control boards.

The new Ohio Environmental Protection Agency began operating in October 1972. The jurisdiction of the Ohio EPA included "laws and regulations pertaining to the prevention, control, and abatement of air and water pollution, public water supply, comprehensive water resource management planning, and the disposal and treatment of solid wastes, sewage, industrial waste and other wastes."[14] Significantly, a single director headed the new agency, ending the practice of having air pollution regulations and orders written by part-time board members, some of whom represented interests adversely affected by pollution abatement rules. Organizationally, at least, Ohio's environmental agency was strong.

In addition, Ohio created a separate entity to handle appeals from actions of its EPA. Except for orders during an air pollution emergency, virtually any regulation, abatement order, permit, or variance can be appealed to the Ohio Environmental Board of Review. Like the Ohio EPA, it too was strong. The review board has three statutory members, and each must have expertise in environmental problems; one member must be a lawyer. All three serve full-time, and membership positions were not parceled out to affected interests.

Withdrawal of the Ohio Implementation Plan

Just as the reorganization of Ohio's pollution programs was completed, the new agency moved to revise the sulfur dioxide emission limitation program. Now that citizen pressure seemed to be subsiding and industry opposition rising, the state EPA began to have second thoughts about its ambitious program. (Several of Ohio's electric utilities had filed suit against the U.S. EPA under provisions for judicial review in the Clean Air Act.) The Ohio EPA consequently sought both to delay compliance from 1975 to 1977 and to revise the implementation plan by making it more detailed through county-by-county analysis.

The U.S. EPA approved state implementation plans on May 31, 1972. By this time there was some doubt that low-sulfur fuel would be available in sufficient quantities to meet national demands. Use of low-sulfur fuel would allow polluters to meet sulfur dioxide emission limitations quickly. But in December 1972, William D. Ruckelshaus, Administrator of the U.S. EPA, stated that nationwide adoption of the alternative of clean low-sulfur fuels to meet emission standards would exhaust supplies, thereby preventing Ohio and other states from meeting their own deadlines. He therefore recommended that compliance dates be delayed in certain cases principally by granting variances, but still insuring that the federal ambient standard would be met by 1975 and that there would be no degradation or backsliding in ambient air quality. The U.S. EPA was not only willing to let Ohio relax its sulfur dioxide regulations, it was encouraging such a change. The U.S. EPA head for Region V (the Midwest) emphatically stated:

> Our studies show there are . . . sufficient supplies to meet sulfur oxide primary ambient air quality standards *provided* State sulfur regulations are set at levels no more stringent than required to meet primary standards.

Unnecessarily stringent sulfur regulations result in fuel shifts which may deny low-sulfur fuels to sources which may require such fuels to meet primary standards. . . .

This policy encourages States to defer application of fuel sulfur regulations to large coal-burning sources where such application is not required to meet primary standards. . . .

We believe much of this projected coal deficit could be eliminated . . . if coal sulfur regulations for large coal users, particularly power plants, could be based on an individual assessment of the impact of each user on ambient air quality. . . .[15]

Instead of following the U.S. EPA recommendation, however, the Ohio EPA requested a simple two-year delay in attaining ambient air quality standards, as permitted by the Clean Air Act. Ohio cited the scarcity of natural gas and low-sulfur oil, the lack of low-sulfur coal, and the insufficient supply of scrubbers. Such problems were already known to federal officials, and they had advised Ohio to modify its plans; but the Ohio EPA felt that these changes should be made only after careful and lengthy analysis, and it requested an across-the-board delay. Although a 1-year extension was possible in the Clean Air Act, the U.S. EPA could not grant Ohio's request for a 2-year delay, because the request had not been included in the implementation plan when it was originally submitted.

However the issue was moot before the U.S. EPA had even answered the request. On June 28, 1973, the U.S. Court of Appeals, Sixth Circuit, ruled in *Buckeye Power Inc. et al.* v. *EPA* that the federal approval of the *Ohio Implementation Plan* was invalid.[16] The court found that the comment period at the state level during the adoption of the implementation plan was inadequate, since the plan, when approved by the U.S. EPA, could be enforced by a federal agency that had conducted no rule-making proceedings of its own on what would be federal regulations. Referring to section 553 of the federal Administrative Procedure Act,[17] the court found that federal approval of the state implementation plan was informal rule making and required "some public participation." This meant that now Ohio electric utilities and other industries could present evidence to the U.S. EPA that Ohio's regulations were unreasonable and impossible to meet.[18] The decision applied only to federal approval of Ohio's plan; the plan was still enforceable at the state level, since state rule making proceedings were not in question.

Far from being a crushing blow to the plans of the Ohio EPA, the decision presented an opportunity to revise an overly optimistic program adopted at a time of intense citizen pressure. In August 1973, the sulfur dioxide portion of the *Ohio Implementation Plan* was formally withdrawn; the Ohio EPA interpreted the nullification of federal approval in *Buckeye Power* as meaning that the plan had never been submitted, thus allowing them to revise. This gave the Ohio EPA, the coal-burning electric utilities, and other Ohio industries the delay they had all been seeking.

Revision of the Sulfur Dioxide Plan

The Ohio EPA had already begun revising the sulfur dioxide emission limitation program before the decision in *Buckeye Power*. The main thrust of the revision was making the emission limitations as source-specific as possible, using dispersion modeling on a county-by-county rather than regionwide basis. The revision was in two parts. For boilers of "less than utility size," a new plan was formulated. This part of the revision, essentially a plan designed for small point sources, was proposed in November 1973, with eased regulations. A different strategy was attempted for boilers of utility size. Instead of rewriting the program, the director of the state EPA issued orders to major electric utilities to initiate an adjudication hearing to test the program. Earlier attempts to rewrite the program had not been successful because negotiations with the utilities had failed. While this part of the sulfur dioxide plan was going through adjudication the revised plan for small point sources was appealed to the Ohio Environmental Board of Review. In September 1974, both review processes were completed—with decisive results.

Consolidated Utilities Cases

On September 6, 1974, hearing examiners issued their report in the adjudication hearing, and it was decidedly negative. Basically, the hearing examiners ruled that: (1) Ohio's ambient standard for sulfur dioxide was "unreasonable"; and (2) that the use of the example-region-worst-case approach and the proportional reduction model was inappropriate because it led to excessively stringent regulations.

The examiners criticized the choice of the federal secondary standards for sulfur oxides as Ohio's only ambient standards for sulfur. In addition, they were very concerned that regulations have an "adequate data base," such as incontrovertible scientific research or good empirical data on ambient air quality, ground-level concentrations of pollutants, stack emissions, and so forth. Consequently, after hearing rather critical testimony from several scientific and medical experts on the health and environmental effects of sulfur oxide pollution, the hearing examiners concluded that the federal primary standards and only the 3-hour secondary standard were derived from an adequate data base; they recommended that the state revise its ambient standards accordingly.

They were not alone in recommending these changes. Evaluating the scientific evidence of the effects of vegetation of sulfur oxides as insufficient, the U.S. EPA repealed the secondary annual standard for sulfur oxides in 1973, retaining only the 3-hour maximum. The annual standard had been based on a single study now regarded as inconclusive. Thus, the hearing examiners reasoned that there was little justification for maintaining Ohio's strict sulfur standards.

The hearing examiners also criticized the techniques used by the Ohio EPA

in writing the state implementation plan. They criticized the proportional
reduction model for being unsophisticated and the example-region-worst-case
approach as requiring more stringent emission standards than necessary in
regions of better air quality. They said that both caused "significant pollution
control costs which are arguably unnecessary . . . " The hearing examiners
stated:

> . . . Ohio's existing limitations upon . . . sulfur dioxide suffer from
> serious deficiencies. Utilization of over-simplified techniques to develop
> these emission limitations obviously stemmed from a feeling on the part
> of Ohio EPA's technical staff (of) time limitation imposed by the Clean
> Air Act Amendments of 1970 and subsequently by perceived pressures
> to develop emissions quickly. This action does not reflect sound
> administrative judgment. If the time limitations demanded by Federal
> law are unrealistic, then they must be abandoned in favor of developing
> emission limitations which accurately reflect the degree of control
> necessary to achieve the proper ambient levels. The application of
> emission limitations which are unnecessarily restrictive to require the
> applicants in this proceeding to expend huge sums of money not
> justified by considerations of adverse health effects or adverse effects
> upon the public welfare is violative of every known criteria for judging
> the reasonableness of administrative action.[19]

These and other recommendations of the *Hearing Examiners' Report* were
presented to the director of the Ohio EPA. In December 1974, Director Ira L.
Whitman issued his orders to the electric companies in the consolidated utilities
case and gave his response to several of the recommendations. Whitman chose
not to change the Ohio ambient air quality standard (the repealed federal
secondary standard), saying that it was needed to protect the public health.
However, he did agree to defer the sulfur dioxide emission regulations for the
electric utilities because of an inadequate data base. The utilities had won a
point.

Rejection of the Revised Plan by the
Environmental Board of Review

Although the director opposed most of the recommendations of the *Hearing
Examiners' Report*, he was clearly mindful of the complaints of the electric
utilities. The Ohio EPA had been working on a revision of emission regulations
to minimize any overkill. In November 1973, the Ohio EPA held public hearings
on the new regulations, which were adopted the next January. The utilities, steel
companies, and several other industries immediately appealed the regulations to
the Environmental Board of Review.

It is not clear why the utilities and their allies should have appealed the new regulations, which dealt with boilers of a smaller size than they used. The new regulations set a sliding scale of emission standards based on location. Such a scheme would ease the pollution control requirements for many small point sources, something the U.S. EPA had been recommending. But for the utilities and the others, the original stringent standards remained unchanged, causing the hearing examiners to call the new regulations in their report "unreasonable" and an "unwarranted differentiation among sources."[20] If the regulations were eased for small polluters, then the burden of air pollution abatement would be placed on the large polluters. The utilities had also been making a unified and uncompromising resistance effort against the sulfur dioxide regulations since 1972, and this litigation fit that strategy.

The Ohio EPA had been trying to "fine tune" the regulations, and here the Environmental Board of Review took issue. By fine tuning, the Ohio EPA meant subregionalization of emission regulations—that is, analyzing air quality on a county-by-county basis. This way a plant in a priority-one air quality control region (those with severe air pollution) could have emission regulations for a priority three location if its county's air pollution was not severe. Fine tuning like this could ease the regulations for at least some plants and still allow Ohio to meet the ambient standards for sulfur dioxide.

However the state review board found subregionalization to be against the law. Citing the Clean Air Act, the board determined that air quality control regions must be created on the basis of meteorological and topographical data and follow urban-industrial concentrations, with political boundaries a second-ary consideration. The board found that these legal requirements had not been met and that subregionalization was more of an "administrative convenience" accommodating the utilities than promoting the goals of the Clean Air Act. The board cited the testimony of Blaine Fielding, counsel for the director of the Ohio EPA, who stated that the "sole motivation" of the director "was to provide, at least insofar as the utility applicants are concerned, a less stringent regulatory program," adding that this was necessary to end the overkill in the regulations.[21] But the board saw fine tuning simply as favorable treatment for the utilities.

The board then concluded that the entire revision effort had been under-taken to accommodate the electric utilities, which maintained their uncompro-mising position. For this reason and because of violations of Ohio administrative law, the board rejected the revised plan. Whereas the hearing examiners had criticized state EPA regulations for being too stringent, the board overturned them for being too lenient. By the end of 1974, therefore, Ohio had no revised sulfur dioxide emission limitation program and the old program was not being enforced. To complicate matters further, the top policy making leadership changed at the Ohio EPA as a result of gubernatorial elections that fall. Democratic incumbent John J. Gilligan lost to former governor James A. Rhodes, who had called the state EPA a "fund-impounding, red-tape-snarled, nitpicking harasser of local governments and private industry."[22]

Federal Intervention

The revised Ohio plan for sulfur dioxide had been submitted to the U.S. EPA for approval; but when the board rejected the attempted revision, the U.S. EPA dismissed it. By 1975, then, there was still no federally approved sulfur dioxide plan for Ohio. The Clean Air Act requires that the administrator of the U.S. EPA write a plan or part of a plan for a state if one is not submitted or acceptable. Thus, in March 1975, when the U.S. EPA should have promulgated its own sulfur dioxide plan for Ohio and had not, the Natural Resources Defense Council threatened to bring a citizen suit to force the administrator to act. In October 1975, the Northern Ohio Lung Association actually filed a citizen suit in federal court to force the administrator to issue a plan; however the U.S. EPA published a plan in November and scheduled hearings in Ohio thereby killing the suit.

The federal EPA hearings in January 1976 brought out the differences between the federal and the state EPAs (the latter now headed by different personnel appointed by the new Republican governor), as well as between the U.S. EPA and Ohio utilities and industry. The debate in 1976 was different from that in 1970. Earlier opposition to environmental regulations took the form of vague predictions of technical problems and economic hardship and argued that scientific evidence of a health hazard from sulfur dioxide was poor at best. The new debate was much more detailed and technically precise, reflecting an experience in dealing with pollution control by both government and industry.

The issues raised in the hearings included the adequacy of the computer simulation model used by the U.S. EPA (especially, the use of air quality estimates instead of recorded data), the federal method for forecasting regional economic growth (a necessary consideration in formulating the regulations so that they would maintain acceptable ambient air quality even as new sources of pollution develop), and the economic impact of the national plan on the Ohio coal industry. The hearings represented a continuation of the dispute about regulatory overkill, that is, whether the standards were more stringent than necessary to attain and maintain the ambient standards. The U.S. EPA held that its regulations were the absolute minimum for meeting the standards; the Ohio EPA and Ohio utilities and industry claimed that the standards still contained much overkill.

To be as accurate as possible and to minimize overkill, the U.S. EPA used a computer simulation model regarded as one of the most sophisticated and advanced air quality dispersion models available. It also used the less stringent federal primary standard. The U.S. EPA explicitly wished to "minimize over-control to the maximum extent possible," by "tailoring" emission standards to an individual source's actual contribution to air pollution. The U.S. EPA tested the emission standards on a county-by-county basis (rather than regionwide) as the Ohio EPA had tried to do in 1973. As before, this "approach was aimed at reducing the potential for overcontrol on sources relative to that which might occur if larger geographical areas were analyzed." It was an explicit attempt to avoid problems associated with the simple strategy of the example-region-worst-case approach and proportional reduction experienced in 1971.

Even with this concern for accuracy, the U.S. EPA still received criticism from all sides at the hearings held in Ohio. Representing environmentalists, Richard Ayres of the Natural Resources Defense Council delivered a very strong dissent. In his view, the U.S. EPA computer simulation model underestimated pollutant levels and therefore led to emission standards too lenient for Ohio's air pollution problem. Ayres summed up his criticism:

> We regard the proposed Ohio plan as . . . a major manifestation of the Ford Administration's program to dismantle the environmental laws for the short-term benefit of the utilities and other industrial groups. Against its better judgment, in our view, EPA has been muscled into proposing a short-sighted plan whose object is to maximize pollutant emissions, limited only to the national air quality standards—a plan that both fails to protect public health and fails to save room for future economic growth in Ohio's cities.[23]

Although it might not be surprising that environmentalists would want a stricter program, the position of the Ohio EPA under new leadership was. The U.S. EPA had previously cautioned Ohio against an overly restrictive plan; but now the advice went in the opposite direction. Dr. John Burr testified for the state EPA. Burr, chief of the Environmental Assessment Section of the Division of Program Development and Review in the Office of Air Pollution Control, maintained that only actual air quality data should be used in setting emission standards, ruling out the use of estimated or predicted emissions in the simulation model. He stated:

> Ohio EPA believes that the use of measured air quality data should be the prime criteria for determining that a problem exists (or does not exist), for assessing the severity of that problem, and should form the primary basis for imposition of emission limiting regulations.[24]

Thus, the Ohio EPA was now criticizing the U.S. EPA for overkill. Burr was clearly negative about the use of the air quality dispersion model. He argued that it should not be used in particular counties unless it was based on actual air quality data from those counties. For the most part, counties that had no air quality data were the ones that were not in violation of ambient air quality standards. Some of these counties had no predicted air quality violations in the model and were, therefore, not scheduled for emission controls in the U.S. EPA plan. However some counties did have predicted violations, although none in 1975, and were scheduled for emission limitations. The alternative that the state EPA offered for these latter counties was maintenance of the status quo on emissions, meaning that a source would not be permitted to exceed the amount of sulfur dioxide that it emitted in some designated previous year. The status-quo regulations would be enforced through granting air pollution permits and variances. The U.S. EPA had promulgated control for thirty-four Ohio counties but the state envisioned controls for only nine, the ones with actual air quality data. The status-quo regulations would cover the other counties. By not allowing for economic growth and rising levels of emissions that would follow the creation of new sources, Ohio may actually have been writing a much more stringent program.

Ohio's position on delaying emission controls for counties without a present air pollution problem was not accepted by the U.S. EPA, which was obligated by the Clean Air Act to improve air quality. The policy differences between the two agencies were concisely stated by John Chicca, chief of the Air Planning Section in the Air and Hazardous Materials Division, U.S. EPA, Region V, in his response to Burr's testimony:

> Now, if I am correct in my analysis of what you are proposing today, with respect to those counties where there may be a potential problem, but you don't have monitoring data to back it up, it would appear . . . that you are essentially saying that the economic risk in overcontrol, at the present time, outweighs the public health risk in not being stringent enough. That would appear . . . not to be a proper striking of the balance from our perspective, and, therefore, we may not be able to implement the full tenor of your remarks . . . [25]

The use and calculation of the growth rate in the model was also severely criticized. Burr felt that the growth rate used by the U.S. EPA contributed to regulatory overkill. Norman Keckler, head of the Akron Regional Air Pollution Control Agency, stated that there were no violations of ambient air quality in Summit County and there was a "negative growth pollution factor" in local emissions, thus making the scheduled federal regulations overly stringent and unnecessary. Keckler also stated that the regulations would terminate some marginal plants within the area and would discourage new industries from locating in Summit County.

Although the differences over the U.S. EPA plan were many and complex, some issues were clear. The U.S. EPA had taken great pains to write a plan that would be as detailed as possible and eliminate any overkill. Criticisms of the plan basically involved charges that it was not detailed enough and that it should have been based, in every case, on hard data and documented violations of ambient air quality. The final promulgation of the U.S. EPA plan was delayed by the U.S. Court of Appeals, Sixth Circuit, while the plan was under challenge by Ohio utilities and other industries. Meanwhile, the Ohio EPA wrote a plan of its own and held hearings in December 1976 and the following January. These hearings became a vehicle for even more criticism of the U.S. EPA Plan.

Reformulation of the Ohio EPA Sulfur
Dioxide Plan

When the new director of the Ohio EPA took over in 1975, he faced the problem of what action to take on the revision of Ohio's sulfur dioxide plan. Knowing that the U.S. EPA was preparing a plan of its own and feeling that the Ohio EPA could not come up with a plan of its own ahead of the federal plan, the director deferred. In December 1976, however, Ohio held hearings on its version of the federal plan with controls for nine counties instead of thirty-four and without federal compliance schedules. The Ohio EPA also adopted the less stringent federal primary ambient air quality standard of an annual average of not more than 80 micrograms per cubic meter.

Once again environmental groups were critical. Catherine Bush, Cuyahoga County League of Women Voters, expressed doubt that the Ohio EPA could enforce its plan:

> Ohio EPA has testified in opposition to the federal plan, calling it "regulatory overkill." This expressed opposition, combined with reluctance on the part of the state government to fund the air pollution control program, makes us uneasy about the Ohio EPA in the role of enforcer of these regulations. They would be the target of mounting pressure by industry to relax air standards including threats to leave the Cleveland area or the state of Ohio and warnings that the building of new facilities and decision on enlarging present installations will be based on whether air pollution laws are enforced.[26]

Bush felt that full responsibility for enforcement should remain with the U.S. EPA. This was mild criticism.

Public officials in Ohio were very critical of the U.S. EPA plan. Representative A.G. Lancione, who represented a coal-mining district in the legislature, roundly opposed the U.S. EPA plan:

> The destruction of the Ohio coal industry will have a profound effect on those workers who rely on Ohio coal companies for their employment, either directly or indirectly . . . The imminent possibility of the Ohio coal industry suffering up to a 75 percent loss in coal production would force the coal industry and its related industries to lay off thousands of workers and cut the families' income by 50 percent or more . . . The devastation of the coal industry would set off a series of economic cut backs that could depress the whole eastern Ohio region. . . .
>
> When one remembers that these consequences could result from the imposition of standards that are, by their very nature, excessive, one is struck by the utter ridiculousness of the forcing of unnecessary sulfur emission standards down the throats of citizens who neither need nor want this undue protection.[27]

The costs to Ohio industry for compliance had long been at issue; but one issue dominated the others at the hearings—the continued use of Ohio coal.

While some Ohio coal could not be used in Ohio if sulfur limitations are enforced, much less is certain. Since some Ohio coal is sold out of state, the exact impact on the Ohio coal-mining industry and jobs was—and is—uncertain. Nevertheless, the deleterious effect on the coal industry from the enforcement of the fedreal plan was a major topic at the Columbus hearings, in part because several hundred coal miners were brought in for the event. Robert S. Ryan, director of the Ohio Energy and Resource Development Agency, flatly stated that there would be a loss of 7000 jobs as a result of implementing the federal plan and a 14 to 20 percent increase in the cost of electricity. The plan, Ryan stated, was "not compatible with responsible energy management...."[28] Although coal can be washed, blended, or made acceptable through the use of scrubbers, there was no general agreement at the hearings on the effect of these techniques in making high-sulfur Ohio coal acceptable. As yet, the Ohio EPA has not adopted its own version of the federal plan.

Federal Plan Upheld

The attempt to write a sulfur dioxide emission limitation program for Ohio reached a conclusion in February 1978, when the U.S. Court of Appeals handed down its decision on the petition for review of thirty-two Ohio industries and utilities.[29] The judges strongly supported the work of the U.S. EPA. The same court that had put the *Ohio Implementation Plan* into suspension in 1973 not only supported the U.S. EPA but even criticized it for not being strict enough. With that, the court dismissed complaints of overkill.

The court supported the use of computer simulation modeling by the U.S. EPA, saying that the model "employs a wiser, more complete and more accurate data base than any prior model yet employed in devising a sulfur dioxide control strategy for a state or county." The court noted that the model did not have "predictive perfection," but said the errors tended to underestimate actual emissions. Generally, the court found that the U.S. EPA plan was less stringent than either the original 1972 Ohio plan or the revised 1974 Ohio plan. Based on these considerations, the court could find no reason for holding the U.S. EPA plan "arbitrary or capricious" and concluded that it was well within the discretion of the administrator of the U.S. EPA to promulgate such a plan.

Finally, the court rejected the state's appeal to delay enforcement further. In its brief, Ohio had protested that the overkill in the federal plan would have serious negative impacts on the Ohio economy, particularly the coal industry. Ohio sought delay to promulgate its own plan, but the court said no: "We reject this suggestion on the basis of a record of delay and default which has left Ohio in the position of being the only major industrialized state lacking an enforceable plan for control of sulfur dioxide." The court added that five years had gone by since the date when all states were to have implementation plans in place. The court simply concluded that there could be no more delay.

Conclusion

With the court's decision, there is finally in Ohio a set of emission regulations for sulfur dioxide that can now be enforced. How can this long, complex, even labyrinthine process of drafting regulations be interpreted? As a case of "implementation beyond capacity," Ohio is a good example. The original ambient standards and emission regulations were very stringent, which quickly led to requests for delay from industry and eventually from the Ohio EPA itself. Jones found a similar pattern of backing away from overly optimistic goals at the federal and state levels. Strong public support has now diminished, and there is even some strong opposition, particularly from the coal industry and coal miners. As an example of nonincremental policy, the sulfur dioxide emission limitation program has involved intense effort to improve administrative and technological capability. In the time since the passage of the Clean Air Act Amendments of 1970, the ability of the U.S. EPA to write a program that could stand up in court has clearly improved. Environmental policy may not be analogous to the space program, but the effort required for both is similar.

Notes

1. See three works by Charles O. Jones: "Speculative Augmentation in Federal Air Pollution Policy-Making," *Journal of Politics* 36 (May 1974):438-463; *Clean Air: The Policies and Politics of Pollution Control* (Pittsburgh: University of Pittsburgh Press, 1975); and "Regulating the Environment" in Herbert Jacob and Kenneth N. Vines, *Politics in the American States*, 3d ed. (Boston: Little, Brown, 1976).

2. Paul R. Schulman, "Nonincremental Policy Making: Notes toward an Alternative Paradigm," *American Political Science Review* 69 (December 1975):1354-1370.

3. Testimony of Jack Wunderle, chief of the Office of Air Pollution Control, Ohio EPA, *Hearings in the Matter of Electric Companies of Ohio, 1974, Combined Cases 73-AV-122, et al.*, pp. 72-74.

4. Ohio Department of Health, Air Pollution Control Board, *Public Hearings Before the Ohio Air Pollution Control Board to Consider the Adoption of Proposed New Regulations AP-5-01 to AP-5-05 and AP-3-01, Inclusive, Prescribing Ambient Air Quality Standards for Sulfur Oxides, Suspended Particulates, Carbon Monoxide, Photochemical Oxidants, and Hydrocarbons, and Other Regulations Relative to the Prevention, Control, and Abatement of Air Pollution in the State of Ohio*, Columbus, Ohio, 23 (November 1970):453.

5. Ibid., pp. 81-82.

6. Ibid., pp. 430-431.

7. Ibid., p. 96.

8. Ibid., pp. 142-143.

9. Ohio EPA, *Particulate Matter and Sulfur Oxide Standards* (adopted 28 January 1972; effective 15 February 1972), sec. AP-3-02 (B).

10. Testimony of Jack Wunderle, *Hearings of Electric Companies Cases*, p. 91.

11. Ohio Energy and Resource Development Agency, *An Evaluation of the Impact of the Proposed USEPA Standards for Ohio*, 1976, pp. 43-45.

12. Clean Air Act, sec. 110, 42 U.S.C. sec. 1857c-5(a)(2)(A)-(H) (1970).

13. J. Clarence Davies III and Barbara S. Davies, *The Politics of Pollution*, 2d ed. (Indianapolis, Ind.: Bobbs-Merrill, 1975), pp. 52-53.

14. Ohio, Environmental Law, Rev. Code (1972), secs. 3745.01-011.

15. Valdus V. Adamkus, Acting Regional Administrator, U.S. EPA, Region V, to John J. Gilligan 25 May 1973, Files of U.S. EPA, Region V, Chicago, Illinois.

16. 481 F.2d 162 (6th cir. 1973).

17. 5 U.S.C. Sec. 553 (1967).

18. *Buckeye Power* v. *EPA*, 170.

19. Ohio EPA, *In the Matter of Consolidated Electric Utilities Cases* (Hearing Examiners' Report), nos. 73-A-P-120 et al., Columbus, Ohio, 6 September 1974, pp. 78-83.

20. Ohio EPA, *Findings and Orders in the Consolidated Utilities Cases*, Nos. 73-A-V-120, et al., 12 December 1974, pp. 67-72.

21. Ohio, Environmental Board of Review, *Buckeye Power, Inc., et al.*, v. *Whitman*, nos. EBR 74-6 through 10, 13 September 1974, pp. 123-135, 179.

22. Gladwin Hill, "Attacks on Environmental Rules Blunted," *New York Times*, 15 March 1976, p. 26.

23. U.S. EPA, Region V, *Hearing on the Proposed Sulfur Dioxide Control Regulation for the State of Ohio*, Columbus, Ohio, 13 January 1976, pp. 164-179.

24. Ibid., p. 31.

25. Ibid., p. 64.

26. Ohio EPA, *Public Hearing Concerning Proposed Repeal of Existing Regulations AP-3-01 to 3-07, AP-3-09 to 3-14 and EP-32-03 and Proposed Adoption of New Regulations EP-11-01 to 11-12 and Amended Regulation EP-32-03*, Cleveland, Ohio, 21 December 1976, pp. 83-85.

27. Ohio EPA, *Public Hearings Concerning the Proposed Repeal of Existing Regulations AP-3-01 to AP-2-07, AP-3-09 to AP-3-14 and EP-32-03, and the Proposed Adoption of New Regulations EP-11-01 to EP-11-12 and Amended Regulation EP-32-03*, Columbus, Ohio, January 11-12, 1976, pp. 31-32.

28. *Ohio EPA Columbus Hearings*, pp. 10-15.

29. *Cleveland Electric Illuminating Company et al.* v. *EPA*, 572 F.2d 1150 (6th cir. 1978).

8

Solar Futures: A Perspective on Energy Planning

Gregory A. Daneke

Introduction

In the aftermath of Sun Day, increasing public concern has been expressed regarding the lack of a coherent solar energy program. As a result, various segments of the federal government have been engaged in a number of solar policy reassessments. However these reassessments have yet to yield a significantly different set of policy perspectives and imperatives. Despite all the attention given to solar energy in recent years (evidenced by geometric increases in solar research funding), it remains a remote promise rather than a practical alternative. This apparent lack of viability is not necessarily attributable to the state of its technology, for most forms of exploiting solar energy have been technically feasible for hundreds of years. The major constraint on solar energy development is price. Price, however, is not a function of inexorable market forces. Price is a function of public policy. In essence, a variety of past policies buttress existing energy resources (oil, coal, and nuclear), thereby reducing the competitiveness of solar energy.[1] This discussion will briefly review these constraints imposed on solar energy through its status as a "policy orphan" and the planning perspectives that subliminally maintain that status.

Planning and Energy Policy

"Planning" has been something of a dirty word in American politics. It is generally considered antidemocratic because it tries to impose the views of an elite minority (planners) on the remainder of society.[2] Despite this and other engrained biases against planning, planning has played and continues to play a major role in the development of policy. There is a growing realization that planning is important in avoiding the debilitating effects of accelerating social change in addition to being useful in times of national emergency (for example, the Great Depression).

These ideas were developed, in part, while the author was a faculty fellow in the Energy and Minerals Division of the U.S. General Accounting Office. The author would therefore like to acknowledge the contribution to his thinking made by Tom Melloy, Farrel Fenzel, and Ken Kazmer. The author would also like to thank Fay Edwards for her helpful comments. However, the views expressed here are not necessarily those of the individuals mentioned, nor of the General Accounting Office.

Today's more widely used planning procedures have changed a great deal from their original states. The turbulent sixties produced unique hybrids such as participatory planning and advocacy planning. Planning has become more systematic, but it has also grown more pluralistic and pragmatic. This is true in most policy areas, with the possible exception of the energy realm. Energy policy makers have tended to rely on antiquated planning concepts, which produce traditional forecasting patterns and shroud normative policy decisions in a market mythology.

Forecasting Energy Futures

The energy crisis, like any crisis, has demanded long-range preemptive policies. A preemptive posture requires adaptive planning that includes forecasting future states of society. Forecasting, particularly that involving technological and sociopolitical uncertainty (factors which prevail in the energy realm), is a very tenuous art. Like other facets of planning, it has grown more sophisticated over the years, drawing heavily on advancements in operations research and econometrics (largely regression analysis). However increased sophistication has not necessarily meant greater accuracy.

As William Ascher demonstrates, larger, more complex forecast models (for example, those with more structural equations) have not fared much better than smaller judgmental forecasts in a range of policy areas, including the economy, energy, transportation, and so forth. This, Ascher explains, is a result of focusing on developing the model itself and paying little attention to the assumptions going into it. Some models depend on earlier models for vital input, and this imposes greater "assumption drag" (the use of outdated or inaccurate assumptions). Another dysfunction brought on by complexity is the glossing over of assumptions that involve spurious relationships. For example, energy demand projections often implicitly assume a causal relationship between energy usage and gross national product. Energy conservation studies have largely exploded this myth.[4]

Beyond the basic problems of clarifying critical assumptions, forecasters rarely, if ever, look at the premises underlying a particular methodology. This is not an unimportant exercise. Quite often the chosen method is ill matched to the mode of inquiry. For instance, math models and/or operations-research techniques are best suited to simple inventory and queuing problems, in which the critical structural relationships are well known and highly stable over time. Econometric models, on the other hand, attempt to distill these critical relationships through empirical observations and statistical extrapolations. In short, math models are matters of form, while econometric models attempt to get at content. In energy modeling these two methods are often mixed without specific reference to the questions asked or the nature of the relationships explored. With specific reference to solar forecasts, the nonmarket nature of solar energy has not been adequately explained or represented. Subsequently both of these common modeling approaches may be inappropriate. Whether one uses an algorithm or a regression line to represent perceived relationships, the forecast will have a certain unwarranted, fatalistic quality. This fatalism stems from the fact that energy policy decisions are often matters of normative choice, particularly when previous choices obliterate natural market forces. In essence, the energy future is somewhat predetermined by existing policy commitments.

Teleological Forecasting

In situations where the future is mostly a matter of normative choice, a different forecasting approach is required. Such an approach might follow what Ian Mitroff and Murray Turoff call a "Singerian system of inquiry" (named for American pragmatist Edgar Singer).[5] Such a system would maintain that change forces are relative to the level of policy commitment. Thus one begins by assuming a certain level of commitment and working backward to discover the types of policy change required to bring about a particular end. This focus on goals or ends gives the enterprise a teleological character (from the Greek, *telos*, meaning both end and essence). The ends themselves might be derived through careful economic and social impact assessment designed to derive future scenarios and/or desired states of the system. Rather than asking what the future will be like, this analysis would ask what the future should be like?

As suggested, this approach to planning is alien to energy policy. Until recently, energy planning was virtually nonexistent, and policy was made largely by default. Even with the creation of the Department of Energy (DOE) and the various national energy plans, the basic approach is one of gradual policy change and business-as-usual. In this context, forecasts merely explore when a particular energy technology will be available if current trends continue.

The teleological approach reopens the issue of policy choice by recognizing that the future is relative to these choices. Mitroff and Turoff point out that:

> Singerian inquiry is virtually absent from the field of technological forecasting and assessment. However, the implication of Singerian inquiry for technological forecasting is that the supposed fundamental polarity of exploratory and normative forecasting completely breaks down.[6]

Moreover, the teleological approach is much more congruent with the general shift in planning from traditional elitism to pluralistic pragmaticism. Forecasting is not merely planning for an inexorable future; rather, it is planning to facilitate the collective creation of alternative futures. This perspective on planning guides the following discussion.

Solar Energy: The Neglected Alternative

Solar energy entails the direct capture or collection of dispersed sunlight and/or the air and water flows created by the sun. In short, solar strategies represent humankind's attempt to augment the natural processes that capture, condense, and store sunlight in the form of coal, natural gas, oil, and so forth. In broadest terms, solar energy involves a wide variety of distinct technologies. The DOE presently considers all the following as solar energy sources:

1. passive design
2. active heating and cooling
3. process heat
4. wind systems
5. solar thermal electric
6. ocean thermal systems
7. biomass conversion
8. terrestrial photovoltaics
9. space satellite power systems[7]

For the past several decades technology, artificial markets, and our life-style have produced an overreliance on concentrated forms of solar energy (that is, oil, gas, and coal). Furthermore, wasteful use patterns (promoted by artificially cheap energy) have produced greater environmental degradation and a presumed dependence on supplemental supplies (primarily nuclear). Energy has consequently become an end in itself and policies have tended to ignore the basic end uses or demands, which initially prompted the quest for increased supplies.

As the expense of centralized, capital-intensive, high-technology systems and fossil fuels increases, postindustrial man may consider returning to the ancient art of collecting less concentrated forms of solar energy. The economic shocks of making this kind of fundamental change in energy use could be traumatic. If society wants to go in this direction, common sense dictates a gradual transition. However, even a gradual transition to solar and other alternative energy systems could be hampered by a panoply of institutional constraints.

Historical Antecedents

Solar energy systems have not always been as exotic as they now appear. Solar energy was the major resource in all ancient civilizations. Beyond its obvious use in agriculture, many cultures developed a number of direct and indirect uses of the sun's energy. As early as 200 B.C., the Persians used windmills to grind various grains. The Pueblo Indians of the Southwest were masters of passive solar design. A variety of solar collection systems were thriving in the United States up to the 1930s. For example, a process-heat plant operated near Phoenix, Arizona, in 1904; solar hot water systems were fairly popular in California and Florida in the 1920s and 1930s; and working windmills were once common sights on the rural landscape. But with the introduction of government-subsidized remote electricity and regulated fuels (such as oil and natural gas), solar usage quickly waned. By the 1950s, solar systems (with the exception of hydropower and photovoltaics for the space program) were virtually abandoned.

A few studies that emerged during this period of "benign neglect" predicted a resurgence of solar energy in the future. One was the famous Paley Commission Report conducted during the Truman administration. This study suggested a major role for solar by the 1970s.[8] A 1959 report issued by the Bureau of Economics and Business Research at the University of Maryland claimed that solar energy systems would soon supplant nuclear ones in cost-competitiveness.[9] But these studies failed to appreciate the overwhelming political and economic power of purveyors of existing energy forms.

The Arab oil embargo (whether real or imaginary) and subsequent events of the early 1970s alerted the nation to the fact that fossil fuels are finite. In the meantime, the prospect of cheap, infinite energy from nuclear power was fading. Under the spector of an impeding energy crisis, solar energy was rediscovered. A portion of solar's new found popularity was, of course, a result of burgeoning environmental concerns. Optimistic sources were touting the coming of the solar age. Yet for solar energy to reassert itself, it must first thread a vast maze of institutional barriers.

The Solar Orphan

Amid the political realities that have promoted the use of fossil and nuclear fuels, solar energy is something of an orphan. It has no natural constituency aside from the infant solar industries and their associated services (for example, plumbers, carpenters, architects, etc.). Although support from organized labor is certainly logical given the labor intensiveness of solar, this support has not been swift in emerging.[10] As late as the mid-1960s, government funding for solar research was virtually nonexistent. By 1972, funding was only 2 million dollars. In 1977, the figure shot up to 290 million, and future allocations will probably average at least 500 million annually. These increases in research funding were meager in comparison with the billions spent in direct and indirect subsidies to other energy resources. (See table 8-1.) It is doubtful that any of the market analogies (such as cost-competitiveness) pertain to this highly convoluted system of government subsidies. Given the lack of large-scale economic and political clout, the solar alternative is substantially disadvantaged in the battle for selected government incentives.

Table 8-1
Estimated Cost of Incentives Used to Stimulate Energy Production

Energy Source	Time Period	Cost in Billions (1976 dollars)
Nuclear fuel	1950-1976	15.3-17.1
Hydro-power	1933-1976	9.2-17.5
Coal	1951-1976	6.8
Oil	1918-1976	77.2
Gas	1918-1976	15.1
Total		123.6-133.7

Source: *Commercializing Solar Heating: A National Strategy Needed*, draft (Washington, D.C.: U.S. General Accounting Office, 1978), p. 11. These figures may be subject to question. For example, the figures on nuclear do not include the full range of potential fuel-cycle subsidies (the uranium depletion allowance, enrichment and waste disposal) nor the impacts of accelerated depreciation, normalized accounting, and limited liability (via Price-Anderson). For a discussion of these items see: Gregory A. Daneke, "The Political Economy of Nuclear Development," *Policy Studies Journal* 6 (Summer 1978).

Tax breaks were initiated for residential applications, but a review of several state-level incentives conducted by the Florida Solar Center concluded that these incentives were so miniscule that they served merely to reduce the penalty associated with solar investment.[11] Most tax breaks were granted to individual homeowners; contractors, developers, and individuals who intend resale were excluded. This discouraged large-scale investments.

Nonetheless, the lack of effective incentives may not have been nearly as critical as the disincentives and institutional barriers to solar development. The lack of performance standards, licensing requirements, and certification provide prime examples of commercial inhibitors.[12] The Environmental Law Institute has also identified a number of unresolved legal issues, which have blocked or hampered solar utilization. These include:

1. solar access, or "sun rights" (for example, codes that would prevent building of units which shade existing collectors)
2. existing building codes (for example, limits on types of structures, citing requirements, and hot water levels)
3. loan and financing problems with regard to solar construction and improvements
4. ERDA (Energy Research and Development Administration) patent policies, which discourage solar innovators from accepting research contracts
5. antitrust issues involving existing utilities and their involvement in solar energy
6. insurance, liability, and warranties involving solar units[13]

Most of these problems are easily resolved through minor policy changes and/or the establishment of basic performance standards. The DOE has had

primary responsibility for spearheading such policy changes, and its record has
been poor. It is a relatively new and amorphous agency and is bound to have
management problems, particularly when developing new programs for a diverse
set of technologies such as solar. However, solar advocates claim that DOE's
planning and management of solar programs have bordered on neglect. Herbert
Epstein, chairman of the American Institute of Architects' energy committee
testified before Congress that, "There is no single focus for solar programs
within DOE, and DOE is not playing a management role for solar programs with
other agencies."[14] Admittedly, managing solar energy would be a fairly difficult
task for even a dedicated and well-staffed bureau; but DOE has had no such
bureau. Denis Hayes suggested that "A good solar program will require
clear-eyed managers and sufficient staff to handle the load. Current renewable
energy programs are deficient in both respects."[15]

The consequences of inadequate staffing, in addition to causing a neglect of
certain critical tasks (such as the development of performance standards for solar
equipment), may have caused DOE to focus on large-scale research and easily
managed projects. Such projects have gone to a few giant firms, thereby losing
the inventiveness of a wide range of participants. Academic researcher, Paul
Craig, contended:

> They (DOE) have developed a system which is just about ideal for
> discouraging innovators who like to operate in a small way. The
> Department also succeeds in discouraging innovative University involve-
> ment. . . . In principle, DOE can deal with unsolicited proposals. In
> practice, though, because of the great emphasis on rigid program plans,
> timelines, and the like, it quite often turns out that proposals simply
> don't fit into any established niche.[16]

In addition to the mode of DOE-promoted research, the substance was also
questioned. Centralized solar systems and space platforms, although considerably less cost-effective than residential applications, were stressed. Arnold Nadler
pointed out that DOE programs did not address germane issues of community
planning for solar development.[17] Barry Commoner summarized the various
indictments of DOE as follows:

> If the DOE approach persists it could be fatal to the hoped-for solar
> transition. By the time the long-term research programs were ready for
> commercialization changes in the existing energy systems will have
> taken place that could well block the introduction of solar energy.[18]

Problems of Planning

Much of the malaise exhibited in solar programs may be the result of a myopic
planning perspective. The majority of solar energy studies have begun by asking
"How much solar energy will the nation have in a given year?" This is a rather
silly question given the high level of policy variability associated with energy

systems, particularly alternative energy systems. To illustrate this point, it may be useful to describe briefly the nature of a few of the major studies. (See table 8-2.)

Over 150 separate assessments of solar potential have been conducted. Most of these forecasts, however, assess only a single technology (for example, wind). The list of comprehensive or multitechnology studies is far smaller, although still lengthy. (See table 8-2.) Yet despite this abundance of sophisticated forecasts, the exact amount of total solar potential remains an open question.

In fairness, while nearly all the comprehensive studies include forecasts, they were primarily designed to test for the level of market penetration (commercial acceptance) under a variety of different sensitivities and under a number of different key assumptions. However their bottom line or estimate of total solar output, has been the factor that attracted the most attention. Here the studies differed widely, thereby tending to exacerbate the problems of solar policy development. For the year 2000, estimates ranged from a 2 percent solar contribution to a 37 percent solar contribution. (See table 8-3.)

The basic reason for these diverse results is that the studies assigned different values to a number of critical factors or assumptions affecting solar development. The most critical factors included:

1. price of alternative fuels
2. total energy demand
3. magnitude and success of solar research and development
4. population growth

Table 8-2
Major Solar Energy Studies

1. *Solar Energy: Progress and Promise* (Washington, D.C.: Council on Environmental Quality, April 1978).
2. Committee on Nuclear and Alternative Energy Systems, *Report of the Solar Resource Group* (Washington, D.C.: U.S. Department of Energy, February 1977).
3. *Status Report: Domestic Policy Review* (Washington, D.C.: Domestic Policy Review Integration Group, August 1978).
4. *Solar Energy: A Comparative Analysis to the Year 2020* (McLean, Va.: The Mitre Corporation, Metreks Division, September 1977).
5. *Market Orientation Program Planning Study* (Washington, D.C.: Energy Research and Development Administration, March 1978).
6. *An Assessment of Solar Energy as a National Energy Resource* (Washington, D.C.: Solar Energy Panel, National Science Foundation/National Aeronautics and Space Administration, December 1972).
7. *Project Independence, Final Report on Solar Energy Panel* (Washington, D.C.: Federal Energy Administration, November 1974).
8. Amory B. Lovins, *Soft Energy Paths: Toward a Durable Peace* (Cambridge, Mass.: Ballinger Publishing, 1977).
9. *Solar Energy in America's Future: A Preliminary Assessment* (Palo Alto, Calif.: Stanford Research Institute, 1977).

Table 8-3
Major Solar Energy Forecasts
(Quadrillion BTUs Displaced)

	Solar Quads/Total Quads		
Study	*1985*	*2000*	*2020*
Council on Environmental Quality		24.5/100	45/105
Committee on Nuclear and Alternative Energy Systems			
Low Case	0/98	.1/146	
High Case	3/98	14/146	
Domestic Policy Review			
Base Case		6/95-132	
Max Case		14.3/95-132	
Mitre Corp.	.09/85	5/113	
ERDA	1.2/95	2.8/117	
Solar Energy Panel, National Science Foundation	.4/117	12/177	109/300
FEA			
Base Case	.8/120	11/180	
Acc. Case	1.4/120	40/180	
Amory B. Lovins	5/95	40/108	70/76
Stanford Research Institute			
Ref. Case	2/99	6/145	11/198
Emph. Case	5/99	15/148	44/204
Low Demand	2/79	7/89	14/102

Note: Does not include hydro-power.

5. conservation
6. consumer awareness
7. gross national product
8. relaxation of institutional constraints

How and why certain value figures were chosen is rarely made explicit in the studies. Quite obviously, these factors involve high levels of socioeconomic and technological uncertainty. Moreover, they are all tremendously influenced by policy change. In short, the studies implied or assumed different levels of policy commitment to solar development.

These hidden assumptions about policy commitments make planning unreliable and self-fulfilling. If one begins by assuming little policy change, solar will not look promising and plans will reflect this pessimism. Since the issues in solar planning are highly normative, solar forecasting may demand a teleological approach.

A Teleological Approach

As suggested previously, teleological forecasting is appropriate when normative policy issues are on the table, for example, the future level of the nation's solar commitment. William Ascher argues that forecasts based on the assumed policy choices of forecast users are meaningless. In addition, he maintains that forecasters ought "... to work backward from desired 'end-states' (such as an acceptable level of air pollution) to the policies required to bring them about."[19] However, working backward from end-states is only one facet of the teleological approach. *Telos* for the Greeks implied the essence of something as well as its end. Teleological forecasting, therefore, involves an attempt to account for the full range of social and environmental implications of a given program. In other words, a teleological forecast is also a technology assessment; but, as Mitroff and Turoff point out, technology assessments have yet to realize the potential of the teleological format.[20] Hazel Henderson attributes this failure to the mythology of market economics and the misconception that technology forecasting is a matter of objective science.[21] Social science, which is at the core of authentic technology assessment, remains suspect.

Problems of inadequate social impact assessment and biased technology forecasting are particularly acute in the energy realm. Energy planners and policy analysts have rarely addressed fundamental questions such as "energy for what?"

Working from End-Goals

A teleological approach begins and ends with a determination of broad-range goals. To start, a distillation of social goals is combined with more basic energy forecasts to form the basis for determining social requirements. Social requirements in turn can be translated into a range of end-goals or end-states. Even in the absence of an elaborate social assessment, establishing hypothetical end-goals may assist policy development. As suggested previously, high levels of technological, socioeconomic, and more importantly political (or normative) uncertainty produce a need for a basic benchmark to facilitate planning.

The teleological approach can be pursued through a variety of methodologies; for example, scenario development,[22] Delphi,[23] or a combination of both may be useful in speculating about those types of activities required to bring about certain predetermined ends. Selecting a group of energy policy experts should help narrow the range of policy alternatives. Having established a reasonable range of activities, more standardized techniques of systematic analysis (for example, optimization, decision, cost-benefit) could be employed to evaluate or rate the various alternatives.

The advantages of the teleological approach are manifold. Initially, a range of end-goals can be considered facilitating marginal comparison. As in zero-base budgeting, incremental increases in the use of different energy sources can be assessed in terms of (1) social utility minus the level of policy change required and (2) the ratio of change to utility.

In addition, market thresholds and other concepts relating to commercialization can be recast in terms of clear objectives and milestones. In this way, perhaps, the use of mythical market assumptions might be avoided. More importantly, the bounds heretofore established by arbitrary assumptions are replaced by opportunities for policy change (for example, raising the price of oil).

The earlier discussion of various solar studies showed that coherent policy development is very difficult without a clear notion of solar potential. These studies tended to ignore the fact that solar potential is as much a matter of normative policy as of technological or market feasibility. In this era of environmental awareness, normative choices must be grounded on a much broader definition of social utility than production economics provides. This is especially true when the entire economic structure of a given policy area is built of consciously designed subsidies and incentives. In these circumstances, policy commitments must be justified on larger social grounds. This requires an exploration of social and environmental matters buffeting end-use choices and establishing the real potential of various energy sources. For a number of reasons, including political commitments to existing energy technologies, the social and/or life-quality assessment of energy sources has been ignored. By and large, the assumption that an energy market exists has included a belief that social preferences somehow get their due.

DOE's performance has been inadequate with respect to developing and using information on social trends and preferences.[24] This pattern is unlikely to continue given the growing importance of social and environmental factors in planning energy futures. Interest groups are increasingly mindful of the environmental effects of nuclear and coal utilization. Meanwhile, the general public is expressing greater concern about end-use economies.

A complete policy analysis of solar energy demands a clarification and incorporation of social values. Social accounting systems are not unique. There are many models of life-quality accounting in such diverse areas as water resource management, community capital facilities planning, and social service delivery assessments.[25] The Water Resource Council's *Principles and Standards for Planning* provides a paradigm for multiple-account systems.[26] Public acceptance is increasingly necessary to program survival in these other policy areas where social science information is becoming more widely used.

The solar energy alternative may be attractive to those sensitive to the private costs and social and environmental impacts of energy utilization. The following section is devoted to discussing the kinds of issues that could emerge with respect to solar energy if social and environmental factors are considered.

Applying Another Perspective

Sources are now predicting that even with a business-as-usual approach, higher rates of energy use will gradually decline as a natural result of price and population factors.[27] With conservation, further reductions are possible. This decline could be accompanied by a growing realization that the United States need not use as much energy as it does to maintain and improve its favorite life-styles. Clark Bullard points out that "it may be possible to gradually reduce the energy required to produce a dollar's worth of GNP to about half."[28] West Germany and Sweden, countries with standards of living equivalent to our own, substantiate this.[29]

Diminished demand for energy will not, of course, make solar energy the major energy source; but it could: (1) divert attention from capital-intensive, high-technology systems (for example, nuclear plants), which are primarily justifiable if one assumes exponential growth in energy demand; and (2) buy time to develop broader uses for existing solar systems and to bring new technologies on line (such as photovoltaics). Nearly 60 percent of all end-use energy consumption is for heating and cooling (most of which involves variations of plus-or-minus 10 degrees). A sizeable portion of this energy use could be provided in fairly short order through the use of existing solar systems (space and water heaters) and heat pumps. Meanwhile, other end-use sectors (such as transportation and industry) could explore other types of solar applications. For example, automobiles could be run on biomass fuels and/or direct solar and wind generated hydrogen. On-site photovoltaics and wind generators could eventually contribute significantly to the nation's remaining electrical needs.

A consequence of this scenario may be that less energy consumption may favorably affect the economics of conventional fuels such as oil. Reduced demand would extend supplies and stabilize prices. In other words, solar energy would still be in competition with currently popular fuel sources, particularly if they remain regulated and/or subsidized. Public policy supports for traditional fuel sources could be balanced by giving solar energy its own set of incentives to make it competitive. Short-term subsidies for solar energy, or, at the very least, removal of institutional constraints, would seem a reasonable policy given the social and environmental benefits associated with solar development.

Compared with coal and nuclear sources of energy, solar energy is environmentally benign.[30] It does not depend on large amounts of other natural resources (such as air, water, and land) to absorb its residuals. Moreover, solar energy does not contribute to breakdown of the ozone layer or to the earth's ambient temperature. In some instances, solar applications may even bring about substantial improvements in the environment. For example, hydrogen is an excellent storage and transfer mechanism for solar energy; it also provides one of the cleanest burning fuels for the internal combustion automobile engine (the major cause of air pollution) and home heating and cooking. In addition, solar systems may free us from some of the potential health and safety threats that may attend continued nuclear development and the economic shocks inherent in easily disrupted, centralized utility systems. Solar installations have little value for weapons development.

Finally, the decentralized capabilities of solar technologies seem more compatible with emerging socioeconomic trends of collective individualism and commercial autonomy than capital-intensive alternatives. In the future, self-reliant communities founded on basic-needs economies could rely entirely on solar energy. The use of solar energy by such communities is consistent with traditional American values such as self-determination, deregulation, and personal freedom. This type of futurology has had virtually no role in formal planning and policy development. Nonetheless, the long-term impacts of evolving social values would seem an essential topic in talking about solar and other energy resources for the year 2000 and beyond. Changing social values are relevant to any discussion of what the nation's energy commitments ought to be.

Conclusions

The point of this chapter is that the form and content of analysis have an important impact on the seeming practicability and attractiveness of policy options. Objective analysis is impossible when current policy choices and future policy preferences influence assumptions of availability and feasibility. The analytical approach with the highest potential for objectivity is the one that examines all policy alternatives in the light of social and environmental as well as economic criteria. Teleological analysis is such an approach. It provides an opportunity to identify long-term ends and a capacity to develop policies for the near term by which to realize those ends. It is more useful than most analytical techniques applied today in that it involves consideration of alternative futures in terms of contemporary life-quality preferences and objective expectations of future social, environmental, and economic conditions.

This chapter has tried to provide evidence of the limited utility of currently popular modes of analysis by focusing on the future of solar energy on the nation's energy agenda. Solar-energy use is economically unattractive in comparison with conventional energy systems when its evaluation is influenced by policy commitments to those conventional systems. Using teleological analysis enables us to consider and evaluate a wider range of possible futures and the means required to realize them. Opening the door in this way to considering a more comprehensive number of choices results in a finding that solar applications have a larger potential utility than indicated using analytical techniques tied to the status quo.

The teleological approach may seem to be an elaborate set of mechanisms designed primarily to promote solar development. This is not the case however.

If solar energy systems fail to pass the "acid test" of social viability and/or policy makers are unwilling to pay the price of development, solar systems cannot be saved from insignificance by the teleological or any other analytical approach. Unlike the hidden biases toward conventional resources, which are latent in most planning perspectives, the teleological approach is at least open to alternate energy futures.

Notes

1. For a historical overview of past energy policies see David Davis, *Energy Politics*, 2d ed. (New York: St. Martins, 1977).

2. Note this and other common biases in: Carl J. Friedrich, "Political Decision-Making, Public Policy and Planning," in Joseph A. Uveges, ed., *The Dimensions of Public Administration*, 2d ed. (Boston: Holbrook Press, 1975).

3. William Ascher, *Forecasting: An Appraisal for Policy-Makers and Planners* (Baltimore: Johns Hopkins University Press, 1978). Note particularly chaps. 5 and 8.

4. See Clark Bullard, "Energy and Jobs" (Paper presented at the Conference on Energy Conservation, University of Michigan, Ann Arbor, November 1977).

5. Ian I. Mitroff and Murray Turoff, "The Whys behind the Hows," *Spectrum* 10 (March 1973):62-71.

6. Ibid., p. 69.

7. See *Solar Energy: A Status Report* (Washington, D.C., Department of Energy, 1978).

8. William S. Paley et al., *Resources for Freedom*, vol. 4 *The Promise of Technology* (Washington, D.C.: U.S. Government Printing Office, 1952).

9. Bureau of Business and Economic Research, *Solar and Atomic Energy: A Survey* (College Park, Md.: University of Maryland, 1959).

10. See *Jobs from the Sun* (Los Angeles, Calif.: California Public Policy Center, 1977); also note Denis Hayes, "Post-Petroleum Prosperity" (Paper presented at the Annual Meeting of the American Association for the Advancement of Science, Washington, D.C., February 1978).

11. *Solar Commercialization at the State Level* (Cape Canaveral, Fla.: Florida Solar Energy Center, 1978).

12. Gregory A. Daneke, "The Political Economy of Nuclear Development," *Policy Studies Journal* vol. 6 (Summer 1978):84-90; see also *Application of Solar Technologies to Today's Energy Needs* (Washington, D.C.: Office of Technology Assessment, 1977).

13. *Legal Barriers to Solar Heating and Cooling of Buildings* (Washington, D.C.: Environmental Law Institute, 1976).

14. Hebert Epstein, "A Statement on Federal Solar Energy Programs"

(Mimeo of testimony read before the Subcommittee on Environment, Energy, and Natural Resources, U.S. House of Representatives, June 12, 1978), pp. 4-5.

15. Denis Hayes, "Statement to Subcommittee." Ibid., p. 3.

16. Paul Craig, Statement to Subcommittee. Ibid., pp. 4-5.

17. Arnold Nadler, "Planning Aspects of Direct Solar Energy Generation," *Journal of the American Institute of Planners* 43 (October 1977):339.

18. Barry Commoner, "Testimony on the Administration's Solar Policy" (Mimeo of testimony read before the Subcommittee on Environment, Energy and Natural Resources, U.S. House of Representatives, June 12, 1978), p. 32. For more regarding limited capital and the solar transition, see Amory Lovins, *Soft Energy Paths* (Cambridge, Mass.: Ballinger, 1977).

19. Ascher, *Forecasting*, pp. 212-213.

20. Mitroff and Turoff, "Whys behind the Hows," p. 67.

21. Hazel Henderson, *Creating Alternative Futures* (Princeton, N.J.: Princeton Center for Alternative Futures and Berkeley Publishing Corp., 1978), pp. 327-338.

22. See Monte Canfield, "Normative Analysis of Alternative Futures: A Methodology Using Scenarios for Policy Analysis" (Aspen, Colo.: Aspen Institute for Humanistic Studies, March 1974).

23. See Norman Dalkey et al., *Studies in the Quality of Life: Delphi and Decision-Making* (Lexington, Mass.: D.C. Heath, 1972).

24. See papers delivered at the following for evidence of this: "Symposium on the Role of the Social Sciences in Energy Policy" (Conference of the American Association for the Advancement of Science, Houston, Texas, January, 1979).

25. See *Water Resources Planning, Social Goals, and Indicators* (Logan, Utah: Technical Committee of the Water Resources Centers of the Thirteen Western States, 1974); there are more examples in Kurt Finsterbusch and C.P. Wolf, etc., *Methodology of Social Impact Assessment* (Stroudberg, Penn.: Dowden, Hutchinson, and Ross, 1977) and Harry Hatry et al., *How Effective Are Your Community Services?* (Washington, D.C.: The Urban Institute, 1977).

26. See Water Resources Council, "Establishment of Principles and Standards," *The Federal Register* 38 (September 1973); also note the discussion of life-quality assessment in water agencies, found in: Gregory A. Daneke, "Life-Quality Accounting and Organizational Change," *The Bureaucrat* 7 (Summer 1978):27-35.

27. Marc Ross and Robert Williams predict that between now and 2010 the demand will grow only one-third as much as it did since 1950. Marc Ross, "Our Present Energy Course" (Working Paper, Department of Physics, University of Michigan, 1978); also note The CONAES Demand Panel, "U.S. Energy Demand: Some Low Energy Futures" in Philip H. Abelson and Allen L. Hammond, eds., *Energy II: Use, Conservation and Supply* (Washington, D.C.: American Association for the Advancement of Science, 1978), pp. 63-72.

28. Clark Bullard, "Energy and Jobs" (Paper presented at the Conference on Energy Conservation, University of Michigan, November 1977), p. 1.

29. Lee Schipper and Allan J. Lichtenberg, "Efficient Energy Use and Well-Being: The Swedish Example," in Abelson and Hammond, *Energy II*, pp. 73-85.

30. See John Harte and Alan Jassby, "Energy Technologies and Natural Environments: The Search for Compatibility," in Jack M. Hollander et al., eds., *Annual Review of Energy* (Palo Alto, Calif.: Annual Reviews, 1978), pp. 101-146.

9

Energy Policy Evaluation: Bureaucratic Performance in the Federal Energy Administration

Robert W. Rycroft

In theory, once public policies have been placed on the political agenda, formulated into programs, and implemented by agencies, the consequences of this process are determined through objective, systematic policy evaluation. The rationale for evaluation is based on the need for performance information giving policy makers an opportunity to exercise their judgment about the implications of choosing among various policy alternatives. Unfortunately, although there can be no doubt that policy studies have made some significant contributions to our understanding of government activities, policy analysis continues to be constrained by difficulties in selecting criteria to define bureaucratic performance or program success.

The problem of criteria selection does not result from any lack of appreciation of the need for objectivity or of the advantages of systematic analysis. The dysfunctional aspects of the politics of evaluation, in which assessments may be biased by evaluators attempting "to make things look good," is well documented.[1] Equally well known are the strengths of applying analytical approaches systematically to the policy-making process as a whole and not to its impacts alone.[2] But despite repeated calls for the use of multiple criteria and broad concepts of bureaucratic performance, most policy analyses limit their scope to a single evaluation standard—usually either economic efficiency or effectiveness. In fact, most policy evaluation is economic analysis; there is a strong orthodox preference for rationalist standards of economy in government that dominates the field of evaluation research.[3] This reliance on criteria focused on policy outputs (efficiency) or outcomes (effectiveness) suffers from three major problems. First, to a great extent the criteria-selection process has been divorced from any theoretical underpinnings other than rational choice theory. This in turn leads to the second difficulty of criteria selection: the relative paucity of political content in criteria that are supposed to evaluate the performance of government. This tendency toward the adoption of apolitical standards reflects the third issue—the risk that rationalist preferences or other value-laden objectives of the researcher will be the basis for choosing criteria.[4]

153

Taken together, the shortcomings of criteria selection pose a major threat to the utility of any evaluation. This is because "the findings of an evaluation study depend upon the criteria chosen, and the standards employed operationally, as much as they depend upon the workings of the program being evaluated."[5] Nowhere is this dilemma more in evidence than in the evaluation of domestic energy policy, where the conventional wisdom of an inadequate set of programs and institutions is based largely on narrow definitions of failure. Typical of this limited focus is the body of literature assessing the policies of the Federal Energy Administration (FEA). As the federal agency responsible for regulating the pricing and allocation of crude oil and its products in the crucial post-embargo (1974-1977) period, the FEA was destined to be a controversial target of evaluation. Out of the studies triggered by this increased federal intervention into oil politics, a consensus has developed that the FEA's administration of the mandatory fuel allocation and pricing programs has been a failure. But this consensus rests almost entirely on evaluations of FEA output efficiency and outcome effectiveness. Little attempt has been made to incorporate criteria designed to evaluate other components of the policy process, such as inputs, decision makers, or feedback. Nor has there been much effort directed toward expanding standards of efficiency and effectiveness beyond the traditional economic model that views the provision of public services as analogous to the production process of a private firm. Finally, with few exceptions, the distributional results of FEA outputs and outcomes have not been made explicit; social equity concerns are deemphasized, if not totally ignored in most analyses of petroleum pricing and allocation. The purpose of this chapter is to respond to these issues by demonstrating the degree to which the findings of an assessment of FEA policies depend on the criteria selected. Following a brief review of the literature of FEA studies, a framework for analysis that includes six evaluative criteria based in the theory of public administration is described. Then the results of applying these standards to the FEA's allocation and pricing programs are outlined and the implications for policy evaluation are discussed.

Evaluations of FEA Performance:
A Review of the Literature

Beginning in the 1970s, there were a number of attempts to consolidate energy and natural-resources responsibilities at the national level. In 1971, for example, an effort was made to merge the Interior and Agriculture departments into a more comprehensive policy-making structure. But it took the stimulus of the energy crisis to overcome considerable bureaucratic and interest group resistance to the creation of a federal energy organization. In December 1973, following months of instability, uncertainty, delay, and contradiction in energy policy, a bill was submitted to Congress proposing the establishment of the FEA. The major rationale for creating the agency was the need, during the energy crisis, to minimize the economic and social impacts of fuel shortages by implementing policies that would control the prices of crude oil and its products and would distribute these fuels among all consuming sectors of society. Pending legislative approval of the new agency, an executive order created the Federal Energy Office (FEO) to develop a framework for the FEA and to manage and coordinate national energy policy in the interim period. The Federal Energy Administration Act took effect in June 1974, and the FEA continued as the foremost energy authority until all national energy responsibilities, including those of the FEA, were combined in the new Department of Energy in August 1977.

The mandatory fuel allocation and pricing programs, designed to prevent economic dislocations, preserve industry competition, and control fuel prices, began in August 1973, with the implementation of Phase 4 price controls on petroleum and its products. The most significant provisions of Phase 4 rules were those creating a two-tier pricing system of old (controlled) and new (uncontrolled) oil. Distribution regulations were added to these rules with the passage of the Emergency Petroleum Allocation Act (EPAA) in November 1973. Under the authority of this legislation, the FEA organized allocation regulations around two programs: crude oil and refined petroleum products. The EPAA also enabled the FEA to structure three sets of pricing rules: those for producers, refiners, and resellers (wholesalers) and retailers. Both allocation and pricing controls were extended for an additional 40-month period by the Energy Policy and Conservation Act (EPCA) of December 1975.

Assessments of FEA policy making cover three distinct periods in the life-cycle of the agency. First, there are evaluations of the agency's youth, which focus on the FEO's interim activities over the 5 months during which the FEA proposal was debated by Congress. A second group of studies analyzes the mature agency in the dynamic crisis-management period (1974-1975), when most of the FEA's programs were actually implemented. Finally, some assessments emphasize the pattern of FEA aging since 1975. These evaluations focus on the conflicts and controversies generated by such factors as increasing agency rigidity and subsequent efforts to reform FEA processes.

Analyses of the FEO have emphasized how its policies were made ineffective by situational factors confronting it. The setting within which the FEO was placed in 1973 was characterized by resource scarcity, system instability, and demands for increased public participation. In combination, these factors helped produce a fragmented energy-policy apparatus hampered by narrow, inflexible decision makers, procedural bottlenecks, and poor information-gathering and policy-coordination capabilities.[6] As could be expected of an agency that functioned for less than 6 months in a highly visible, highly political environment, the FEO also suffered from a number of organizational problems that raised efficiency issues. Most of the difficulties cited by analysts as constraints on efficient FEO performance were associated with either personnel or program factors. In the first 60 days of its existence, for example, the most damaging personnel problems for the FEO were high turnover rates among employees who had been delegated from other agencies and the lack of energy expertise among some officials who were transferred to the new organization. At later stages, morale problems developed when the oil embargo ended and the FEO lost its crisis spotlight. The FEO also went through a difficult change in leadership when John Sawhill replaced William Simon as energy czar.

The program problems of the FEO have been summarized as attempting to do too many things on too many fronts. According to this analysis, the fragmentation that characterized FEO policy making led to rules and regulations based on projections of conditions in existence prior to the energy crisis. In addition, the FEO has been accused of manifesting so-called typical bureaucratic behavior patterns by adopting limited objectives, invoking rigid operating procedures, and evaluating the future in terms of the "worst-possible" event. That is, the agency was caught up in efforts to avoid the dire predictions of massive unemployment, brownouts, and industrial closings as a result of the energy crisis.[7] While the worst outcomes were avoided, one analyst has concluded that "the policies of the FEO did not achieve a just and efficient petroleum allocation among products, regions, refiners, or time periods." But the same study also found that "the inefficiencies and inequities of price controls, and their ultimate failure to limit oil-company profits, were not the fault of the FEO." Rather, the analysis points the finger of blame at the policy of controlling the price of oil products to the extent that demand exceeded supply.[8] To summarize, evaluations of FEO performance are in general agreement that the interim agency was ineffective in dealing with energy shortages (to the extent that it may have exacerbated supply problems), inefficient in program development, and a failure in trying to create a more equitable system of distributing the costs of the oil embargo.

Studies of the mature FEA are equally critical of the agency's actions. These evaluations have tended to focus on the counterproductive nature of bureaucratic growth in the new agency. Thus, the claim has been made that the FEA's frequent attempts to broaden its regulatory reach (by advocating agency expansion into coal regulatory policy, for example) hampered its effective administration of petroleum pricing and allocation. The agency also has been criticized for its apparent inability to respond to the changing conditions of the energy supply-demand dilemma. In particular, the FEA's pricing and allocation rules were targets of negative evaluations because they were tied to base periods (1972-1973) that had limited relevance to economic and technical conditions once the embargo ended.[9] At least three other objections to the FEA's 1974 and 1975 implementation of the mandatory fuel allocation and pricing programs are found in the literature: the tendency for FEA rules to lead toward the bureaucratization of the oil industry by placing excessive compliance burdens on petroleum firms; the issue of regulations denying consumers the benefits of competition by restricting ease of entry into sectors of the oil industry and by inhibiting industry planning and financing activities through constant rule modification to fit market conditions; and the inadequate level of executive branch oversight of the FEA and limited legislative and judicial countervailing power over agency policies.[10]

Because analyses of the mature agency feature more complete information about policy products and impacts than is the case with the generalized studies of the temporary FEO, FEA studies over the period 1974-1975 are more explicit in their delineation of evaluative criteria. In most instances, however, these standards of program success are limited to the criterion of effectiveness, usually defined in terms of agency attainment of legislatively established goals. A typical evaluation of the FEA's ineffectiveness in reaching goals, such as the EPAA's mandate to preserve an economically sound and competitive petroleum industry, is the conclusion that allocation regulations "may not be the appropriate method of securing these high priority objectives," since the allocation program "might be justified only as an experimental solution for present energy problems, problems which may demand further complex federal efforts to attain significant goals."[11]

Studies of the aging FEA have substantial analytical data and extensive administrative experience on which to build their evaluations. In the most ambitious study to date, President Ford's Task Force on Reform of Federal Energy Administration Regulation undertook an assessment of allocation and price controls as part of a major effort aimed at regulatory reform. On the basis of a 6-month investigation, the task force concluded that FEA regulation resulted in administrative costs to the taxpayer of some $47 million per year just to maintain the agency's programs. Furthermore, compliance costs for the industry to respond to these rules were estimated to be in excess of $500 million annually. But the study found that these costs did not generate the expected benefits to consumers, because FEA policies discouraged the construction of new refinery capacity necessary to meet future demand for refined petroleum products; encouraged inefficiencies in the distribution of petroleum products; created barriers to the importation of cheaper foreign products; and created incentives toward utilization of domestic refining capacity at levels where the incremental costs of production and prices to consumers were substantially increased.[12] For these reasons, the task force recommended elimination of product price and allocation rules for refiners and resellers and adoption of a set of standby controls in the event of a supply interruption. As this summary of findings implies, the task force report is based almost entirely on economic cost-benefit analysis; its only major concession to political issues is a discussion of procedural problems with regulatory programs. Beyond some general comments regarding equity, the task force report makes no effort to apply evaluative standards other than traditional economic efficiency and effectiveness criteria.

Ignored by this assessment and others of its type are such issues as oil company overcharges, recently estimated by DOE auditors to amount to some $1 billion during the period between 1973 and 1976. Thus even this comprehensive evaluation is limited by analytical blind spots of the sort that are typical of assessments of FEA performance.

A Framework for Evaluating FEA Policies

Determining the most appropriate performance criteria is a difficult task. The list of possible standards is long and the issue area of energy policy has not developed enough to provide many hints. The approach adopted here is based on the assumption that no single evaluative criterion adequately assesses performance or program success, because it limits analysis to one set of measures of one policy process component. Instead, to illustrate how the choice of criteria influences evaluation, a systems framework covering the entire policy process (inputs, decision makers, outputs, outcomes, and feedback) is used. As illustrated in table 9-1, this framework couples policy process components and evaluative criteria as follows: inputs are evaluated by the criterion of responsibility, decision makers by the standard of representativeness, outputs by both efficiency and equity, outcomes by effectiveness, and feedback by responsiveness. Each of these criteria is firmly grounded in the theory of public administration.

The case for applying the criterion of representativeness to public policies is based on the theory that "better," more democratic decisions are made by diverse groups, not elites. Moreover, representative decision making increases public participation and may even reduce minority group alienation.[13] For present purposes, representativeness is defined as the passive sociological correspondence of FEA bureaucrats to the origins of the broader society.[14] Thus, a representative agency is one that employs a ratio of minority groups approximating their proportion of the population served by it. Three dimensions of representation may be applied to an evaluation of FEA policy: the level of representativeness, operationalized as the ratio of the percentage of FEA personnel in various indicator categories (race, sex, and so forth) to the percentage of the population for the same categories; the integration of representatives, focused on the degree to which all groups in the FEA are socially mixed; and the distribution of representatives, using such factors as the income and job rankings of groups throughout the agency to determine the degree to which personnel have been stratified or segmented into the organization.[15]

The conceptualization of the standards of efficiency and equity outlined in table 9-1 represents a modification of the traditional economic model, which defines efficiency as the ratio between resources (inputs) and products (outputs) and equity as the distribution of these products. Here efficiency is approached instead as the ratio of resources to bureaucratic effort. Equity is then defined as

Table 9-1
A Framework for Evaluating Federal Energy Administration Policies

Criteria	Applied to FEA Policies	Measures
Representativeness Sociological correspondence of decision makers to the origins of the broader society	To what degree do FEA decision makers mirror the dominant forces in society representing a reasonable cross-section of occupations, classes, and the like?	Correspondence between the race and sex of FEA decision makers and those of society as a whole
Efficiency Ratio of agency expenditures to effort	To what degree do greater inputs of FEA resources result in higher levels of bureaucratic efforts at the point where the agency and the oil industry interface?	Ratio of FEA manpower expenditures to the number and type of violations detected and the penalties assessed in the compliance and enforcement program
Equity Equal distribution of agency effort	To what degree are FEA outputs uniformly and non-discriminately distributed across the client oil industry?	Number and type of compliance and enforcement actions taken against various industry sectors and types of firms
Effectiveness Correspondence between the impact of agency effort and agency goals	To what degree do FEA efforts result in changes in the social conditions which serve as goals for the agency?	Correspondence between observed outcomes—such as refinery capacity—and executive, legislative, and bureaucratic goals established for the FEA
Responsiveness Correspondence between agency decisions and public preferences and interest group demands	To what degree do FEA decisions reflect the unarticulated, individualized expressions of public opinion and the articulated and aggregated demands from organized interests?	Correspondence between FEA decisions—on such issues as price controls—and public polls, and the number and type of agency responses to oil companies through the exceptions and appeals program
Responsibility Internal and external controls on agency actions	To what degree are the FEA's powers limited by bureaucratic or societal controls?	Levels of constraints on FEA performance from internal and external sources, of both an informal and formal nature

the equal distribution of this effort across the client community (in this case, the oil industry). Effort, as used here, refers to the nature and intensity of government-community contact. Indicators of effort include such things as agency investigative case loads, numbers and types of rule violations detected, and amounts of penalties assessed for such violations.[16] This is a narrower concept than the economic notion of product, which usually is defined in more general terms (the protection of public health and welfare, for example) but which ultimately relies on proximate indicators (such as the number of agency investigators per violation) that are more accurately characterized as indicators of government effort than as public sector products. The choice of bureaucratic effort as the focus of efficiency and equity standards has several advantages for policy evaluation. First, such an approach enables a clear analytical distinction to be drawn between efficiency and effectiveness measures: efficiency relates resources to efforts; and effectiveness relates efforts to goals. Second, governmental effort has important distributional elements to which the criterion of equity applies. How an organization distributes its effort among various components of its client community is significant for a number of reasons: there is a major symbolic aspect to governmental distribution efforts; some governmental efforts have a direct relationship to other output indicators; and efforts are what government agencies really produce, and their distribution is important.[17]

Bureaucratic responsiveness is an attempt by public bodies to match their decisions to constituency preferences. These preferences are manifested through two modes of policy feedback: unarticulated, individualized expressions of public opinion; and articulated group demands from organized interests. The first concern is therefore the degree to which FEA programs have been sensitive to shifts in public opinion, as revealed in national surveys. Since there is no simple test for responsiveness, this evaluation centers on answering such questions as: does the agency follow public opinion, try to discover public preferences, and do its best to inform the public about policy alternatives? Is there much opposition to, and criticism of, agency performance? Does the agency respond to criticism? Does it change its behavior to answer criticism?[18] The second major focus is answering the question of responsiveness to whom? Here emphasis is on a determination of the manner in which the FEA responds to organized interests (primarily the oil industry), which aggregate and articulate demands and supports for the agency. The exceptions and appeals component of the mandatory fuel allocation and pricing programs—the major government-community interface where the FEA was able to respond to industry-initiated requests—is the activity subjected to analysis.[19]

Throughout the effort to restructure national energy policy around the FEA, a recurring organizational question has been: to what degree are the agency's powers controlled? In other words, how is the agency made responsible to the executive, Congress, and the courts? And what are the restraining mechanisms, such as bureaucratic professionalism, which operate within the agency? This is the traditional responsibility criterion that is at least implicitly applied to evaluations of every new agency's performance.[20] Responsibility can be applied to FEA programs by defining the criterion in terms of the location and form of bureaucratic control. The location of control can be either punitive restraints imposed by external sources or internal self-control exercised by the bureaucrats themselves. Regardless of the location of responsibility, two forms of administrative control have been significant: formal reliance on established rules and informal manipulation of values or norms of agency personnel. Thus four categories of bureaucratic responsibility may be identified and applied to an evaluation of FEA performance: internal formal, internal informal, external formal, and external informal.[21]

The Performance of the FEA

The framework used in this chapter considers FEA fuel allocation and pricing programs as a policy process composed of five parts (decision makers, outputs, outcomes, feedback, and inputs) measured by six evaluative criteria (representativeness, efficiency, equity, effectiveness, responsiveness, and responsibility). Table 9-2 illustrates the operationalization of these concepts and the relative performance of the FEA according to each standard. The summaries of the evaluation of FEA performance outlined are taken from a more comprehensive study.[22]

Representativeness

This study found FEA decision makers unrepresentative of the general population, especially in the highest policy-making positions of the agency. In particular, the early (FEO) stages of the agency's development were characterized by extremely low minority-group representation. Moreover, the FEA's integration of minority representatives was found to be lower than the measure for the entire federal service and lower than at least two organizations performing similar functions (the Department of the Interior and the Federal Power Commission). Both the level and integration of minority representatives in the FEA were seriously limited by the crisis environment within which early staffing efforts took place and by conflict of interest problems (which restricted the hiring of personnel with oil industry backgrounds, for example) inherent in the agency's regulatory responsibilities.

With regard to the distribution of FEA minority representatives, the agency was found to be a stratified bureaucracy, evidencing maldistributions of minority employees into lower income, status, and responsibility positions. Such

Table 9-2
An Evaluation of Federal Energy Administration Performance

Policy Process Component	Evaluative Criterion	Empirical Indicators	Dimensions	FEA Performance
Decision makers	Representativeness	Correspondence between the social origins of bureaucrats and the larger society	Level	Unrepresentative
			Integration	Unrepresentative
			Distribution	Unrepresentative
Outputs	Efficiency	Ratio of manpower expenditures to bureaucratic effort	Pattern	Inefficient
	Equity	Equal distribution of bureaucratic effort	Pattern	Inequitable
Outcomes	Effectiveness	Correspondence between the impact of bureaucratic effort and agency goals	Executive	Ineffective
			Legislative	Moderately effective
			Bureaucratic	Effective
Feedback	Responsiveness	Correspondence between agency decisions and public preferences and group demands	Public opinion	Moderately responsive
			Interest demands	Responsive
Inputs	Responsibility	Internal and external controls on agency performance	Internal Informal	Irresponsible
			Internal Formal	Irresponsible
			External Informal	Irresponsible
			External Formal	Moderately responsible

maldistributions are typical of the American federal bureaucracy, posing the traditional threat of an elite corps of policy makers who may be insensitive to the problems and attitudes of low-income, minority groups.[23] These findings have broad implications for energy policy in general and for the fuel allocation and pricing programs in particular. In a period (1974-1975) in which the number of participants in the energy policy system was undergoing rapid expansion, there were still segments of the population that did not have equal access to the major energy institutions. Especially relevant among the many issues of social equity resulting from this disparity in accessibility were such things as the need for federal agencies to help low-income families cope with shortages and sharp price increases in energy.[24] Thus, the FEA's unrepresentativeness may have been related to the lack of responsiveness (discussed in greater detail further) the agency occasionally demonstrated toward public opinion from lower-income and less educated segments of society. An example of such a linkage could have been the agency's resistance to incorporating lower-class attitudes favoring gasoline rationing as a policy alternative over decontrol and price increases advocated by the FEA during 1975.[25]

Efficiency

From the first days of the FEA, resource expenditures in manpower for the compliance and enforcement program were a policy issue. The crisis environment within which the agency was created required a crash effort to develop audit procedures and enforcement guidelines. These administrative difficulties were exacerbated by what some FEA compliance personnel termed a "policy of deregulation" that emphasized the temporary nature of many regulations.[26] Long after the FEA was able to assume full control of the compliance effort (in mid-1974) the agency still was operating well below authorized strength. Internal evaluations in 1975 indicated that perhaps as much as twice the existing manpower level would be necessary to perform required audits in a timely manner. Thus, the overall level of manpower resources and their confused early administration could be characterized as inadequate and a barrier to efficient agency policy making. Just as significant were the symbolic aspects of reduced personnel levels that lowered the visibility of the agency to the public.

Not only was the level of compliance manpower insufficient, but the manner in which it was allocated among regions and programs constrained agency efficiency. Throughout 1974 and 1975 there were major differences between regional compliance office strengths; those regions with the lowest actual-to-authorized manpower ratios (regions 6, 7, and 8, in particular) had compliance authority for major sectors of the oil production and refining industries. This misallocation of expenditures is explained by the FEA's early emphasis on identifying violations at the retail level. Because the retail sector was the source of most complaints in 1974, compliance personnel were concentrated in the eastern regions, where most of the 225,000 wholesale and retail firms were located. This emphasis, however politically expedient, was not warranted. Although retail enforcement uncovered 18,000 violations and refunded some $51 million, this was "nickel-and-dime" enforcement compared to violations in the production and refining sectors. For example, the refinery audit and review program alone, with less than 25 percent of the manpower of the retail effort, recovered over five times the refunds to the marketplace. Moreover, the potential impact of unresolved cases in 1975 was even greater in the refining sector, totalling over $700 million. But despite recommendations that the FEA redirect its compliance effort toward refinery and producer investigations, the agency moved rapidly in 1975 to increase its manpower commitments to an audit of utilities suppliers.[27]

Finally, there appears to have been little relationship between expenditure levels for FEA regional offices and effort levels within various programs. For example, most refunds and penalties from investigations of crude oil producers were outputs from regional offices that had neither high manpower allocations nor high concentrations of the production industry within their boundaries (especially regions 7, 8, and 9). The primary cause of this uneven enforcement effort was a lack of uniform operating procedures in each of the FEA's regions. In effect, each regional office established its own interpretation of whether a violation was subject to penalty. There were inadequate or nonexistent guidelines regarding the conduct of audits, the determination of the intent of violations, and the collection of penalties until at least September 1975. In combination, these factors led to a highly inefficient implementation of the compliance and enforcement component of fuel allocation and pricing programs.[28]

Equity

Two issues dominate evaluation of FEA compliance and enforcement efforts according to the criterion of equity. The first concerns the degree to which the nonuniformity in FEA regional enforcement led to the agency's treating different sectors of the oil industry differently. The second focuses on the amount of discriminatory FEA enforcement that existed—the degree to which, for example, the agency demonstrated a pattern of more extensive enforcement against small firms rather than large oil companies.

With respect to the impact of nonuniform enforcement on equitable FEA policy outputs, the agency's early emphasis on investigating retail and wholesale firms preempted widespread audits of other sectors of the oil industry. By far the largest number of investigations, over half the refunds, and almost all the penalties were assessed against retailers and wholesalers before 1976. Moreover, in the one exception to this retail emphasis—the discovery of violations in the refinery audit and review program totalling over $400 million—the refineries were not assessed penalties nor were they required to make any refunds. Instead, these companies were allowed to write off the value of these violations against "banked costs" (potential legal price increases that the market could not yet absorb). Thus, while the FEA collected over $60,000 in penalties from crude oil producers and propane marketers for violations involving about $1 million, the agency did not penalize refiners at all for violations of almost half a billion dollars.[29] The symbolic value of this policy was not lost on either the industry or the agency's own enforcement personnel. One unfortunate result of this inequitable situation was that, combined with the general lack of adequate enforcement guidelines, many regional compliance offices chose not to force rules on sectors of the industry they perceived as being singled out for regulatory sanctions. As one FEA compliance official testified before Congress in mid-1975, "we made our own decision in the region that we were not going to assess penalties on small firms when the large, major firms were not being penalized by the refinery audits."[30]

These comments raise the second issue of FEA output equity, discrimination against smaller, independent firms in favor of integrated, major petroleum companies. Not only did FEA emphasis on retail investigations discriminate against small firms, by definition, but the entire crude-oil-producer investigation effort focused on independents. Moreover, FEA manpower allocations to large petroleum refineries were consistently below authorized levels to the extent that there were often fewer than four auditors assigned to major refining operations.[31] Whereas these program practices had the effect of providing a pattern of more sanctions being directed against smaller firms, other factors also influenced this situation. Most importantly, the complexity of FEA rules guaranteed that the company with the largest legal staff and the most sophisticated computer capabilities had the greatest potential for successful compliance. Taken together, these factors led to FEA outputs being distributed across the client industry in a nonuniform, discriminatory fashion that had the effect, if not the intent, of favoring large oil companies over small firms.[32]

Effectiveness

The FEA operated under three distinct sets of goals. At the executive level, Project Independence and related programs emphasized increasing domestic production of all forms of energy, reducing reliance on insecure foreign oil imports, and providing products at the lowest possible prices. A different focus was taken by the congressional mandate to the FEA. As outlined in the EPAA, the EPCA, and other legislation, the agency was to preserve an economically sound and competitive petroleum industry, permit refineries to operate at full capacity, and distribute crude oil and refined petroleum products equitably among all geographical regions and among all sectors of the oil industry. Finally, the FEA pursued its own informal goals giving more importance to maintaining organization continuity and defending agency functions from encroachment. It is these three sets of goals—executive, legislative, and bureaucratic—that form the basis for a comprehensive assessment of FEA goal attainment.

The FEA was not able to reach the broadly defined executive goals outlined in Project Independence and subsequent presidential energy policy statements. Most significantly, despite FEA rules designed to provide incentives for increasing the production of crude oil (such as the two-tier pricing system), oil production steadily decreased after 1973. A similar lack of effectiveness was demonstrated by the import fees designed to reduce oil imports: despite the introduction of supplemental fees, the nation imported more oil in mid-1975 than it had prior to the 1973 crisis. Moreover, federal energy policies were totally unable to hold down the prices of these imports. Nor were efforts to hold the line on domestic oil prices particularly effective.[33]

Agency policies were slightly more effective in attaining the goals of the EPAA. There is evidence, for example, that the old oil entitlements program, which allowed all refiners equal access to lower-priced, controlled oil, was successful in equalizing the costs of crude oil to refiners, thereby improving the competitive positions of small and independent firms. The agency also appears to have been moderately effective in its efforts to distribute fuels equitably by region. And despite some early problems, FEA rules had at least mixed success in equitably distributing fuel prices among regions. Each of these legislative goals was reached, however, at some cost. The use of entitlements to bolster industry competitiveness led to increased crude costs and the addition of another layer of complex federal regulations with their greater administrative and compliance burdens. Furthermore, the entitlements program did little to reduce the competitive disadvantages that were hurting nonbranded independent gasoline retailers by 1973. Finally, the FEA was ineffective in attaining the legislative goal of enabling refineries to operate at full capacity, at least in part because of the related and conflicting objective of expanding refinery capacity.[34]

Because the FEA was established as a temporary agency with a 2-year legislative mandate, the issue of its attempts to maintain itself as an organization unit was controversial. But despite repeated attempts to terminate the agency's regulatory responsibilities, the FEA survived to be incorporated into the Department of Energy.[35] In fact, the FEA's budget and personnel levels increased rapidly during its brief lifetime: the agency grew from less than 1900 to more than 3400 employees in a 3-year period. Thus, although opposition to the FEA increased over the years, opponents were unsuccessful in their attempts to reduce its regulatory reach.

Responsiveness

For the purposes of this study, "the test of a responsive administrative system in a democracy is how well national and community preferences, and the policies and actions of the bureaucratic agencies, suit each other."[36] To examine the responsiveness of FEA policies to public opinion it is necessary to focus on those policy areas where opinion data are available and where only the FEA had administrative authority. Such areas include the deregulation of price controls, the regulation of production and utilization sectors of the oil industry, the regulation of corporate profits, import controls, competition in the oil industry, and the regional distribution of fuels. At first, the public's attitudes toward price controls on petroleum and its products were fairly accurately reflected in FEA policies. Immediately following the 1973 crisis, public opinion generally supported existing controls. However by mid-1974, when the FEA began to move toward advocacy of a decontrol policy, its actions started to deviate from public opinion. As the impact of the energy crisis faded and the FEA pressed for an end to emergency controls in late 1974, public opinion continued to resist the return of oil to so-called free-market conditions. A large portion of the public, for example, continued to prefer rationing over price increases as a method for dealing with energy shortages as late as January 1975.[37] But by August 1975, public opinion on the issue of deregulation of oil had come to mirror the FEA position: a majority favored decontrol if it would encourage domestic production. These data suggest that the FEA did not exhibit a high degree of responsiveness to public opinion on the issue of oil pricing. Nor was the agency highly responsive to public demands for greater federal intervention into oil exploration or utilization activities. On other issues, however, the FEA was more responsive. For example, the implementation of oil import fees appears to have reflected public opposition to the use of imports as solutions to fuel shortages. Furthermore, the FEA was willing to go along with strong public opinion favoring government control of corporate profits. Finally, the FEA's responsiveness to demands from both the public and the oil industry to do something about interregional and interfuel shortages was moderately successful in reducing the worst ratios of supplies to projected needs. In particular, FEA efforts to issue emergency allocations to eastern and midwestern states were well founded on political grounds; oil-heat users in these regions were more likely to favor government regulation of energy use.

FEA responsiveness to interest group demands was structured through the Office of Private Grievances and Redress, composed of three elements: the Oil Import Appeals Board, the Office of Special Redress Relief, and the Office of Exceptions and Appeals. However, of these three available feedback mechanisms, only the Office of Exceptions and Appeals appears to have functioned as intended. The Oil Import Appeals Board responded to only a very narrow sector of the petroleum industry (usually resellers of gasoline or crude oil), and the ombudsmanlike Office of Special Redress Relief was virtually inactive. In part, this limited utilization of extraordinary assistance mechanisms may be traced to the broad responsiveness function performed by the Office of Exceptions and Appeals. Because the FEA enjoyed extensive freedom from the constraints of the Administrative Procedures Act in its administration of the fuel allocation and pricing programs (Congress had taken the position that the emergency nature of these programs warranted additional agency flexibility), the agency was allowed a broad range of discretionary authority with which to select the most appropriate due-process response for a given situation. As a result, a range of exceptions and appeals criteria evolved, including the narrowly defined standard of serious hardship and the more flexible concept of gross inequity. Within this framework, agency responses to industry demands were restrained; but the FEA was responsive to a broad spectrum of firms with a wide variety of complaints.[38]

Responsibility

Internal informal controls on FEA performance, emphasizing the professional aspects of public service as sources of administrative responsibility, were limited by the temporary nature of the agency's legislative mandate and by conflict-of-interest threats involving agency personnel. From its creation, the FEA suffered from organizational problems that began with recruitment of personnel. FEA officials testified before Congress that they faced "severe problems" in recruiting personnel because of uncertainty surrounding the agency's tenure. Retention of personnel was even more difficult: the FEA's turnover rate of 38 percent at one time was one of the highest in the entire federal government. Most damaging was the difficulty in securing expertise in such complex fields as petroleum extraction, conversion, and refining, while assuring administrative responsibility through the strict observance of government conflict-of-interest rules. In particular, the oil industry backgrounds of FEA personnel were a sensitive political issue. Although the limited available data indicate that the FEA was not captured by the oil industry, these issues constrained the achievement of bureaucratic responsibility by using internal informal controls.[39]

Internal formal restraints on FEA policies were weakened by the absence of strong presidential leadership and the lack of an effective agency hierarchy. The FEA was created during a period in which presidential politics were dominated by the Watergate scandal. In the absence of high-level supervision, hierarchical control was limited, there were few clear delineations of agency responsibilities, delegation of authority was blurred, and performance rewards and sanctions were vague.

External informal controls, focusing on increasing public participation in the administrative process, were also not sufficient. For the FEA, the primary avenue through which citizens were involved in decision making was the advisory committee. The agency created advisory groups to cover almost every FEA activity; but two fundamental problems developed with this set of bureaucratic controls. First, some interest groups, such as the Consumers Union, complained that they had insufficient resources to monitor FEA actions. Second, even when groups were successful in aggregating and articulating their recommendations, the FEA often did little to heed their comments. Thus, the FEA's Environmental Advisory Committee threatened a mass resignation in 1976, when their recommendations continued to be ignored by the agency.

The principal means to secure responsibility in the FEA was the external formal reliance on congressional control and the rule of law enforced by adjudication in the courts. Congress controlled FEA policies through four methods: statutory determinations of the structures and functions of the agency, budgetary appropriations, investigations by committees and by the General Accounting Office, and publicizing FEA actions. Judicial controls were more limited because the agency had been granted broad discretionary authority to deal with the energy crisis and because the courts interpreted the agency's regulatory authority very generously.[40]

Implications for Policy Evaluation

The case of the FEA provides an excellent example of how the choice of evaluative criteria influences the findings of a policy evaluation. Criticized as an inefficient and ineffective bureaucracy by analysts using narrow analytical foci, the FEA is a classic case of a regulatory agency created for purposes other than the mere economic allocation of resources. The FEA was established in part as an overseer of oil industry competition, in part as a receptor of interest group demands, and in part as a political symbol of federal government action in the wake of the energy crisis. Thus, FEA policies were largely inefficient, inequitable, and unrepresentative, but they also can be seen as moderately effective, responsive, and responsible, depending on the criteria selected. Care should therefore be taken in defining FEA policy failure in terms of any single standard. Consideration should be given to concepts such as representativeness, equity, responsiveness, and responsibility in future research assessing the content of public policies.

Notes

1. See C.H. Weiss, *Evaluation Research: Methods of Assessing Program Effectiveness* (Englewood Cliffs, N.J.: Prentice-Hall, 1972), pp. 10-23.

2. See Y. Dror, *Public Policymaking Reexamined* (Scranton, Penn.: Chandler, 1968), p. 41.

3. A. Schick, "Beyond Analysis," *Public Administration Review* 37 (May/June 1977):258-263; and R.A. Ball, "Equitable Evaluation through Investigative Sociology," *Sociological Focus* 10 (January 1977):1-14.

4. R.W. Rycroft, "Selecting Policy Evaluation Criteria: Toward a Rediscovery of Public Administration," *Midwest Review of Public Administration* 12 (June 1978): forthcoming.

5. G.P. Whitaker, "Who Puts the Value in Evaluation?" *Social Science Quarterly* 54 (March 1974):759.

6. W.O. Doub, *Federal Energy Regulation: An Organizational Study* (Washington, D.C.: U.S. Government Printing Office, 1974), pp. 13-19.

7. P. MacAvoy, B.E. Stangle, and J.B. Tepper, "The Federal Energy Office as Regulator of the Energy Crisis," *Technology Review* 77 (May 1975):39-44.

8. R.B. Mancke, *Performance of the Federal Energy Office* (Washington, D.C.: American Enterprise Institute for Public Policy Research, 1975), pp. 16-21.

9. A.M. DiLeo, "An Introduction to the Mandatory Petroleum Allocation Regulations," *Louisiana Bar Journal* 22 (September 1974):107-110.

10. S.A. Wakefield, "Allocation, Price Control and the FEA: Regulatory Policy and Practice in the Political Arena," *Rocky Mountain Mineral Law Institute* 21 (1975):282-284.

11. C.A. Wagner, "National Energy Goals and FEA's Crude Oil Allocation Program," *Virginia Law Review* 61 (May 1975):937.

12. P. MacAvoy, *Federal Energy Administration Regulation* (Washington, D.C.: American Enterprise Institute for Public Policy Research, 1977), pp. 139-146.

13. H. Kranz, "Government by All the People: The Why and How of a More Representative Public Service," *Good Government* 89 (Fall 1972):4.

14. F.C. Mosher, *Democracy and the Public Service* (New York: Oxford University Press, 1968), p. 12.

15. See V. Subramaniam, "Representative Bureaucracy: A Reassessment," *American Political Science Review* 61 (December 1967):1010; D. Nachmias and D.H. Rosenbloom, "Measuring Bureaucratic Representation and Integration," *Public Administration Review* 33 (November 1973):591-593; and K.J. Meier, "Representative Bureaucracy: An Empirical Analysis," *American Political Science Review* 69 (June 1975):529-531.

16. See R.W. Rycroft, "Bureaucratic Performance in Energy Policy-Making: An Evaluation of Output Efficiency and Equity in the Federal Energy Administration," *Public Policy* 26 (Fall 1978): forthcoming.

17. B.D. Jones, "Distributional Considerations in Models of Government Service Provision," *Urban Affairs Quarterly* 12 (March 1977):291-312. See also B.D. Jones and C. Kaufman, "The Distribution of Urban Public Services,"

Administration and Society 6 (November 1974):337-360; and M.V. Pauly and T.D. Willett, "Two Concepts of Equity and Their Implications for Public Policy," *Social Science Quarterly* 53 (June 1972):8-19.

18. R.C. Fried, *Performance in American Bureaucracy* (Boston: Little, Brown, 1976), p. 55.

19. R.W. Rycroft, "Energy Policy Feedback: Bureaucratic Responsiveness in the Federal Energy Administration," *Policy Analysis* 5 (Winter 1979): forthcoming. See also V.B. Ermer, "Strategies for Increasing Bureaucratic Responsiveness," *Midwest Review of Public Administration* 9 (April/July 1975):121-132; and D.A. Taebel, "Bureaucratization and Responsiveness: A Research Note," *Midwest Review of Public Administration* 7 (July 1973):199-200.

20. R.W. Rycroft, "Bureaucratic Responsibility in the Federal Energy Administration," *The Bureaucrat* 6 (Fall 1977):19.

21. C.E. Gilbert, "The Framework of Administrative Responsibility," *Journal of Politics* 21 (August 1959):382. See also N.J. Powell, *Responsible Public Bureaucracy in the United States* (Boston: Allyn and Bacon, 1967), p. 6.

22. See R.W. Rycroft, "The Federal Energy Administration: A Case Study of Energy Policy-Making" (Ph.D. diss., University of Oklahoma, 1976).

23. See C.H. Levine, "Unrepresentative Bureaucracy: Or Knowing What You Look Like Tells You Who You Are (and Maybe What to Do about It)," *The Bureaucrat* 4 (April 1975):94.

24. See Energy Policy Project of the Ford Foundation, *A Time To Choose: America's Energy Future* (Cambridge, Mass.: Ballinger, 1974), p. 334.

25. See *General Public Attitudes and Behavior Toward Energy Saving: Highlight Reports* (Princeton, N.J.: Opinion Research Corporation, 1975).

26. See U.S. General Accounting Office, *Problems in the Federal Energy Administration's Compliance and Enforcement Effort* (Washington, D.C.: U.S. Government Printing Office, 1974), pp. 1-4.

27. U.S. Senate, Committee on the Judiciary, *Federal Energy Administration Enforcement of Petroleum Price Regulations* (Washington, D.C.: U.S. Government Printing Office, 1975), pp. 13-24.

28. Rycroft, "Bureaucratic Performance."

29. See U.S. House of Representatives, Committee on Interstate and Foreign Commerce, *FEA Enforcement Policies* (Washington, D.C.: U.S. Government Printing Office, 1975), p. 201.

30. U.S. Senate, Committee on the Judiciary, *Federal Energy Administration*, p. 64. See also U.S. Senate, Committee on Government Operations, *Enforcement and Compliance of FEA Oil Price Regulations* (Washington, D.C.: U.S. Government Printing Office, 1975), pp. 1-5.

31. "Fact Sheet on Federal Energy Administration Compliance Activities," Washington, D.C., Federal Energy Administration, 1975.

32. Rycroft, "Bureaucratic Performance."

33. U.S. Federal Energy Administration, *Report to Congress on the Economic Impact of Energy Actions* (Washington, D.C.: U.S. Government Printing Office, 1975), pp. 27-50.

34. See Rycroft, "Federal Energy Administration."

35. See K.E. House, "Getting Entrenched: Energy Agency Spends Much Energy to Insure a Long Life, Foes Say," *Wall Street Journal*, March 9, 1976.

36. Fried, *Performance in American Bureaucracy*, p. 49.

37. Opinion Research Corporation.

38. Rycroft, "Energy Policy Feedback." See also W.F. Cockrell, "Exceptions to Federal Regulation for Management of the Energy Crisis," *Oklahoma Law Review* 28 (Summer 1975):530.

39. See *Report on the Use of Presidential Executive Interchange Personnel With Oil Industry Backgrounds by the Federal Energy Office* (Washington, D.C.: U.S. General Accounting Office, 1974).

40. Rycroft, "Bureaucratic Responsibility," pp. 23-31.

10 The Formulation and Implementation of Energy Policies

Richard J. Tobin and
Steven A. Cohen

During the 1950s and 1960s, most public officials devoted little attention to the availability, use, or interrelatedness of energy resources. By the early 1970s, however, this neglect could no longer be tolerated. Shortages of natural gas, sharply rising prices for imported oil, and concern for the safety and environmental impacts of coal and nuclear power combined to insure that energy would be on the national government's policy agenda. For the first time, federal officials found themselves faced with a need to formulate and implement policy responses to the so-called energy crisis, which had become one of the nation's major problems. This chapter focuses on how effective the formulation and implementation of energy policies can be given the nature of the problem.

The Nature of the Energy Issue

As Americans enter the 1980s, they have reached a historic turning point. Resources that were once considered plentiful now appear in short supply. In an age of scarcity, the United States, the most consumptive nation in the world, is faced with a major challenge: to begin the process of somehow reducing its use of nonrenewable resources. In many ways energy is the most important of these resources and is one on which everyone depends. This point is especially salient for Americans, because no nation has so closely tied its well-being and economic viability to the availability of large amounts of energy as has the United States. Most of the energy consumed in the United States is produced by finite, nonrenewable fossil fuels.

The full extent of the country's dependence on exhaustible energy supplies is indicated by the fact that most Americans gear their life-styles to the use of oil and natural gas, which account for nearly three-quarters of all the fuel consumed in this country. Although they are the most popular, world and domestic reserves of these two fuels may be exhausted within a short period of time. As the National Academy of Sciences has suggested: "World resources of petroleum and natural gas, discovered reserved and undiscovered recoverable resources will be seriously depleted by the end of the century if present trends of world production and consumption continue."[1]

This situation is aggravated because total energy consumption is increasing rapidly, at a pace that exceeds the rate of population increase. As the data in table 10-1 indicate, the amount of energy consumed per person in the United States has almost tripled since the beginning of this century. By the end of this century, it is estimated that Americans will be using over 80 percent more energy than they consumed in 1974.[2] One might hypothesize that these increases are the result of industrialization and that all industrialized nations consume great amounts of energy. Although this is partially true, all the increased consumption cannot be attributed to the maintenance of industrialized society. Other data reveal that the United States consumes much more energy per capita than most other industrialized countries. In fact, due to the large population of the United States, the high level of per capita consumption reported in table 10-2 makes this country the largest consumer of energy in the world. Americans represent only a small fraction of the world's population; but they consume almost one-third of all energy resources produced each year.

Two further issues compound the problem of high levels of consumption in the United States. First, to sustain their energy habit, Americans must import nearly half of all the petroleum they use. Much of this petroleum comes from politically unstable areas of the world, where unrest might lead to disruption of production or distribution. In addition, reliance on foreign supplies dangerously limits the country's freedom of action in international affairs and precipitously increases its balance-of-payments deficit.

Second, high levels of consumption often lead to environmental degradation. In the words of one analyst, "Energy production and consumption combine to form the world's greatest environmental insult."[3] Strip mining can permanently scar the earth's landscape and deep mining often leads to water pollution because of acid drainage. Devastating spills are possible whenever oil is transported, and air pollution results whenever coal and oil are burned. Thermal

Table 10-1

Energy Consumption and Population in the United States, 1860-1976

Year	Total Quads[a]	Population (in millions)	Quads per Person
1900	9.6	76.0	.126
1920	21.3	105.7	.201
1940	25.0	131.7	.190
1960	44.6	179.3	.249
1970	67.1	203.2	.330
1976	74.2	220.0[b]	.337

Sources: Richard Corrigan, J.O. Kirchten, and Robert Samuelson, "Jimmy Carter's Energy Crusade," *National Journal* 9 (April 30, 1977):659; and *The American Almanac* (New York: Grosset & Dunlop, 1973), p. 5.

[a]A quad equals one quadrillion (10^{15}) British thermal units or the amount of energy in approximately 170 million barrels of oil.

[b]Estimated.

Table 10-2

Energy Consumption per Capita in Selected Industrialized Nations, 1972

(tons of oil equivalent)

	Per-Capita Consumption
Canada	8.38
United States	8.35
Sweden	5.31
Netherlands	4.68
West Germany	4.12
United Kingdom	3.81
France	3.31
Japan	2.90
Italy	2.39

Source: J. Darmstadter, J. Dunkerly, and J. Alterman, *How Industrial Societies Use Energy: A Comparative Analysis,* A Resources for the Future book published by The Johns Hopkins University Press (Baltimore: The Johns Hopkins University Press, 1977), p. 5.

pollution and radioactive contamination can result from the use of atomic power. These are only a few examples; the list could be extended for pages. For environmental reasons alone, therefore, many people want different patterns of energy development and use.

Not only are the levels and consequences of consumption a source of concern, but so are the causes. The consumptive habits of Americans are tied to industrial development. Prior to industrialization the major sources of energy were renewable resources such as wind, wood, and animal and human labor. The creation and maintenance of the earth's vast industrial machine has required—and continues to require—more energy than that obtainable from easily exploited renewable sources.

Industrialization may be a primary cause of extensive energy use, but it is not the only factor. Throughout most of the post-World War II era, public policies have greatly encouraged a high rate of energy consumption. To cite only a few examples, federally sponsored home mortgages in the 1950s and 1960s almost exclusively financed construction of new, single-family suburban dwellings. The interstate highway system further encourages low-density settlement patterns and energy-intensive truck and automobile transport over rail transport. Government regulation of interstate shipments of natural gas insured that gas prices did not reflect actual costs, thereby encouraging consumption.

Certain public policies foster high levels of consumption, and the marketplace does too. Americans are overwhelmed with energy-intensive products that most of the world's population has never seen. Many of the products are produced and used in ways that waste energy. In one study, for example, it was found that it takes more energy to package them to produce items in plastic milk bottles, nonreturnable beverage containers, and frozen prepared foods.[4]

Another study found that in major areas of energy use (residential, commercial, industrial, and transportation), Americans usually consume more energy than others to accomplish similar purposes.[5] In Sweden where the climate is much more severe, residents use less than three-quarters as much energy to heat their homes, which are approximately the same size as Americans' on a per-capita basis. Most Germans are able to heat their water for less than 40 percent of the energy that Americans use. These significant differences are not limited to the residential sector. Many people in other countries are able to operate their businesses, manufacture their goods, and transport themselves in private automobiles much more efficiently than Americans. The reasons for these differences are not as important as the fact that a peculiar style of commercial, residential, and technological development in the United States has resulted in high levels of energy consumption.

This evidence has led some to conclude that Americans must make a major transition "from a period of abundant cheap oil and gas to a period when these resources will be in short supply."[6] However, the scope and complexity of the energy problem ensure that it will be difficult both to formulate and to implement viable policies.[7]

Problems with the Formulation of Energy Policies

A government's attempts to formulate solutions to problems usually involve at least two broad but closely interrelated steps. In the first, a government decides what should be done, and in the second it actually drafts the necessary legislation that will lead to implementation.[8] Each step has its own problems and constraints. At the first stage policy makers must decide which decision-making approach will lead to the most desirable policy outcomes. Once this decision is reached such things as attitudes toward the issue, policy agendas, and the nature of congressional decision making will affect efforts to legislate a solution.

Problems with the First Step

When faced with most problems, governments at all levels typically employ incremental decision making. In this mode, previous actions are believed the best guide to future choices; change is likely to be very gradual; and policies that remedy existing problems are preferred over policies that address future goals. The appeal of incrementalism is closely linked to the ease of its use. With incremental decision making, few analytic resources are needed; risks and uncertainty are minimized; and sunk costs and standard operating procedures are respected. Pehaps of greater importance is that incremental decision making "is politically expedient because it is easier to reach agreement when the matters in dispute among various groups are only modifications of existing programs rather than policy issues of great magnitude, . . ."[9]

Despite its widespread popularity, incremental policy making is not without its flaws. When policy formulators rely on the incremental approach, they may not consider all possible alternative responses to a problem. In fact, they usually consider only how existing policies can be modified or improved. If reliance on existing policies (or on slight variations of these policies) will not bring about a needed major change, then incremental approaches will not produce appropriate responses.

A neglect of some alternatives often characterizes incremental decision making, but such a neglect would be unlikely with a rational or comprehensive approach. Rational policy formulators commit themselves to a process that seeks to set and achieve long-term goals after a thorough analysis of the situation and a full consideration of all possible alternatives and their consequences. Unlike the incremental approach, rational formulators do not give existing policies any special preference and, in fact, are entirely willing to change or discard them in favor of policies that maximize the attainment of desired objectives.[10]

Given the complexity of many problems and beliefs that large-scale changes are needed, some assert that separate problem elements cannot be addressed individually, because a solution to one segment may make it more difficult to deal with others. A holistic approach may therefore be necessary, but it is unachievable through normal incremental decision making. Rational decision making offers an alternative that can approximate holistic thinking and enable policy makers to articulate optimal policies, or so it is argued.

Despite the ease in describing the process, it is very difficult for public policy to be formulated in a rational manner. Decision makers often do not have the necessary resources, such as time and money, to conduct a comprehensive analysis of a particular policy issue. Even when attempts at such analysis are made, they are frequently abandoned in the face of other problems that demand immediate attention. In addition, in many policy areas it is nearly impossible to specify goals and alternative courses of action adequately. In these cases, a high level of uncertainty forces the cost of information so high that incrementalism, speculative augmentation, or even guessing become more reasonable approaches to policy making than the rational method.

In sum, the intelligent policy formulator faces a crucial choice. He can develop a plan that will bring about incremental changes; but such a choice would probably not allow him to achieve long-range goals. Alternatively he can rely on a rational approach; but he would have to acknowledge that the American political system is not particularly amenable to rational decision making.

Problems with the Second Step

After formulators have selected and applied a decision-making approach, they must translate this choice into legislation that reflects their goals. The difficulties in this translation process in the energy area are enormous as Presidents Nixon, Ford, and Carter discovered. The experiences of each of these presidents illustrate the pitfalls of the second step of policy formulation; but President Carter's experiences provide the basis of the following analysis since his efforts are the most recent.

After several months of highly intensive effort in early 1977, the Carter administration developed what appeared to be a relatively rational approach to the nation's energy situation. The national energy plan was supposed to bring about large-scale changes in the way Americans use energy. Carter hoped to decrease consumption of oil and natural gas by increasing their costs and by penalizing their users. Conversions to coal, the country's largest available energy resource, would eventually be mandatory for most major fuel users. Businesses and individuals would be encouraged to conserve fuel through a series of tax credits and programs designed to promote the installation of insulation. To emphasize the need for such changes, the president claimed that the seriousness of the nation's energy problems required a response that would be equivalent to a declaration of war. With this introduction, the president sent his proposals to Congress in April 1977.

Regardless of the president's desires, his plan had an uneven record of success in Congress, and much of the original design was never enacted. Many reasons can be offered to explain this failure, but three seem to be of special importance.

First, there are a number of conflicting opinions about the seriousness of the energy problem. Although the president tried to place the highest priority on energy, his efforts met with skepticism and disbelief among many members of the public. For example, while public concern for energy was at record levels during the Arab oil embargo of late 1973 and early 1974, by early 1977 (shortly after the president's speech) this concern had diminished to a point where nearly 50 percent of all Americans believed no shortages of energy existed. An even higher percentage felt that President Carter was exaggerating the seriousness of the problem.[11] Other public opinion data help to explain this widely shared attitude. In one Gallup Poll conducted in the spring of 1977, only half the respondents were aware that the United States imported oil. As far as the causes of the energy problem, another poll from 1977 found that 70 percent of those questioned agreed that oil companies had conspired to exacerbate fuel shortages.[12]

Just as many members of the public are skeptical about the energy problem, so too are many congressmen. President Carter continually stressed the need for immediate congressional action on his energy program; but few congressmen agreed with this assessment. Few members of the public were clamoring for action; there were no external events to produce a sense of urgency; and the alleged consequences of inaction simply did not develop.

Many congressmen also accused the administration of misrepresenting or withholding information about the extent of the energy problem. Such criticisms are easily explained. The fact that information on energy is often in the hands of people overseas or under the tight control of highly competitive, multinational energy firms means that much is unknown about the scope or dimensions of the problem. In addition, the quality of available information on energy is not always certain. One sure result of this situation is the need to extrapolate from limited and, perhaps, questionable data. Extrapolations can never be more than estimates, and this creates opportunities for widely divergent interpretations of the same data.

Second, even if the president's concern had been persuasive, there still was no guarantee that energy would readily find a place on Congress's policy agenda. This agenda includes a collection of political questions that are considered "within the range of legitimate concerns meriting the attention of the polity."[13] An item receiving a place on the agenda is likely to remain on it for an extended period. As Roger Cobb and Charles Elder explain it, items remain on an already crowded agenda because policy makers assume that older problems merit more attention because of their longevity; because policy makers are more familiar with them; and because the time policy makers have available to them for individual items is often too limited to permit them to do anything of major consequence.[14]

Legislative behavior was entirely consistent with this analysis during the 95th Congress (1977-1978). Old problems received the most attention as congressmen reviewed existing laws on taxes, labor, welfare, education, clean air, clean water, minimum wages, social security, food stamps, congressional ethics, and the criminal code, to name only a few. The point is that new items must compete with existing ones to achieve a salient place on Congress's agenda. Indeed, it often takes several years' effort or a dramatic event like the Arab oil embargo before a new item becomes the subject of extensive discussion.[15] Thus President Carter's efforts in 1977 and 1978 benefited from the efforts of his two predecessors. At the same time, however, achievement of agenda status does not guarantee that Congress will devote undivided attention to an issue. As President Carter discovered, his many requests for congressional action on energy during the 95th Congress were often met with complaints that Congress was too busy with other equally compelling problems.

Third, the nature of congressional decision making virtually assures that major differences will exist between a president's proposals and eventual legislative outputs. One can safely generalize that congressmen like to handle familiar issues with clear precedents at the expense of unfamiliar items without such precedents. From a congressman's perspective, familiar issues allow him to use what has been labeled routine formulation, which is a "repetitive and essentially changeless process of reformulating similar proposals within the issue-area that has a well-established place on the agenda of government."[16] In Charles Jones's words, "people are most satisfied when tomorrow brings the same expectations and responsibilities as today."[17] In other words, President Carter's desire for far-reaching legislative responses was inconsistent with expectations of congressional behavior.

Another characteristic of congressional decision making is a preference for policies that do not upset the status quo as defined by existing legislation. Although presidents can perceive a need for significant shifts in policy, creating support for such shifts may not be easy in the face of a preference for incremental decision making among many congressmen. Inherent in any call for major change is an unmistakable message that something is amiss with the policies that incumbent legislators have already formulated and enacted. One effect of this kind of message is to lead key congressmen to defend their prior achievements or to argue that only minor changes are needed to remedy the problem.

Efforts to alter significantly the status quo also conflict directly with well-organized interest groups that are generally satisfied with current policies. These groups can be excluded from the initial phase of policy formulation but not from the legislative arena, which provides an ideal setting for interest-group access. Proponents of the status quo only have to succeed at one point in the legislative process to modify or defeat proposals for change. In contrast, advocates of change must succeed at every stage in both the House and the Senate.

For proposals on energy, the chances of total success at every stage are remote. When President Carter sent his energy proposals to Congress, he had hoped that both chambers would consider them as a single package. The House of Representatives consented but the Senate did not. It referred different segments of the plan to separate committees, and each took several months to develop its own proposals, many of which conflicted with the president's. That the president had succeeded in getting the House to consider his energy plans together was remarkable in itself. Few congressional committees are without some responsibility for energy, and few are willing to abdicate this responsibility. One survey in 1976 found that twenty-three committees and fifty-one subcommittees had jurisdiction over some aspect of energy. The implications of this situation are magnified when one realizes that congressional leaders have no way to coordinate the activities of all their committees. As a result, one analyst has remarked that a "unified and integrated executive program [for energy is] unlikely to be judged as such by any one congressional unit."[18]

These few comments about congressional behavior do not exhaust the possibilities. Nonetheless they do offer a partial explanation for President Carter's lack of success in Congress with his energy plan. Much of his original proposal was never adopted. By the time Congress adopted its own version of an acceptable energy program in late 1978 (after 18 months of debate), the program differed greatly from the comprehensive plan that the president and his advisors had developed. Indeed, one commentary called the congressional energy package a "shrunken and shredded version" of the president's.[19] One reason for such a claim is that Congress had relied heavily on existing policies and in many instances had tried to modify them only marginally.

More important than the form of the legislation is its impact. One goal of the president's plan had been to reduce the consumption of oil and natural gas. Immediately after Congress had acted, however, some predicted that the new legislation would have few of the intended consequences. The president had hoped to discourage the consumption of oil by industries and electric utilities by imposing a tax on its use; but this proposal failed to win congressional support. There was even some speculation that the new legislation could actually lead to a greater use of imported oil, because deregulation might encourage industrial users to switch to oil as a result of the increased costs for gas.[20] Thus, an attempt to formulate a rational response to reorient the nation's energy habits had been substantially modified.

Problems with the Implementation of Energy Policies

Whether policy formulation proceeds along rational or incremental lines, past experience suggests that the original intent of any policy is transformed when bureaucracies charged with implementation begin their efforts. Indeed, the outcomes of any implementation process are likely to be very different from those anticipated by the individuals who formulated the policy. It is not surprising, then, to find a significant gap between plans formulated in the executive branch, Congress's legislative outputs, and the energy policies that bureaucrats seek to accomplish. The possible explanations for these discrepancies are many, but among the more important ones are such things as: (1) the nature of the policy issue, its political environment, and the policy-formulation process accompanying the issues; (2) the capabilities of organizations responsible for policy implementation; (3) interorganizational communications and relations; and, (4) the socioeconomic and general political environment.[21]

The Nature of the Policy Issue

The nature and type of policy issue can be conceptualized as an independent variable that acts on the policy-formulation process[22] and as an intervening variable that acts, in turn, on the dependent variable, policy implementation. In this case, the implementation of energy policy is the dependent variable. The energy issue is a "high stakes" conflict-laden one, producing policy-formulation processes characterized by bargaining and compromise. Its wide scope and significance guarantees the active involvement of powerful and conflicting interest groups, each attempting to achieve policies they favor or to prevent policies they oppose. For example, automobile manufacturers are apprehensive that mandatory conservation will require them to produce smaller cars, which may lead to smaller profits. Similarly, conservation might mean diminished profits for oil companies. Many electric utilities are unenthuasiastic about the pollution control problems associated with the need to burn larger amounts of coal. Residential consumers and industrial consumers may favor opposing policies. Liberals may favor an activist governmental approach while conservatives may favor only marginal incursions by government. The involvement of such disparate interests typically leads to policies that represent the lowest common denominator; that is, the result is a policy potpourri that every powerful interest can tolerate but one that may serve no coherent overall purpose.

It is likely, moreover, that in the case of energy policy the difficulties that Congress experienced in its attempt to produce a cohesive energy policy will be repeated in the implementing agencies. Interest groups that were unable to convince Congress to support their positions will shift their efforts to the bureaucracies and attempt to influence the implementation of the very policies they were unable to influence earlier.[23] In addition, if a policy results from a series of compromises designed to ameliorate conflict rather than to solve specific policy problems, it should be expected that the policy will be better at easing conflict than it will be at solving problems. The cohesion and logic of the policy design will probably be unable to survive the distortions of the bargaining process. Participants in this process often display more concern for their own individual interests than with the overall coherence of the policy being designed. Consequently, the incoherent policy that often results from such a process is not surprising.

Organizational Capabilities

Each organization that may perform policy-implementing tasks should be identified in attempting to determine the likelihood that a program will be implemented successfully. Having identified these organizations, two questions must be asked: Can they do it? Are the organizations able to accomplish their assigned tasks?

Whatever energy strategies are adopted, the major organizations involved in implementation will include labor unions, power companies, automobile manufacturers, energy-research institutes, coal and oil companies, state and local units of government, the Environmental Protection Agency, and the U.S. Departments of Energy, Transportation, and Housing and Urban Development. A simple count of the organizations likely to be involved in carrying out the various components of a comprehensive national energy program indicates that the prospects for successful implementation are discouraging. As Jeffrey Pressman and Aaron Wildavsky suggest in their case study of a federal employment program in Oakland, California, when the number of organizations performing policy-implementing tasks increases, the problems of implementation increase as well.[24]

If a national energy program is to be implemented, each of the affected organizations must be capable of performing specific, assigned tasks. Each must be provided with sufficient resources to motivate and coordinate the behavior required to achieve these tasks. One of the resources needed to coordinate activity is prior experience. Government energy agencies are generally new organizations, however, facing many problems in their efforts to coordinate and implement policy. Richard Corrigan reported evidence of this in his analysis of early reaction to the U.S. Department of Energy (DOE), when he noted that the department's image is threatened by the widespread perception that it is inexperienced and disorganized.[25]

Although DOE suffers from a lack of coordinating experience, it is not entirely correct to say that the agency is new. Many existing agencies with long-standing attachments to various interests and policies were combined to create the DOE. As illustrations, the Energy Research and Development Administration had close links with atomic energy interests, and the Federal Power Commission had been closely associated with electric power companies. As a result, the leaders of DOE have found it necessary to convince members of the old organizations that they now belong to an organization with a new mission. If the leadership fails in this effort, the new DOE may find itself with the worst feature of old agencies (bureaucratic inertia) and the least desirable feature of new agencies (inexperience). Indeed, a preliminary assessment of DOE suggests that such a situation may exist. Creation of the department was heralded as an important step in solving the nation's energy problems; but such projections are now widely discounted. It appears likely that much of the energy of new components of the organization will be wasted in attempts to coordinate and motivate activities of older segments of the organization. This attempt to gain control over existing activities makes it difficult to devote resources to new policy initiatives such as a national energy plan.

The DOE may therefore have difficulty implementing its energy policies; but these difficulties pale in comparison with the problems that other implementing organizations face. As an example, many of the private organizations likely to be involved in implementing new energy policies have traditionally encouraged production and consumption. In some instances these organizations are being asked to aid efforts to conserve energy—a role reversal that most are poorly equipped to undertake. For gas, oil, coal, and electric companies, there is very little competitive advantage to be gained by advising customers to cut their use and purchases of energy resources.

Interorganizational Relations and Communications

Bureaucracies do not necessarily follow the orders of legislatures and executives. The latter groups are often assigned policy-making roles, but policy is also made in the process of administration. If this is the case, then it is important that those administering an executive or legislative policy understand and support it. If they do not, they will have many opportunities to modify or emasculate a policy. Members of such organizations must be motivated or inspired to perform certain tasks. For example, to implement a national energy policy, DOE officials must motivate their own members and the members of many other organizations. Or, to be more exact, officials in DOE must convince the leaderships in other organizations to motivate their members. Each bureaucratic organization must be convinced that the implementation of an energy policy furthers its purposes. To accomplish this goal, resources must be provided, coercion applied, arguments articulated, bargains forged, and attitudes and behaviors modified.

Although this describes what should be done, reality limits what DOE can do. At the national level, the energy agency cannot enforce its will on other federal agencies and is limited to bargaining and cajolery because it rarely has authority over these other agencies. At the subnational level, DOE has few incentives to offer state and local governments and, unless specific legislative authority is provided, probably will have very little control over them.

Even if DOE could achieve acceptable levels of interorganizational coordination, it would still have problems with communication. Each agency involved in implementation will interpret and reformulate the policy tasks given to it because of such factors as its clientele, its organizational biases, and even its hostility toward the lead agency. To say the least, the interpretative phase is the key component of policy making. If this point is kept in mind, then the significance of congressional compromise on energy policy is magnified. Compromises can effectively deter much conflict in legislative arenas; but the result is often vaguely worded laws that are written to allow many interpretations. Unfortunately, Congress can avoid conflict through compromise and vagueness, but bureaucrats charged with implementation are not afforded such luxury. They must interpret and apply uncertain and ambiguous policy edicts. The outcome, of course, can be bureaucratic programs that bear little relation to executive or legislative intent. The large number of organizations involved with energy policies obviously increases the chances for poor communication and misinterpreted directions.

Still other problems are likely to affect interorganizational communications. Because many types of energy policy making are new areas of endeavor for American governments, communication messages and networks will initially be confused and disorganized. Communication initially will be difficult, as personnel in the lead agency seek out and make contact with those key actors in implementing organizations capable of carrying out specific tasks. A certain amount of experimentation and evaluation will be necessary to determine which communication set-ups work and which do not. In addition to difficulties that arise from disorganized communication networks, problems will also result from genuine confusion about how to deal with a new policy area. As an illustration, the reader may recall that in the early days of the Carter administration officials provided ambiguous messages about the urgency of the energy problem. The American people watched President Carter on television, cardigan clad at fireside, appealing for support for his energy program on February 2, 1977. Later, on April 20, 1977, he declared that the nation's energy program would be the "moral equivalent of war." During this initial media blitz the public was also told that it would be asked to make great sacrifices for the good of the nation. Shortly after this publicity campaign, however, the administration began to downplay the amount of sacrifice that would be required; and when the complete Carter energy plan was unveiled, the sacrifices required were considerably less than those required in wartime.

President Carter was not alone in his uncertainty about how to respond to the energy situation. Presidents Nixon and Ford also had difficulty in selecting appropriate and convincing messages. The presidents' problem stems in part from confusion about the proper pitch required to sell the energy crisis and the very nature of the energy situation itself. Shortages of certain energy resources appear to be on the horizon, and the possibility of resource depletion will have to be confronted; but the actual exhaustion of these resources will occur in the future. The urgency of the situation results from the long lead times that are required to find acceptable substitutes for nonrenewable energy sources. Despite the apparent urgency, it is difficult to start preparing for war (or its so-called moral equivalent) long before the actual fighting begins. It is also difficult to convey the urgency of the energy situation when oil and natural gas are still flowing relatively freely and cheaply. In addition, congressional action to date has not reflected the belief that immediate and comprehensive action is necessary or even desirable. Instead, Congress has created the distinct impression that urgency is of little import.

The uncertainty surrounding the energy policy arena is reflected not only in ambiguous communications but also in confused bureaucratic energy politics. Given their limited experience and knowledge, it is difficult for policy formulators and key implementing agencies to assess organizational interests and capabilities. Questions arise with no certain answers: Can automobile manufacturers meet fuel efficiency goals? Will local governments enforce energy-efficiency regulations? Which federal agencies are best qualified and most interested in performing specific tasks? Can state utility commissions be convinced to adopt policies that encourage conservation? The inability to give definitive answers to such important questions insures that energy policies can be implemented only in an atmosphere of extreme uncertainty. This uncertainty will affect interorganizational relations and make it difficult for an organization to calculate its interests vis-à-vis a particular policy and policy-implementing task.

The Socioeconomic and General
Political Environment

Social, political, and economic variables largely determine the kinds of policies that can be implemented. These variables establish the parameters for acceptable public policies. For example, policies tend to be implemented when the public: (1) can afford their cost (economic environment); (2) believes they are needed and ought to be implemented (social environment); and (3) perceives that it is legitimate for government to attempt to meet a particular need (political environment).

The economic environment is particularly critical to the implementation of energy policies. The availability of energy resources and the nation's economic health are tightly interwoven. Spiraling prices for energy have already had a devastating effect on many families and businesses. If prices continue to rise rapidly, larger amounts of everyone's income will be allocated to pay for energy instead of such things as food, housing, or new industrial equipment. Such cost increases for energy will not be well received; but Americans will have little choice except to pay higher prices if they expect government to implement suitable long-range energy policies.

Conservation, a policy that some analysts favor, could be encouraged through appeals to conscience or to one's sense of patriotism; but examination of the social environment of the energy situation explains why such methods will probably be unsatisfactory. The social environment, or the attitudes and beliefs of the citizenry toward a policy issue, is an important determinant of the implementability of any policy. If the public is thoroughly convinced that a problem is serious and that major changes are imperative, policy implementors will find their tasks easier to do. For energy policy this is especially true. Public acceptance of the energy problem and of the required changes are probably the major keystones to success. As the earlier data on public attitudes toward energy indicated, however, many Americans remain unconvinced that they should change their patterns of energy consumption. For example, when asked how they might respond to the waste and scarcity of energy, few Americans demonstrate a strong commitment to change their current behavior. Many people, in fact, see no need to change their energy-related habits. In one national opinion survey conducted in early 1977, half the respondents blamed other people for waste and felt that voluntary conservation would not be a realistic solution. Of those people who had thought about the energy question, most would prefer a technological fix requiring little effort on their part and few changes in their personal behavior.[26] In addition, more recent data suggest that the prospects for personal change are becoming even more unlikely. Between February and April of 1978, the number of Americans who indicated that the energy situation was the most important problem facing the nation dropped from 23 percent to only 8 percent according to two Gallup Polls.[27] These data provide policy makers with discouraging prospects, and they would be ill advised to rely on strategies that require extensive public cooperation.

Finally, the political environment establishes limits for the legitimate activities of governments. By definition, the political environment determines political feasibility. If a policy is proposed in a favorable social and economic climate but the elites controlling the political agenda and decision arena oppose it, it is unlikely that the policy will be implemented.[28] Policies formulated under these conditions tend to be symbolic and designed to placate rather than bring about substantive change. It is important to note, however, that the economic environment tends to influence the social environment; and both economic and social conditions influence political feasibility.

Conclusions

As this chapter has demonstrated, the formulation and implementation of public policy is much more difficult than the simple articulation of desirable goals. Moreover, policies that are eventually implemented often tend to be quite different than the ones originally proposed. Such distortions are especially likely when massive impacts, irreconcilable interests, and great scope and conflict characterize the policy issue. Of the complete range of domestic issues, only the issue of the economy as a whole can claim greater scope and engender greater conflict than the energy issue. For these reasons, making and applying comprehensive energy policies will be difficult if not torturous. Individual components that distribute benefits throughout society, such as subsidies for home insulation, may be made and implemented with little difficulty. In contrast, energy policies that regulate economic and commercial activity, that redistribute wealth and resources, or that call for certain interests to sacrifice will be much harder to enact and administer. In a society where private interests are intimately involved in decision making, one should expect unrelenting interest group activity in the formulation and implementation of such regulative and redistributive energy policies.

Based on these observations at least one conclusion is inescapable: the United States is unlikely to have, either easily or quickly, any semblance of a comprehensive energy policy in the near future. Barring any sudden display of charismatic leadership, the energy policies likely to emerge over the next decade will be short term, noncomprehensive, poorly coordinated, tolerable to major economic interests, and unlikely to require great individual sacrifices. For the policies that do emerge, there is likely to be an uneven record of implementation.

Notes

1. *Mineral Resources and the Environment* (Washington, D.C.: National Academy of Sciences, 1975), p. 81.

2. *The Washington Post*, January 9, 1976, p. D16.

3. Charles J. Hitch, "Energy in Our Future," *The Key Reporter* 42 (Summer 1978):2.

4. *The Washington Post*, June 9, 1975, p. B8.

5. U.S. Congress, Joint Economic Committee, Joint Committee Print, *Achieving the Goals of the Employment Act of 1946–Thirtieth Anniversary Review*, vol. 2, *Energy, Paper No. 2, Energy and Economic Growth*, 95th Cong., 1st sess. (1977), pp. 30-37.

6. Executive Office of the President, Energy Policy and Planning, *The National Energy Plan*, Washington, D.C., 1977, p. 7.

7. The reader is reminded that not all people agree on the nature of causes of the energy problem. In fact, one forum of scholars concluded in 1978 that the notion of an impending energy crisis is "bunk." The report about the University of Miami's International Scientific Forum on an Acceptable Energy Future is in the *Buffalo Evening News*, November 29, 1978, p. 1.

8. James E. Anderson, *Public Policy-Making* (New York: Praeger, 1975), p. 70.

9. Ibid., p. 13.

10. Ibid., p. 10.

11. These public-opinion data are reported in "Public Perceptions of the Energy Problem," *Resources*, no. 57 (January-March 1978):2, 21-22.

12. Ibid., p. 22.

13. Roger W. Cobb and Charles D. Elder, *Participation in American Politics: The Dynamics of Agenda-Building* (Baltimore: Johns Hopkins University Press, 1972), p. 14.

14. Ibid., p. 89.

15. Separate components of energy (oil, coal, natural gas) have long been the subject of congressional concern. Only in recent years, however, has Congress tried to develop an overall policy that considers the interrelationship among the resources.

16. Charles O. Jones, *An Introduction to the Study of Public Policy*, 2d ed. (North Scituate, Mass.: Duxbury Press, 1977), p. 56.

17. Ibid., p. 54.

18. Ibid., p. 75.

19. Richard Corrigan and Dick Kirschten, "The Energy Package—What Has Congress Wrought," *National Journal* 10 (November 4, 1978):1760.

20. Ibid.

21. See Carl E. Van Horn and Donald S. Van Meter, "The Implementation of Intergovernmental Policy," in Charles O. Jones and Robert D. Thomas, eds.,

Public Policymaking in a Federal System (Beverly Hills, Calif.: Sage Publications, 1976), pp. 39-62.

22. See Theodore Lowi, "Four Systems of Policy, Politics and Choice," *Public Administration Review* 32 (July-August 1972):298-310.

23. For an excellent treatment of shifting arenas of conflict, see E.E. Schattschneider, *The Semi-Sovereign People* (New York: Holt, Rinehart & Winston, 1960).

24. Jeffrey L. Pressman and Aaron B. Wildavsky, *Implementation* (Berkeley, Calif.: University of California Press, 1973).

25. Richard Corrigan, "The Department of Energy's Continuing Confusing Shakedown," *National Journal* 10 (February 4, 1978):184. More than six months later the situation was just as bleak. According to one report, a "widely held view on Capitol Hill and in industry circles is that chaos rules, that low morale and old-boy satrapies are endemic" in the DOE. See *Washington Post*, September 5, 1978, p. A2.

26. "Public Perceptions of the Energy Problem," p. 22.

27. Reported by the *New York Times*, May 21, 1978, p. 36.

28. Public opinion helps to structure the social environment, which, in turn, influences elite attitudes and behavior. In this way public opinion influences the political environment. See V.O. Key, *Public Opinion and American Democracy* (New York: Alfred A. Knopf, 1961), pp. 150-151 and William C. Mitchell, *The American Polity* (New York: The Free Press, 1962), p. 198.

11 Lessons Learned

David Howard Davis

The ten other chapters of this book, with subjects ranging from Washington's corridors of power to Minnesota's northern forests and from the silence of arid deserts to the roar of Niagara Falls, teach a variety of lessons about energy and environmental policy and about the analysis of these policies.

The Primacy of Politics: This rubric is assumed throughout the book. Should it be? Are politics truly dominant over economics, technology, social relations, or other factors?

The brief for the primacy of economics is strong in energy policy. An economist would argue that energy—that is, coal, oil, electricity, or whatever—is a scarce resource that should be allocated efficiently, just as apples, automobiles, houses, diamonds, and theater tickets are scarce resources that should be allocated efficiently. For the most part an economist would favor a market solution. Thus the energy consumer, whether individual or industrial, would buy gasoline to power his automobile or coal to heat his factory, using price as a guide. Where prices signal changes, the consumer shifts from one fuel to another, or conserves more fuel, or switches to a less energy-intensive activity. Of course, the market is not perfect. Distribution of electricity or gas is a natural monopoly (that is, two or more firms cannot efficiently compete). Information may be inadequate or a cartel may extract monopoly prices. In these cases, the economist would agree to the need for government regulation as a substitute for competition; but essentially he would see energy as an economic problem. Environmental pollution proves less amenable to an economic solution, for here price does not capture the full cost of production. Some costs are to be borne by people who breath air contaminated with taconite fibers or carbon monoxide or by miners who breath the dust in a coal mine or radon in a uranium mine. The polluter ought to bear the burden internally, not spew it forth onto the public and his employees. If that raises the price of his product, fine. Then consumers will shift to less polluting products and society as a whole will be better off.

The scientist might make a case that technology is the key to energy and environmental policy. Science and engineering can solve the problems. They can drill deeper oil wells, build cheaper solar panels, and design more efficient stack scrubbers. The barriers to technical solutions are high costs, laws such as city building codes, institutions such as the Environmental Protection Agency or the Federal Energy Regulatory Commission, and the attitudes of overzealous environmentalists or profit-hungry petroleum companies.

While the brief for social factors not funneled through political institutions is not as strong as the briefs for the primacy of economics and technology, it still deserves exposition. Lynn White blames the Judeo-Christian heritage for modern man's abuse of the environment.[1] This religious tradition imbued western man with a linear rather than cyclical view of time. The new belief was that history was heading somewhere, not just repeating itself. There was the idea of progress. There was man's God-ordained conquest of nature. Compounding the march of progress, as Christianity replaced paganism, trees, rivers and mountain tops lost the nymphs, demi-gods, and elves who had protected them from the woodcutter, the farmer and the miner. Amory Lovins makes a reciprocal argument with respect to energy.[2] He maintains that people should forsake their foolish energy gluttony. They should take the soft paths of solar, wind, and wood rather than the hard paths of central power stations and giant refineries.

Without necessarily rejecting any of these three approaches to understanding energy and environmental policy, this book focuses on political explanations. Politics stands over all. After the market has allocated scarce resources, government intervenes to alter the allocation. After scientists and engineers design a facility, government approves or disapproves its site, output, or even existence. Social attitudes toward energy consumption or environmental protection filter through interest groups, political parties, legislatures, courts, and administrative agency hearings.

Research Designs

Having explored the shared assumption that politics is primary, it is now in order to ask how these ten chapters apply political science and what political science contributes to understanding energy and environmental policy.

In terms of methodology, three chapters look broadly at many cases and four look intensely at single cases. To use the jargon of the discipline, three are quantitative and four are case studies. The three quantitative chapters—water planning in western New York, representation in the Four Corners states, and utility rates in forty-seven states—use quantitative methods to reduce their data to manageable proportions. The data for water planning and Four Corners are from public opinion surveys. The former survey had 1,000 respondents and the latter had 6,600–6,500 citizens and 100 state senators. They represent popular and elite attitudes. In contrast, data for the public utility rate study are economic and institutional variables compiled from industry and government publications.

The water planning and utility rate studies used multiple-regression, a powerful statistical tool. The utility rate study explained 54 percent of the variance with seven independent variables ($R^2 = .54$). The results for the water planning study were lower. Thirteen independent variables explained 20 percent of the variance ($R^2 = .20$).

The four case studies—reorganization in Illinois, the Reserve Mining Company lawsuit, air pollution in Ohio, and the Federal Energy Administration—narrate relevant facts and analyze them in terms of political science theory. In doing so they describe political terrain in which citizens, administrators, and politicians make policy and give a feel for the process. Of these four, the FEA chapter is the least descriptive and the most theoretical.

The goal of the methodology is, of course, to test theory with facts. The ten chapters utilize a fairly standard range of political science theory: group, institutions, attitudes, and so forth. Not surprisingly, the discipline's old favorite—group theory—proves most popular in this book. It is the foundation of the water planning, Illinois reorganization and Reserve Mining Company studies. Other chapters use it to a lesser extent. Although the intellectual source may be Bentley, Herring and Truman, the theory has been filtered through other authors, for citations to these founding fathers are scarce. Institutional models of legislatures and bureaucracies comprise the second most popular theoretical focus, for example in the utility rate, Four Corners, and Illinois studies. Citations here are to Wahlke, Eulau, Bernstein, Downs and Rourke (although strangely, not to Weber). Attitude is the third most popular theoretical framework as in the water planning and Four Corners chapters. Citations are to Miller and Stokes, Verba and Nie, and Luttbeg. The energy policies chapter considers the practicality of the rational decision-making mode; this is a secondary theme in many other chapters. The FEA chapter examines the economic model explicitly; other chapters do so with less awareness.

The theories omitted are perhaps as revealing as those used. Despite its wide use in teaching undergraduates, none of the ten chapters uses the systems model of David Easton, with its familiar arrows, boxes, and feedback loop. This omission suggests that this pretentious model is too vague and amorphous to be carefully applied step by step to a specific energy or environmental case.

Also conspicuously missing is Marxism or some related elite model. This seems strange in view of frequent popular criticism of the power of big oil companies and of industry's disregard of the environment. If the Rockefellers and the Mellons secretly rule America, they must do so, at least in part, through Exxon and Gulf.

Review of the ten chapters' research design defies synthesis. Where appropriate, the studies use statistical techniques; but statistics are often inappropriate. Case studies permit more specificity; however specificity prevents generalized conclusions. As always with political science, replication and control groups are unattainable. Theoretical assumptions used throughout the book vary. As mentioned previously, group theory is popular, and elite theory is eschewed. In short, these ten studies exhibit the research-design characteristics and problems typical of the discipline.

Theoretical Links between Energy
and Environmental Policy

This book, like many others, examines both energy and the environment. But should these two be yoked together? What features do they share besides the initial E? Are they one issue area or two? Having asked the big question, it seems necessary to fumble about briefly trying to define the term "issue area." The most common issue areas in political science, such as housing, health, agriculture, and education, are based on industries. For housing and agriculture this seems easily apparent. Health and education are not immediately thought of as industries, since they are run by higher-status professionals prone to rhetoric about responsibility and public service. Other common political science issue areas cut across industrial lines. Tariffs, labor relations, and foreign affairs are traditional topics of the discipline. In all cases analysis focuses on relevant institutions and participants. Who gets what, when, and how? Frequently the conclusion is that a subgovernment exists, described as a triangle of a private interest group, a sympathetic congressional committee, and the relevant executive branch agency. The president, the public, and political parties participate occasionally, but for the most part conflict is resolved within the subgovernment.

Theodore Lowi offers a different approach.[3] He suggests four arenas: distributive, redistributive, regulatory, and constituent. Lowi maintains that the arena determines the political style. For example, distributive policies are characterized by logrolling, whereas redistributive policies are characterized by bargaining. Congress is much more likely to amend regulative bills than distributive bills.

To what extent do energy and environment fit either approach? Energy clearly fits the industrial mode, but does environment fit it too? No one doubts that manufacturers produce pollutants at the same time they produce steel, houses, or meat. The pollution is unwanted but it is still a product. Indeed the energy industry itself is an enormous polluter, spewing forth coal dust, smog, radiation, and so on. Nevertheless this mechanical linkage does not do much to explain a political linkage between energy and the environment. Energy and the environment are both pervasive, but they each pervade differently in policy terms. Energy goes in; pollution comes out. If the two are forced into the industrial definition their scope becomes excessive. The issue-area approach no longer simplifies. It smothers.

What of Lowi's four categories, do they reveal a twinship of energy and environmental policy? They do not. Various energy and environmental laws fit at least three of Lowi's four categories. The Federal Water Pollution Control Act distributes billions of dollars annually, paying 75 percent of the construction costs of municipal waste-water treatment plants. In contrast, the Clean Air Act is almost entirely regulative. Energy legislation displays the same division as environmental. The Natural Gas Policy Act of 1978 (part of the so-called National Energy Act) is classically regulative, its passage characterized by bargaining (rather than logrolling) and a prominent role for trade associations. At the same time its NEA companions, the Public Utilities and the fuel acts of 1978, distribute financial assistance to energy-impacted states and municipalities. The Department of Energy budget distributes $4 billion dollars for research, development, and commercialization. According to Lowi, taxes are redistributive. This would place the Energy Tax Act of 1978 in a third category. Thus Lowi's typology, like the traditional industry issue area, fails to show the twinship between energy and the environment.

Economic Links between Energy and Environmental Policy

If energy and the environment do not fit the same issue area, perhaps economic factors explain their twinship. The chief reason for government intervention in the economy is market failure: monopoly, economies of scale, entry barriers, imperfect information, externalization, collective goods, and equity.

Monopoly certainly explains some government preemption. Regulation of public utilities such as electric and natural gas distribution is needed because these are natural monopolies. Two or more firms cannot efficiently compete; therefore government controls price and quantity. The OPEC cartel is the opposite. Here, thirteen governments have banded together to create a monopoly. The Interstate Oil and Gas Compact that controlled petroleum from 1938 until recently is a domestic example of a petroleum cartel. Yet, when applied to the environment, this form of market failure, monopoly, is irrelevant. Monopoly is not a useful concept in analyzing the environment.

Economy of scale is a second form of market failure that leads to government intervention. Massive hydroelectric projects such as the Hoover, Fort Peck and TVA dams were beyond the scope of private business during the 1920s and 1930s. More recently, the $8 billion Trans-Alaskan Pipeline System required special legislation and government midwifery. But in energy, economy of scale is the exception. True, some projects are very expensive; but they are still within the scope of private business insofar as raising necessary capital. The proposed natural gas pipeline along the Alaskan highway will cost $14 billion. The joint American-Canadian pipeline consortium plans to raise the capital privately. Moreover, economies of scale for energy projects are now generally well within the capabilities of a private firm. For instance a 1,000 megawatt (Mw) electric generating plant is more efficient than two 500-Mw plants; but that is the top. Because of transmission limits, a 2,000-Mw plant is no more efficient than two 1,000-Mw plants. Superficially, environmental cleanup may seem to share some of these characteristics. It is often cheaper to have a single sewage treatment plant than many small ones. Controlling air pollution may be simpler from one large electric plant than many small coal furnaces. Yet this is essentially a mechanical coincidence rather than a commonality. The expanse and solitude of a park or wilderness is a better example. Backpacking in the desert loses much of its appeal if a dune buggy roars by. The Alaskan caribou needs a range of thousands of square miles. Less will lead to its eventual extinction. In sum, economy of scale falls short in linking energy and environmental policy.

Barriers to entry often call for government intervention in energy. The oil and nuclear industries are oligopolistic. The natural gas and electric industries are monopolistic. On the other hand most of the barriers to entry are governmental: franchises, regulation, entitlements, and so forth. The utility rate and the FEA studies include numerous examples. In analyzing the environmental sphere, two views of the problem of barriers are equally valid: (1) the question is irrelevant; (2) there are no barriers to entry, and indeed, that is the problem. Since time immemorial, government has given carte blanche to any polluter to dump anything into the air or water. Either of these two views leads to the same conclusion, that barriers to entry are important for energy policy and irrelevant for environmental policy.

Imperfect information is a common form of market failure. For example cunsumers may not know which automobile is most efficient or which air conditioner has the lowest life-cycle costs. The Energy Policy and Conservation Act of 1975 (sections 502 and 322) sought to remedy this ignorance through mandatory labeling. As with the forms of market failure discussed before, this particular form of market failure is not relevant to environmental issues.

A fifth form of market failure, externalization, does link the two policy areas. Many of the costs of energy are borne externally by coal miners with black lungs, people breathing smog, children exposed to radiation, and tax payers supporting extra police, schools, and social workers in boom towns. Much of this externalization takes the form of pollution. The environmentalist solution is to internalize the costs as much as possible. Thus workman's compensation raises the cost for industries prone to accidents. When consumers face the higher prices they may find a substitute, thereby making the socially optimal choice. Many environmentalists favor internalizing cost in this manner. For example an effluent charge is a tax for the right to pollute a river. If the charge is set appropriately, it will show consumers in dollars how much the environment is being damaged. The polluter can measure this against alternative means of controlling pollution.

The market cannot cope with a collective good. A collective good (or public good in the economist's terminology) cannot be denied to noncontributors. Clean air is an example. Because air blows about for many miles, A cannot breath clean air while his neighbor, B, breaths smog. The air will be either clean or polluted for everyone in an airshed. In contrast, sanitation workers can pick up A's trash and leave B's (perhaps because B did not pay). Solid waste is not a collective good. It is divisible, whereas air is indivisible. Water occupies an intermediate position. Once in a lake, river or ocean it flows about, making it a collective good. Yet since access can be controlled through permission to use beaches, docks, and riverbanks, it has many private goods features. The environment is primarily a collective good, therefore; but energy is much less so. Research is the clearest case. If a company invents a new, cheaper way to refine oil, its competitor will gain the benefit without having paid for the research unless the first company can protect its invention by secrecy or patents. Patent law is a way to convert a collective good into a private good by government coercion. Thus market failure due to the nature of collective goods is widespread for environmental but rare for energy issues.

Equity is the last form of market failure to be considered. This concern permeates energy: gasoline allocation in 1974, crude oil price controls, natural gas regulation, lifeline rates for electricity. Equity is less of a concern in the environment. The benefits of clean water are far from equitable. Members of the middle class benefit most for they own lake front cottages, or boats, or automobiles to drive to distant parks. The poor cannot afford cottages, boats, and automobile excursions. The prospect of making Newark Bay, the East River, or the St. Louis waterfront suitable for recreation is remote. The rich do not benefit much from clean water either, since they tend to fly to pristine northern lakes or the warm Caribbean for their clean water. Air pollution is a different story. The air tends to be dirtiest in the central cities where the poor live. Moreover, air blows about so the burden is less certain. The beneficiaries of clean air change daily with the weather, whereas the beneficiaries of clean water do not.

Not all agree that equity should be labeled an economic criterion. In a free-market system inequity is not necessarily a failure. If the poor have less electricity, gasoline, boats and cottages, that has nothing in particular to do with energy or environment. According to this line of reasoning, equity (that is the distribution of wealth and income) is not an economic issue but a political one.

Reviewing these seven forms of market failure reveals little commonality between energy and the environment. Only in terms of externalization was the overlap significant and that was because both dealt with pollution. This was the mechanical linkage found irrelevant earlier in this chapter. Having found economic criteria related to market failure unsatisfactory, what of political criteria?

Political Links between Energy and Environmental Policy

Notwithstanding any rigorous analytic scheme, energy and the environment are tightly linked in the popular mind. Public opinion, the personnel in the two fields, and society's resolution of the problems share much. Analysis of the commonality reveals more about political techniques of the 1960s and 1970s than about any underlying logic. Both issues leapt suddenly into popular consciousness within 5 years of each other. Earth Day, April 22, 1970, transformed concern with ecology from a tiny band of biologists, bird watchers, and backpackers into a mass movement. To the surprise of many, President Richard Nixon and the Republican Party joined the bandwagon. The so-called energy crisis also sprang forth suddenly. The Arabs began their boycott on October 17, 1973, and within weeks every American had felt its effect. Public demand led quickly to gasoline allocation, new laws, and new government agencies.

Personnel in energy and the environment were often the same. Robert Presthus maintains that certain ambitious men and women (whom he labels "upward mobiles") jump from one new organization to another.[4] Their goal of career advancement overpowers considerations such as subject specialization or institutional loyalty. Thus it is no surprise to find the same individuals who joined the Environmental Protection Agency when it was established in 1970 now working at DOE.

Society's way of resolving both environmental and energy problems reflects its era. As heirs of the New Deal, Americans look toward the national government. It is an age of big government. The legislative response to the environmental movement was the National Environmental Policy Act of 1969, the Clean Air Act of 1970, and Federal Water Pollution Control Act of 1972. The response for energy was the Emergency Petroleum Allocation Act of 1973, the Energy Policy and Conservation Act of 1975, and the National Energy Act of 1978. Administrative reorganization followed the same path. For the environment it was the Council on Environmental Quality and the Environmental Protection Agency. For energy it was the FEA, the Energy Research and Development Administration, and the DOE. In both cases resolution gravitated to government and within government to the national level. Far from the public having faith in American business to supply energy, the public positively distrusted private business. Senator Henry Jackson's 1974 hearings on the multinational oil companies is illustrative. Having opted for the government over the private sector, the public prefers the national to the state or local level. Notice, for example, that the analysis of water planning in western New York is based on Section 208 of the Federal Water Pollution Control Act; that analysis of air pollution policy in Ohio is based on the Clean Air Act; and that the Reserve Mining Company had to find a new disposal site because the U.S. Environmental Protection Agency had forbidden discharging taconite tailings into Lake Superior.

Implementation of national government policy through the states represents a different solution to problems having diverse conditions. The older version of American democratic theory, epitomized in the Tenth Amendment to the U.S. Constitution, exalted the federal system because it allowed each of the states to resolve its own problems according to its particular situation. This assumption underlies the study of representation in the Four Corners states. The corollary of the diversity proposition was that each state could experiment. When a program proved successful, other states could copy it or the national government could adopt it. For instance, New York and Wisconsin electricity programs of the 1920s became the models for TVA, rural electrification, and other New Deal programs in the 1930s. The newer version of federalism is for the national government to establish the program and for the states to administer it. This is a far cry from the older version.

State government abdication of revenue raising is one reason for this. In the past thirty years the national government budget has increased more than twelve-fold, while the number of personnel is virtually the same. Much of the difference represents grants to the states or assumption of state transfer payments. The national government is a superior revenue raiser because (1) it relies on personal and corporate income taxes whereas the states rely on sales taxes and the municipalities rely on property taxes, both more onerous to the voter; and (2) inflation boosts its revenues through deficits and pushes taxpayers into higher brackets.

An unexamined assumption that the national government should deal with other governments rather than nongovernment organizations is a second reason for the new version of the federal system. Most citizens would have objected to Exxon allocating gasoline in 1974, even though Exxon probably could have done a better job than the ad hoc energy offices the fifty states hastily assembled. Similarly, the government built thousands of miles of highways during the 1950s and 1960s while the railroads decayed. The Federal Water Pollution Control Act pays 75 percent of the cost of municipal waste-water treatment facilities but does not do so for industrial facilities. Consequently, industry piggy backs onto municipal plants even when it would be more efficient to do its own treatment. To take an example from this book, the impetus for reorganizing Illinois's energy bureaucracy can be viewed as imitation of concurrent organization of the national level as the U.S. Department of Energy was being established in 1977.

State implementation can cynically provide opportunities for manipulation. The National Energy Act provides two contrasting examples: natural gas supply and public utility rates. The Natural Gas Policy Act, one of five laws that constitute the so-called National Energy Act, provides that, at their option, states, rather than the national government, can classify wells into two dozen or so categories. Since the law is complex and ambiguous, opportunities for discretion are rife. It came as no surprise that Texas, Louisiana, and six other producing states were ready immediately to assume these duties. On the other hand, President Carter sought to impose proconsumer national standards on the state public utility commissions. When this failed, the face-saving compromise was to adopt the president's standards but not to make them mandatory.

Coercion is the final commonality that energy and the environment share.

Force is, of course, the ultimate sanction of government. Having set a certain price for crude oil or natural gas, the government can enforce these prices. Land condemnation operates for both. Building a hydroelectric dam or expanding a park means buying land that the owners are not always willing to sell; hence, government exercises its right of eminent domain. A court sets the price; the agency pays it and then evicts the owners. Powerful as this element of coercion may be, it does not really yoke together energy and environmental policy. Coercion too nearly approaches universality to serve as a useful category.

Reviewing the three areas that might link energy to environmental policy—theory, economics, and politics—shows that the linkage is weak. Energy and the environment share little besides the initial E. Using the traditional political science definition of issue area found the environment fitting poorly into the industry mold. Neither did Lowi's four arenas uncover commonalities. Both fit two or three arenas. The economic perspective proved little more useful. Most forms of market failure did not apply to the environment. Externalization was the exception and that did not particularly link the two topics.

It was the political links between energy and the environment that proved the strongest. The evolution of popular attitudes, personnel in government and interest groups, and institutional techniques, especially of the national government, were the strongest links between energy and the environment.

Political science often stands in envy of disciplines such as physics and economics with their more general theories. In contrast, the study of policy seems untidy. Each situation seems unique. Studies cannot be replicated. Data defy quantification. Conditions change constantly. Theory is elusive and unsettled. Perhaps a better comparison is to geography, where mapping the terrain remains the core of the discipline. Political scientists might better be named political explorers, setting out to observe the hills and valleys, survey the mountains and plumb the depths of the policy process. Each analyst can envision himself as a Columbus of policy. Just as Columbus sailed his wind-powered ships westward to discover a pristine, wilderness America, a political scientist can seek to find and chart new territory. While navigating unknown regions, the political scientist can console himself with the memory that Columbus's great voyage could not begin until Spain achieved political security and stability in 1492—a fifteenth-century example of the primacy of politics.

Notes

1. Lynn White, "The Historical Roots of Our Ecological Crisis," *Science* 155 (March 10, 1967):1203-1207.

2. Amory Lovins, *World Energy Strategies* (Cambridge, Mass.: Friends of the Earth, 1975).

3. Theodore J. Lowi, "Four Systems of Policy and Choice," *Public Administration Review* 32 (July-August 1972):298-310.

4. Robert Presthus, *The Organizational Society* (New York: Random House, 1962).

Glossary of Abbreviations

DBED	Department of Business and Economic Development
DMM	Department of Mines and Minerals
DNR	Department of Natural Resources
DOE	Division of Energy
EPA	Environmental Protection Agency
EPAA	Emergency Petroleum Allocation Act
EPCA	Energy Policy and Conservation Act
ERDA	Energy Research and Development Administration
FEA	Federal Energy Administration
FEO	Federal Energy Office
FPC	U.S. Federal Power Commission
HEW	U.S. Department of Health, Education and Welfare
IERC	Illinois Energy Resource Commission
MEPA	Minnesota Environmental Policy Act of 1973
NEPA	National Environmental Policy Act of 1969
PCA	Pollution Control Agency
PUC	Public Utilities Commission

About the Contributors

Paul Anderson is a visiting instructor of political science at Texas A&M University. He will receive the Ph.D. degree from Purdue University in 1979.

Steven A. Cohen has held a Rockefeller Foundation Fellowship in public policy. He received the Ph.D. degree from the State University of New York at Buffalo. He is an assistant professor at West Virginia University.

Leon S. Cohen is an associate professor of political studies and public affairs at Sangamon State University. During the period of research on energy reorganization he was also director of the Illinois Legislative Studies Center at SSU and coordinator of the Illinois Legislative Staff Internship Program.

Jonathan Czarnecki received the Ph.D. degree in political science from the State University of New York at Buffalo.

Gregory A. Daneke teaches policy analysis and public management in the School of Natural Resources at the University of Michigan. He served as a faculty fellow with the Energy and Minerals Division of the U.S. General Accounting Office in 1979. He is the author of numerous works including the forthcoming text *Administrative Policy and the Public Interest: An Introduction to Policy Analysis.*

David Howard Davis is on the staff of the Congressional Research Service at the Library of Congress. After receiving the Ph.D. degree from Johns Hopkins University in 1971, he taught at Rutgers and Cornell Universities. In 1973-1974, he was a NASPAA public administration fellow at the U.S. Environmental Protection Agency. He recently served at the U.S. General Accounting Office. Professor Davis is the author of *Energy Politics.*

Helen Ingram is professor of political science on leave from the University of Arizona to Resources for the Future, where she is a senior fellow. She has written widely in the fields of natural resources and the environment.

Sheldon Kamieniecki is assistant professor of political science at California State College at San Bernardino. He received the Ph.D. degree from the State University of New York at Buffalo in 1978. His research and teaching interests are in political behavior and public policy, particularly environmental policy.

Nancy K. Laney has a Masters of Public Administration from the University of Arizona. Formerly employed by the Arizona State Senate, she is presently a member of the Governor's Commission on the Arizona Environment. Ms. Laney is coauthor of the forthcoming book, *Policy, Representation and the Four Corners States.*

John R. McCain is finishing his doctoral dissertation at the University of Arizona in political science. He is presently working as a staff policy analyst for the Arizona Groundwater Management Study Commission.

Kenneth E. Mitchell was a research associate with the Illinois Legislative Studies Center at Sangamon State University during the research for this book. He is currently assistant director of the Illinois General Assembly's Joint Committee on Administrative Rules. He holds a Master's degree in Sociology from the University of Illinois at Chicago Circle.

Albert J. Nelson is an assistant professor of political studies at Sangamon State University. He received the Ph.D. degree at the University of Oregon in 1974, specializing in American politics on the state and local levels, legislative and executive politics, and public policy.

Thomas M. Pelsoci is an assistant professor of political science at Cleveland State University. His research areas are in energy/environmental and regulatory policies, and he teaches public administration, urban politics, and policy analysis.

Robert W. Rycroft is an assistant professor in the Graduate School of International Studies at the University of Denver. He was previously a Compton visiting fellow in the Center of International Studies at Princeton University and a research fellow in the Science and Public Policy Program at the University of Oklahoma. He has been involved in applied energy policy analysis for over 6 years.

Richard J. Tobin is assistant professor of political science at the State University of New York at Buffalo. He has published in the *Western Political Quarterly*, the *American Journal of Political Science*, and the *American Politics Quarterly*. He is also the author of *The Social Gamble: Determining Acceptable Levels of Air Quality* (1979).

Dr. Norman J. Vig is associate professor and chairman of the Department of Political Science at Carleton College. He is author of *Science and Technology in British Politics* and coauthor and editor of *Politics in Advanced Nations.*

About the Editor

Michael Steinman is an associate professor of political science at the University of Nebraska in Lincoln. His work has been published in *Social Science Quarterly, Urban Affairs Quarterly, Public Personnel Management, Policy and Politics,* and other journals. He is the coeditor of *Problems in Administrative Reform* (forthcoming). He spent 1978-1979 directing a project for the Office of the Governor in Nebraska culminating in the identification of state research-and-development priorities and administrative reforms to promote them. His primary teaching and research interests are public administration and public policy. He received his doctorate from the University of Chicago in 1971.